REGENTS CRITICS SERIES

bought
March 3, 1972
30
collab

General Editor: Paul A. Olson

THE AUTHOR'S CRAFT
AND OTHER CRITICAL WRITINGS
OF ARNOLD BENNETT

Other volumes in the Regents Critics Series are:

The Author's Craft
and Other Critical Writings
of Arnold Bennett

Edited by

SAMUEL HYNES

UNIVERSITY OF NEBRASKA PRESS · LINCOLN

Acknowledgments for the use of copyrighted material appear on
page 275.

Regents Critics Series

The Regents Critics Series provides reading texts of significant literary critics in the Western tradition. The series treats criticism as a useful tool: an introduction to the critic's own poetry and prose if he is a poet or novelist, an introduction to other work in his day if he is more judge than creator. Nowhere is criticism regarded as an end in itself but as what it is—a means to the understanding of the language of art as it has existed and been understood in various periods and societies.

Each volume includes a scholarly introduction which describes how the work collected came to be written, and suggests its uses. All texts are edited in the most conservative fashion consonant with the production of a good reading text; and all translated texts observe the dictum that the letter gives life and the spirit kills when a technical or rigorous passage is being put into English. Other types of passages may be more freely treated. Footnoting and other scholarly paraphernalia are restricted to the essential minimum. Such features as a bibliographical check-list or an index are carried where they are appropriate to the work in hand. If a volume is the first collection of the author's critical writing, this is noted in the bibliographical data.

PAUL A. OLSON

University of Nebraska

Contents

III. HERESIES

Introduction

I

One of the early entries in Arnold Bennett's journal is a meditation on heredity. Thinking about his various ancestors—the puritanical farmers, the town dwellers, the illegitimate child of a famous engineer—Bennett wondered that this mixture should have combined to produce him, "a writer, an artist pure and simple, yet with strong mercantile instincts." [1] These two apparently contradictory sides of Bennett's nature—the artist and the merchant—have puzzled his critics, and have sometimes led to oversimplifications of a complex man, usually at the expense of the artist in him. Philistines have claimed Bennett as one of their own, and persons of pure aesthetic principles have deplored his mercantile streak, and overlooked the rest. Ezra Pound's portrait of Bennett as Mr. Nixon in "Hugh Selwyn Mauberley" is characteristic of this sort of simplifying treatment:

> In the cream gilded cabin of his steam yacht
> Mr. Nixon advised me kindly, to advance with fewer
> Dangers of delay. 'Consider
>   'Carefully the reviewer.
>
> 'I was as poor as you are;
> 'When I began I got, of course,
> 'Advance on royalties, fifty at first,' said Mr. Nixon,
> 'Follow me, and take a column,
> 'Even if you have to work free.
>
> 'Butter reviewers. From fifty to three hundred
> 'I rose in eighteen months;
> 'The hardest nut I had to crack
> 'Was Dr. Dundas.

1. *The Journal of Arnold Bennett* (New York, 1933), p. 113. All references are to this, the first one-volume edition.

'I never mentioned a man but with the view
'Of selling my own works.
'The tip's a good one, as for literature
'It gives no man a sinecure.

'And no one knows, at sight a masterpiece.
'And give up verse, my boy,
'There's nothing in it.'[2]

Pound's ear seldom failed him, and he got a good deal of Bennett
into his poem. Anyone who has read Bennett's books of practical
advice to authors—*Journalism for Women*, or *How to Become an Author*
—will recognize the prudent, matter-of-fact tone of the literary
businessman with "strong mercantile instincts." This was the
Bennett who managed his writing life like a one-man factory; who
watched production and measured it against costs; who set his
fees by the word and by the hour, and gave exactly ten shillings'
worth of work for ten shillings pay; and who read the small print
of his contracts and badgered his agent for better terms. This
Bennett was an efficient and successful manufacturer of literature,
and he earned enough by his industry to live a splendid and expensive life, in which the steam yacht that Pound resented was only one
delight.

Mr. Nixon is a recognizable likeness of Bennett, but only in the
sense that a good caricature is a likeness; the poem does not acknowledge the other side of Bennett's nature, the side that made him
"an artist pure and simple." One can discover this Bennett by
reading *The Old Wives' Tale* or *Clayhanger* or *Riceyman Steps*, but he is
also in the critical writings. Bennett once boasted in a review that
he had "never pretended to look at things from any other standpoint
than that of a creative artist," and though the evidence of his
business correspondence would seem to contradict this,[3] there is a
sense in which it is true. He saw no reason why an artist should not
prosper, and he decided early in life that he would work best in

2. Ezra Pound, "Hugh Selwyn Mauberley (Life and Contacts)," *Poems
1918–21* (New York, 1926 and 1954), p. 194.

3. See James Hepburn (ed.), *Letters of Arnold Bennett*, Vol. I (London: Oxford
University Press, 1966). This volume contains Bennett's letters to his agent,
J. B. Pinker.

opulent surroundings; but he nevertheless thought of himself as an artist, and when the occasion dictated, he spoke like one. For example, in 1910, in a review of Sturge Moore's *Art and Life*:

His value is that he would make the English artist a conscious artist. He does, without once stating it, bring out in the most startling way the contrast between, for example, the English artist and the Continental artist. Read the correspondence of Dickens and Thackeray, and then read the correspondence of Flaubert, and you will see. The latter was continually preoccupied with his craft, the two former scarcely ever—and never in an intelligent fashion. I have been preaching on this theme for years, but I am not aware that anybody has been listening. I was going to say that I was sick of preaching about it, but I am not. I shall continue . . . .[4]

The most striking thing about this passage is the number of ways in which it echoes the views, and even the phrases, of Edwardian writers with whom Bennett is not usually associated: Henry James, for instance, and Joseph Conrad, and especially Ford Madox Ford. The idea of the "conscious artist," the comparison of English and Continental attitudes, the admiration for Flaubert and the contempt for Thackeray—all these are in Ford's *The English Novel*, and similar opinions are scattered through the essays and introductions of James and Conrad. These shared ideas define a small but important group of Edwardian writers, those "Europeanized" novelists who were trying to raise the English novel to the level of an art form by connecting it to a European tradition. It is important to note that Bennett merits a place among them.

Certainly Bennett thought of himself in that way, as a novelist in the European realistic tradition that derived from French and Russian masters: he consciously modeled his *Old Wives' Tale* on Maupassant's *Une Vie*, and he was constant in his admiration for Turgenev and Dostoievsky. Like James and Conrad and Ford he was a "good European" in a time of English insularity; he lived for several years in France (*The Old Wives' Tale* was conceived in Paris and written near Fontainebleau), married a French wife, and had a wide acquaintance among French intellectuals, including Ravel

4. "Books and Persons," *New Age*, VI (March 24, 1910), 494.

and Gide. His knowledge of modern French writing, painting, and music was extensive, and his responsiveness to new movements was quick and generous. In all this (except perhaps the wife) he was very much the Edwardian *avant-garde* artist.

Mr. Nixon and the Conscious Artist were both abiding parts of Bennett's nature, and Bennett himself saw no incompatibility between them. He nurtured both characters, and wrote in both voices. "Do you want me to do my best and most serious work," he asked a magazine editor, "or do you want me to adopt a popular standard?"[5] He could and did do both, altering the level according to the demand, and to avoid competing with himself. (He was so copious a writer that he had to vary his work so as not to flood the market; in a letter to his agent he described himself aptly as "an engine for the production of fiction."[6]) Bennett's own account of his work done during 1908 gives a fair example of the variety of things that he was able to do, almost simultaneously: "*Buried Alive*, 3/4 of *The Old Wives' Tale*, *What the Public Wants*, *The Human Machine*, *Literary Taste: How to Form It*; about half a dozen short stories, including *A Matador in the Five Towns*; over 60 newspaper articles. Total words, 423,500."[7] A popular novel, a serious novel, a play, a book of popular philosophy and one of literary advice, newspaper sketches and a serious story, articles for journals ranging from *T. P.'s Weekly*, a popular penny paper, to the intellectual-socialist *New Age*—all this came from one man, and in one year. And all of it was equally expressive of Bennett's nature: merchant and artist spoke antiphonally, and with equivalent authority.

It is this equivalence that gives Bennett his unique quality, both as a novelist and as a critic. It means that he brought to his work, and to his judgments of other men's work, two kinds of standards: the standards of the craftsman, who respects good work and does his own as well as he can; and the standards of the artist, who aspires to create a permanent and living work of the imagination, and measures all art by that aspiration. As a craftsman, Bennett acknowledged many levels of literary work—he could write sympathetically

5. *Letters*, p. 184. The letter is dated April 30, 1913.
6. *Letters*, p. 50 (April 27, 1904).
7. *Journal*, p. 311.

about Turgenev or about the latest romance with equal facility and careful judgment. He asked only that the work be well done of its kind, and that the writer use his tools well, whatever task he set them to. He deplored the misuse of language wherever he found it, in a novel by Virginia Woolf or an ad for the Piccadilly Hotel, and scolded the misusers in his articles. When a piece of work was well done, he praised it generously, though he was always careful to distinguish the literary artist from the merely popular writer; he never confused his standards.

Bennett's receptiveness to the more popular kinds of writing was more than a matter of commercial interest; he was naturally drawn to the mass audience, those semi-educated members of his own class whose hunger for literature was greater than their taste. "The public," he said, "is a great actuality, like war," [8] and it was that great actuality that he sought to reach. He addressed his "pocket philosophies" to those readers, explaining how to gain mental efficiency, how to develop literary taste, how to live with a wife; he addressed reviews and articles to them through their penny papers; but he also wrote novels for them. He believed, he said, in the democratization of art—that a gifted writer could reach this public, and remain an artist. "There is a theory," he wrote,

> that the great public can appreciate a great novel, that the highest modern expression of literary art need not appeal in vain to the average reader. And I believe this to be true—provided that such a novel is written with intent, and with a full knowledge of the peculiar conditions to be satisfied; I believe that a novel could be written which would unite in a mild ecstasy of praise the two extremes—the most inclusive majority and the most exclusive minority. [9]

It was Bennett's peculiar fortune to belong both to the majority and to the minority: Five Towns and Paris, merchant and artist were so mixed in him that he could understand at once the many and the few. One can see both views expressed in his first book of criticism, *Fame and Fiction* (1901). The title itself suggests the majority

8. *The Author's Craft* (see below, p. 43).
9. "The Average Reader and the Recipe for Popularity" (see below, p. 58).

interest, and the subtitle confirms it: "An Enquiry into Certain Popularities." The book is about popular success: what makes a best seller? Bennett looked at the most popular novels of the turn of the century, considered their virtues and weaknesses, and judged them by generous but firm literary standards. Most of the writers discussed are now forgotten—writers like Miss Braddon, Charlotte M. Yonge, Rhoda Broughton, Sarah Grand, Marie Corelli, and Silas Hocking; but in their day they were all better known, and better read, than Conrad or James—or Bennett. In his book Bennett analyzed the bases of their success, and noted such excellences as his examples had. But in his final judgments, he spoke as an artist, and noted their shortcomings. It is significant that Bennett, at the beginning of his career, should have thought it worth while to study popular success; but it is equally significant that in his criticism he maintained the distinction between success and art.

The last three essays in *Fame and Fiction* are of a different sort: if the rest of the book belongs to the world of Mr. Nixon, these essays are by the Conscious Artist. The subjects are Gissing, George Moore, and Turgenev—three masters of the realistic tradition to which Bennett in his serious work belonged. None of them was a proper example of *fame*—they were rather, as Bennett described them, "a small nondescript class of the non-popular or misunderstood." They wrote art novels for that "most exclusive minority," the serious novel readers. But Bennett wanted to bring them to the majority; and in the case of the long essay on Moore he could only do so by putting the essay in his book, since he could not persuade any periodical to publish it.

The twofold interest expressed in the contents of *Fame and Fiction* continued throughout Bennett's life. During the Edwardian years he was the principal English publicist of new European ideas, through his columns in the *New Age*; but he was also the friend and admirer of popular writers. His *New Age* articles are sprinkled with the names of forgotten authors whose books Bennett had liked; and after the war, when Bennett was probably the best-known, highest-paid, and busiest novelist in England, he yet found time to write an indignant letter to the *Nation*, defending Charles Garvice, a popular novelist who had been mauled in a review. Garvice,

Bennett insisted, was "a thoroughly competent craftsman," and if that was not the highest human achievement, neither was it to be despised.[10]

II

By his own account, Bennett's career as a critic began in the early 1890's, when he sent an unsolicited review of some French book to the *Illustrated London News*.[11] It is appropriate that his first criticism should have been of a French book, for Bennett was always a Francophile. It is also appropriate that it should have been a review in a popular paper, for Bennett prided himself all his life on being a professional reviewer. In 1903 he estimated that he reviewed "a book and a fraction of a book" every day, including Sundays, and nearly thirty years later he noted with pride that he had reviewed a thousand books in three years. During the Edwardian years when he wrote "Books and Persons" for the *New Age*, he was widely read and admired by the modern, the radical, and the young. In the twenties his influence was even greater: "Bennett was the only man in my literary lifetime," Hugh Walpole said, "who could really make the fortune of a new book in a night."[12]

A good deal of Bennett's income came from his journalism, and his rates for his *Evening Standard* pieces were high (he eventually got up to two shillings a word), but he did not review simply for money. For the first eighteen months of his association with the *New Age* he wrote his weekly articles for nothing, and he was never paid more than a guinea a week for the column. He was, as he said, a born reviewer, and he would rather review for nothing than not review at all.

One can perhaps explain this compulsion in terms once more of the merchant and the artist. Bennett took a professional interest

10. "Mr. Garvice's Novel," *Nation*, XXVI (March 13, 1920), 807.

11. Bennett told this story twice—in *The Truth About an Author* (London, 1903), and in an article in the *Evening Standard* (July 10, 1930). However, James Hepburn argues that very probably "the first reviewing was done in the *Illustrated London News*, over the initials A. B., on 18 November 1893 and 24 March 1894" (*Letters*, p. 13); neither of these reviews is of a French book.

12. Hugh Walpole, Preface to *Essays and Reviews by Arnold Bennett* (London, 1938), p. 1. This is a dealer's catalog of Bennett manuscripts.

in his own trade; he liked to know what was going on, and he liked to record his responses at once. If he could not publish his views, he would write them in his journal; but being a professional, he preferred publication and payment. He wrote, not as a pundit, but as a working journalist—rapidly and to the occasion; he seems never to have revised, and never to have lingered over his copy. What emerged were the direct and frank opinions of a gifted professional writer who was deeply involved in the literary life of his time—a record both of the man and of the moment. Few are what one would call formal essays; the principal exception, the essay on George Moore, was the one that Bennett could not sell.

Bennett's great period as a critic was the time before World War I—the years from *Fame and Fiction* to *Books and Persons*. These were years of great cultural and social ferment in England, when what we know as modern England was taking form. The suffrage movement, the Fabian Society, the Labour party, airplanes, radio-telegraphy, psychoanalysis, postimpressionism, movies, were all parts of the Edwardian scene. Conrad, Forster, Wells, and Galsworthy were doing their best work, and Lawrence and Joyce and Virginia Woolf were beginning to publish. Bennett, in the midst of all this and aware of most of it, was also at his peak; between 1907 and 1915 he wrote *The Old Wives' Tale* and the *Clayhanger* trilogy, and at the same time kept up a stream of lively articles, including the brilliant weekly pieces for the *New Age*. But his time of brilliant production ended when the Edwardian Age ended—in August, 1914.

The war drew Bennett's energies away from literature, to government propaganda, and he never quite regained his place among the artists, nor his authority among the young. The change was partly a change of generations, and partly a change in Bennett's public role. Joyce, Eliot, and Mrs. Woolf dominated the postwar literary scene, and their work made Bennett's kind of realism seem a part of the rejected Edwardian past. The Victorian restraints and shibboleths against which Bennett had directed his ironic barbs were gone, replaced by the easy manners of the twenties. The battles for recognition of European art had been won. In this England, Bennett could not reach forward to the *avant-garde*.

And Bennett had changed, too. He had become wealthy, the friend of peers and owner of a yacht. He had not written a first-rate novel in ten years, and his literary journalism was no longer printed in the serious journals. He was famous—his name on billboards sold papers, and people turned on the street to stare at him— but he was no longer much admired by the intellectuals or by the young; he had become a symbol of what was old-fashioned in fiction.

The relations between Bennett and the younger generation were most dramatically expressed in his quarrel with Virginia Woolf.[13] The quarrel began just after the war, and continued intermittently until Bennett's death. Bennett charged Mrs. Woolf with failure to create characters; Mrs. Woolf replied that Bennett was obsolete. As literary quarrels go, it was not a particularly vituperative one; the principals continued to meet at dinner parties, and maintained civil communications. Still, it had unfortunate effects. By insisting that the quarrel was a generational one, Mrs. Woolf helped to separate her own generation of writers from a tradition from which they might have learned; her arguments made the realistic methods of Bennett seem useless to younger writers, and incompatible with her own "modern" methods.

Another consequence is more difficult to assess. Mrs. Woolf's dismissal of Bennett contained a strong element of class snobbishness: Bennett's passion for plain subjects, and his correspondingly plain style, seemed to her gross and vulgar, and she patronized him. Bennett, wounded, responded by affirming his own vulgarity: "She is the queen of the high-brows," he wrote, "and I am a low-brow." Of course he was nothing of the kind, either socially or artistically; but he had been despised in public by a lady, and voluntary vulgarity was one defense against her. The cost to himself was great; by accepting the public role of Mr. Nixon, he abdicated his place among the conscious artists, and abandoned his lifelong faith that the two roles—the merchant and the artist—could coexist in one skillful and serious writer.

13. For detailed accounts of the Bennett-Woolf quarrel, see Irving Kreutz, "Mr. Bennett and Mrs. Woolf," *Modern Fiction Studies*, VIII (Summer, 1962), 103–115, and Samuel Hynes, "The Whole Contention Between Mr. Bennett and Mrs. Woolf," *Novel*, I (Fall 1967), 34–44.

Though Bennett in his last years proclaimed himself a low-brow, and wrote for a popular newspaper, he did not cease to be a shrewd judge of new writing. He recognized that *Jacob's Room* was "packed and bursting with originality"; he praised *Ulysses*, the novels of D. H. Lawrence, and the poems of Robert Graves; he liked Graham Green's *The Man Within* and Richard Hughes' *High Wind in Jamaica* (both first novels), and Hemingway's *Farewell to Arms*. He found space to notice Edward Dahlberg's *Bottom Dogs* and Svevo's *Confessions of Zeno*. Until he died he remained what he had been for three decades—the best literary journalist in London.

III

It is not easy to summarize Bennett's critical principles, for he was essentially a pragmatic critic, concerned with the particular problems in the book before him. His general essays—like "What Is a Good Novel?"—do not go far beyond a few basic principles: that novels should be well constructed, that characterization is of the first importance, that all fiction is essentially moral. His streak of North Country common sense made him impatient of literary frills and obscurities: he couldn't see the point of *The Waste Land*, nor could he figure out what *A Passage to India* was all about; and though he praised *Ulysses*, he complained of its "pervading difficult dullness." He was a forthright man, and he disliked the evasions of literary gentility; of A. C. Benson, the most genteel of Edwardian writers, Bennett remarked: "Whenever I read Mr. Benson I feel that vulgarity, of which he is so afraid, is a most precious quality," and he found Henry James' "colossal cautiousness" very trying.

Much of this sounds like pure Mr. Nixon, and if it were all of Bennett's criticism there would be no reason to read this book. But Bennett was sensitive as well as sensible, as many essays here collected demonstrate. He saw and praised the brilliant simplicity of Chekhov's style, he appreciated the Rabelaisian humor of Joyce (at a time when few critics saw how funny *Ulysses* is), and he revered the delicacy of Turgenev. In the essays on these writers, and on others that he admired, the artist in Bennett spoke most directly. But Bennett was concerned that merchant and artist should not be separated; he took it as his goal to "unite in a mild ecstasy of praise the two extremes—the most inclusive majority and the most exclusive minority," and to achieve that goal the two voices had to speak as one. One can discern this intention in Bennett's critical writings as well as in his fiction; it is there in the extraordinary range of his interests, and it is there in the character-istic Bennett style—a blunt, no-nonsense kind of prose, which is nonetheless capable of epigrammatic sharpness and wit. No one would argue that Bennett always succeeded in this intention, either in his novels or in his essays, but at his best he did succeed in a way that no one else did in Bennett's time, or has since. No other English writer in this century has come so close to reaching the audience that Bennett aspired to, that great actuality, the public.

A Note on the Texts

Most of these essays first appeared in daily or weekly papers. Many of them were later gathered into collections, and when Bennett did so he sometimes revised, removing topical references and moderating his tone. The revised versions seem to me to lack the vigor and flavor of the original, rapidly written pieces, and I have gone back to the original sources for my texts.

There is one exception. *The Author's Craft* was first published in the *English Review* as "The Story Teller's Craft." Bennett took more than usual care in writing these four long essays—perhaps because they were to appear in a solemn literary monthly—and they are more deliberate, more "written" than the journalistic pieces are. When he prepared these essays for book publication he reworked the text, polishing it and improving continuity. I have taken that revised version, the text of the first edition of 1914, as definitive.

Parts I and III of this book are organized by date of publication. The many short items in Part II made strict chronological order-ing impractical and untidy, and I have therefore grouped together the writings on a single author there, and have arranged the groups according to the date of birth of the subject.

Source notes at the end of each selection give both the first peri-odical publication and the first appearance in book form.

The selections have been reprinted as they appeared in the source, with editorial changes restricted to the correction of obvious typographical errors. Foreign-language quotations are translated in footnotes. Editorial deletions are indicated by three asterisks (∗ ∗ ∗) to distinguish them from the author's own ellipses.

SAMUEL HYNES

Northwestern University

I. THE AUTHOR'S CRAFT

The Author's Craft (1913)

I

A young dog, inexperienced, sadly lacking in even primary education, ambles and frisks along the footpath of Fulham Road, near the mysterious gates of a Marist convent. He is a large puppy, on the way to be a dog of much dignity, but at present he has little to recommend him but that gawky elegance, and that bounding gratitude for the gift of life, which distinguish the normal puppy. He is an ignorant fool. He might have entered the convent of nuns and had a fine time, but instead he steps off the pavement into the road, the road being a vast and interesting continent imperfectly explored. His confidence in his nose, in his agility, and in the goodness of God is touching, absolutely painful to witness. He glances casually at a huge, towering vermillion construction that is whizzing towards him on four wheels, preceded by a glint of brass and a wisp of steam; and then with disdain he ignores it as less important than a mere speck of odorous matter in the mud. The next instant he is lying inert in the mud. His confidence in the goodness of God had been misplaced. Since the beginning of time God had ordained him a victim.

An impressive thing happens. The motor-bus reluctantly slackens and stops. Not the differential brake, nor the foot-brake, has arrested the motor-bus, but the invisible brake of public opinion, acting by administrative transmission. There is not a policeman in sight. Theoretically, the motor-bus is free to whiz onward in its flight to the paradise of Shoreditch, but in practice it is paralysed by dread. A man in brass buttons and a stylish cap leaps down from it, and the blackened demon who sits on its neck also leaps down from it, and they move gingerly towards the puppy. A little while ago the motor-bus might have overturned a human cyclist or so, and proceeded

3

nonchalant on its way. But now even a puppy requires a post-mortem: such is the force of public opinion aroused. Two policemen appear in the distance.

"A street accident" is now in being, and a crowd gathers with calm joy and stares, passive and determined. The puppy offers no sign whatever; just lies in the road. Then a boy, destined probably to a great future by reason of his singular faculty of initiative, goes to the puppy and carries him by the scruff of the neck, to the shelter of the gutter. Relinquished by the boy, the lithe puppy falls into an easy horizontal attitude, and seems bent upon repose. The boy lifts the puppy's head to examine it, and the head drops back wearily. The puppy is dead. No cry, no blood, no disfigurement! Even no perceptible jolt of the wheel as it climbed over the obstacle of the puppy's body! A wonderfully clean and perfect accident!

The increasing crowd stares with beatific placidity. People emerge impatiently from the bowels of the throbbing motor-bus and slip down from its back, and either join the crowd or vanish. The two policemen and the crew of the motor-bus have met now in parley. The conductor and the driver have an air at once nervous and resigned; their gestures are quick and vivacious. The policemen, on the other hand, indicate by their slow and huge movements that eternity is theirs. And they could not be more sure of the conductor and the driver if they had them manacled and leashed. The conductor and the driver admit the absolute dominion of the elephantine policemen; they admit that before the simple will of the policemen, inconvenience, lost minutes, shortened leisure, docked wages, count as less than naught. And the policemen are carelessly sublime, well knowing that magistrates, jails, and the very Home Secretary on his throne—yes, and a whole system of conspiracy and perjury and brutality—are at their beck in case of need. And yet occasionally in the demeanour of the policemen towards the conductor and the driver there is a silent message that says: "After all, we, too, are working men like you, over-worked and under-paid and bursting with grievances in the service of the piti-less and dishonest public. We, too, have wives and children and privations and frightful apprehensions. We, too, have to struggle desperately. Only the awful magic of these garments and of the garter which we wear on our wrists sets an abyss between us and you." And the conductor writes and one of the policemen writes, and they keep on writing, while the traffic makes beautiful curves to avoid them.

The still increasing crowd continues to stare in the pure blankness of pleasure. A close-shaved, well-dressed, middle-aged man, with a copy of *The Sportsman* in his podgy hand, who has descended from the motor-bus, starts stamping his feet. "I was knocked down by a taxi last year," he says fiercely. "But nobody took no notice of *that*! Are they going to stop here all the blank morning for a blank tyke?" And for all his respectable appearance, his features become debased, and he emits a jet of disgusting profanity and brings most of the Trinity into the thunderous assertion that he has paid his fare. Then a man passes wheeling a muck-cart. And he stops and talks a long time with the other uniforms, because he, too, wears vestiges of a uniform. And the crowd never moves nor ceases to stare. Then the new arrival stoops and picks up the unclaimed, masterless puppy, and flings it, all soft and yielding, into the horrid mess of the cart, and passes on. And only that which is immortal and divine of the puppy remains behind, floating perhaps like an invisible vapour over the scene of the tragedy.

The crowd is tireless, all eyes. The four principals still converse and write. Nobody in the crowd comprehends what they are about. At length the driver separates himself, but is drawn back, and a new parley is commenced. But everything ends. The policemen turn on their immense heels. The driver and conductor race towards the motor-bus. The bell rings, the motor-bus, quite empty, disappears snorting round the corner into Walham Green. The crowd is now lessening. But it separates with reluctance, many of its members continuing to stare with intense absorption at the place where the puppy lay or the place where the policemen stood. An appreciable interval elapses before the "street accident" has entirely ceased to exist as a phenomenon.

The members of the crowd follow their noses, and during the course of the day remark to acquaintances: "Saw a dog run over by a motor-bus in the Fulham Road this morning! Killed dead!"

And that is all they do remark. That is all they have witnessed. They will not, and could not, give intelligible and interesting particulars of the affair (unless it were as to the breed of the dog or the number of the bus-service). They have watched a dog run over. They analyse neither their sensations nor the phenomenon. They have witnessed it whole, as a bad writer uses a *cliché*. They have observed—that is to say, they have really seen—nothing.

II

It will be well for us not to assume an attitude of condescension towards the crowd. Because in the matter of looking without seeing we are all about equal. We all go to and fro in a state of the observing faculties which somewhat resembles coma. We are all content to look and not see.

And if and when, having comprehended that the *rôle* of observer is not passive but active, we determine by an effort to rouse ourselves from the coma and really to see the spectacle of the world (a spectacle surpassing circuses and even street accidents in sustained dramatic interest), we shall discover, slowly in the course of time, that the act of seeing, which seems so easy, is not so easy as it seems. Let a man resolve: "I will keep my eyes open on the way to the office of a morning," and the probability is that for many mornings he will see naught that is not trivial, and that his system of perspective will be absurdly distorted. The unusual, the unaccustomed, will infallibly attract him, to the exclusion of what is fundamental and universal. Travel makes observers of us all, but the things which as travellers we observe generally show how unskilled we are in the new activity.

A man went to Paris for the first time, and observed right off that the carriages of suburban trains had seats on the roof like a tramcar. He was so thrilled by the remarkable discovery that he observed almost nothing else. This enormous fact occupied the whole foreground of his perspective. He returned home and announced that Paris was a place where people rode on the tops of trains. A French woman came to London for the first time—and no English person would ever guess the phenomenon which vanquished all others in her mind on the opening day. She saw a cat walking across a street.

The vision excited her. For in Paris cats do not roam in thoroughfares, because there are practically no houses with gardens or
"areas"; the flat system is unfavourable to the enlargement of cats.
I remember once, in the days when observation had first presented
itself to me as a beautiful pastime, getting up very early and making
the circuit of inner London before summer dawn in quest of interesting material. And the one note I gathered was that the ground
in front of the all-night coffee-stalls was white with egg-shells!
What I needed then was an operation for cataract. I also remember
taking a man to the opera who had never seen an opera. The work
was *Lohengrin*. When we came out he said: "That swan's neck was
rather stiff." And it was all he did say. We went and had a drink.
He was not mistaken. His observation was most just; but his perspective was that of those literary critics who give ten lines to point-
ing out three slips of syntax, and three lines to an ungrammatical
admission that the novel under survey is not wholly tedious.

But a man may acquire the ability to observe even a large number
of facts, and still remain in the infantile stage of observation. I
have read, in some work of literary criticism, that Dickens could
walk up one side of a long, busy street and down the other, and then
tell you in their order the names on all the shop-signs; the fact was
alleged as an illustration of his great powers of observation. Dickens
was a great observer, but he would assuredly have been a still
greater observer had he been a little less pre-occupied with trivial
and unco-ordinated details. Good observation consists not in multi-
plicity of detail, but in co-ordination of detail according to a true
perspective of relative importance, so that a finally just general
impression may be reached in the shortest possible time. The
skilled observer is he who does not have to change his mind. One
has only to compare one's present adjusted impression of an intimate
friend with one's first impression of him to perceive the astounding
inadequacy of one's powers of observation. The man as one has
learnt to see him is simply not the same man who walked into one's
drawing-room on the day of introduction.

There are, by the way, three sorts of created beings who are
sentimentally supposed to be able to judge individuals at the first
glance: women, children, and dogs. By virtue of a mystic gift with

which rumour credits them, they are never mistaken. It is merely not true. Women are constantly quite wrong in the estimates based on their "feminine instinct"; they sometimes even admit it; and the matrimonial courts prove it *passim*. Children are more often wrong than women. And as for dogs, it is notorious that they are for ever being taken in by plausible scoundrels; the perspective of dogs is grotesque. Not seldom have I grimly watched the gradual disillusion of deceived dogs. Nevertheless, the sentimental legend of the infallibility of women, children, and dogs, will persist in Anglo-Saxon countries.

<h1 style="text-align:center">III</h1>

One is curious about one's fellow-creatures: therefore one watches them. And generally the more intelligent one is, the more curious one is, and the more one observes. The mere satisfaction of this curiosity is in itself a worthy end, and would alone justify the business of systematised observation. But the aim of observation may, and should, be expressed in terms more grandiose. Human curiosity counts among the highest social virtues (as indifference counts among the basest defects), because it leads to the disclosure of the causes of character and temperament and thereby to a better understanding of the springs of human conduct. Observation is not practised directly with this high end in view (save by prigs and other futile souls); nevertheless it is a moral act and must inevitably promote kindliness—whether we like it or not. It also sharpens the sense of beauty. An ugly deed—such as a deed of cruelty— takes on artistic beauty when its origin and hence its fitness in the general scheme begin to be comprehended. In the perspective of history we can derive an aesthetic pleasure from the tranquil scrutiny of all kinds of conduct—as well, for example, of a Renaissance Pope as of a Savonarola. Observation endows our day and our street with the romantic charm of history, and stimulates charity —not the charity which signs cheques, but the more precious charity which puts itself to the trouble of understanding. The one condition is that the observer must never lose sight of the fact that what he is trying to see is life, is the woman next door, is the man in the train—

and not a concourse of abstractions. To appreciate all this is the first inspiring preliminary to sound observation.

IV

The second preliminary is to realise that all physical phenomena are inter-related, that there is nothing which does not bear on everything else. The whole spectacular and sensual show—what the eye sees, the ear hears, the nose scents, the tongue tastes and the skin touches—is a cause or an effect of human conduct. Naught can be ruled out as negligible, as not forming part of the equation. Hence he who would beyond all others see life for himself—I naturally mean the novelist and playwright—ought to embrace all phenomena in his curiosity. Being finite, he cannot. Of course he cannot! But he can, by obtaining a broad notion of the whole, determine with some accuracy the position and relative importance of the particular series of phenomena to which his instinct draws him. If he does not thus envisage the immense background of his special interests, he will lose the most precious feeling for interplay and proportion without which all specialism becomes distorted and positively darkened.

Now, the main factor in life on this planet is the planet itself. Any logically conceived survey of existence must begin with geographical and climatic phenomena. This is surely obvious. If you say that you are not interested in meteorology or the configurations of the earth, I say that you deceive yourself. You are. For an east wind may upset your liver and cause you to insult your wife. Beyond question the most important fact about, for example, Great Britain is that it is an island. We sail amid the Hebrides, and then talk of the fine qualities and the distressing limitations of those islanders; it ought to occur to us English that we are talking of ourselves in little. In moments of journalistic vainglory we are apt to refer to the "sturdy island race," meaning us. But that we are insular in the full significance of the horrid word is certain. Why not? A genuine observation of the supreme phenomenon that Great Britain is surrounded by water—an effort to keep it always at the back of the consciousness—will help to explain all the minor phenomena of British existence. Geographical knowledge is the mother of discernment, for the varying physical characteristics of the earth are the sole direct terrestrial influence determining the evolution of original vital energy.

All other influences are secondary, and have been effects of character and temperament before becoming causes. Perhaps the greatest of them are roads and architecture. Nothing could be more English than English roads, or more French than French roads. Enter England from France, let us say through the gate of Folkestone, and the architectural illustration which greets you (if you can look and see) is absolutely dramatic in its spectacular force. You say that there is no architecture in Folkestone. But Folkestone, like other towns, is just as full of architecture as a wood is full of trees. As the train winds on its causeway over the sloping town you perceive below you thousands of squat little homes, neat, tended, respectable, comfortable, prim, at once unostentatious and conceited. Each a separate, clearly-defined entity! Each saying to the others: "Don't look over my wall, and I won't look over yours!" Each with a ferocious jealousy bent on guarding its own individuality! Each a stronghold—an island! And all careless of the general effect, but making a very impressive general effect. The English race is below you. Your own son is below you insisting on the inviolability of his own den of a bedroom! . . . And contrast all that with the immense communistic and splendid façades of a French town, and work out the implications. If you really intend to see life you cannot afford to be blind to such thrilling phenomena.

Yet an inexperienced, unguided curiosity would be capable of walking through a French street and through an English street, and noting chiefly that whereas English lamp-posts spring from the kerb, French lamp-posts cling to the side of the house! Not that that detail is not worth noting. It is—in its place. French lamp-posts are part of what we call the "interesting character" of a French street. We say of a French street that it is "full of character." As if an English street was not! Such is blindness—to be cured by travel and the exercise of the logical faculty, most properly termed common sense. If one is struck by the magnificence of the great towns of the Continent, one should ratiocinate, and conclude that a major characteristic of the great towns of England is their shabby and

higgledy-piggledy slovenliness. It is so. But there are people who
have lived fifty years in Manchester, Leeds, Hull and Hanley without
noticing it. The English idiosyncrasy is in that awful external
slovenliness too, causing it, and being caused by it. Every street is a
mirror, an illustration, an exposition, an explanation, of the human
beings who live in it. Nothing in it is to be neglected. Everything in it
is valuable, if the perspective is maintained. Nevertheless, in the
narrow individualistic novels of English literature—and in some
of the best—you will find a domestic organism described as though
it existed in a vacuum, or in the Sahara, or between Heaven and
earth; as though it reacted on nothing and was reacted on by nothing; and as though it could be adequately rendered without
reference to anything exterior to itself. How can such novels satisfy
a reader who has acquired or wants to acquire the faculty of seeing
life?

V

The net result of the interplay of instincts and influences which
determine the existence of a community is shown in the general
expression on the faces of the people. This is an index which cannot
lie and cannot be gainsaid. It is fairly easy, and extremely interesting,
to decipher. It is so open, shameless, and universal, that not to look
at it is impossible. Yet the majority of persons fail to see it. We hear
of inquirers standing on London Bridge and counting the number of
motor-buses, foot-passengers, lorries, and white horses that pass over
the bridge in an hour. But we never hear of anybody counting the
number of faces happy or unhappy, honest or rascally, shrewd or
ingenuous, kind or cruel, that pass over the bridge. Perhaps the
public may be surprised to hear that the general expression on the
faces of Londoners of all ranks varies from the sad to the morose;
and that their general mien is one of haste and gloomy preoccupation.
Such a staring fact is paramount in sociological evidence. And the
observer of it would be justified in summoning Heaven, the legis-
lature, the county council, the churches, and the ruling classes,
and saying to them: "Glance at these faces, and don't boast too
much about what you have accomplished. The climate and the
industrial system have so far triumphed over you all."

VI

When we come to the observing of the individual—to which all human observing does finally come if there is any right reason in it—the aforesaid general considerations ought to be ever present in the hinterland of the consciousness, aiding and influencing, perhaps vaguely, perhaps almost imperceptibly, the formation of judgments. If they do nothing else, they will at any rate accustom the observer to the highly important idea of the correlation of all phenomena. Especially in England a haphazard particularity is the chief vitiating element in the operations of the mind.

In estimating the individual we are apt not only to forget his environment, but—really strange!—to ignore much of the evidence visible in the individual himself. The inexperienced and ardent observer, will, for example, be astonishingly blind to everything in an individual except his face. Telling himself that the face must be the reflection of the soul, and that every thought and emotion leaves inevitably its mark there, he will concentrate on the face, singling it out as a phenomenon apart and self-complete. Were he a god and infallible, he could no doubt learn the whole truth from the face. But he is bound to fall into errors, and by limiting the field of vision he minimises the opportunity for correction. The face is, after all, quite a small part of the individual's physical organism. An Englishman will look at a woman's face and say she is a beautiful woman or a plain woman. But a woman may have a plain face, and yet by her form be entitled to be called beautiful, and (perhaps) *vice versa*. It is true that the face is the reflection of the soul. It is equally true that the carriage and gestures are the reflection of the soul. Had one eyes, the tying of a bootlace is the reflection of the soul. One piece of evidence can be used to correct every other piece of evidence. A refined face may be refuted by clumsy finger-ends; the eyes may contradict the voice; the gait may nullify the smile. None of the phenomena which every individual carelessly and brazenly displays in every motor-bus terrorising the streets of London is meaningless or negligible.

Again, in observing we are generally guilty of that particularity which results from sluggishness of the imagination. We may see the phenomenon at the moment of looking at it, but we particularise in that moment, making no effort to conceive what the phenomenon is likely to be at other moments.

For example, a male human creature wakes up in the morning and rises with reluctance. Being a big man, and existing with his wife and children in a very confined space, he has to adapt himself to his environment as he goes through the various functions incident to preparing for his day's work. He is just like you or me. He wants his breakfast, he very much wants to know where his boots are, and he has the usually sinister preoccupations about health and finance. Whatever the force of his egoism, he must more or less harmonise his individuality with those of his wife and children. Having laid down the law, or accepted it, he sets forth to his daily duties, just a fraction of a minute late. He arrives at his office, resumes life with his colleagues sympathetic and antipathetic, and then leaves the office for an expedition extending over several hours. In the course of his expedition he encounters the corpse of a young dog run down by a motor-bus. Now you also have encountered that corpse and are gazing at it; and what do you say to yourself when he comes along? You say: "Oh! Here's a policeman." For he happens to be a policeman. You stare at him, and you never see anything but a policeman—an indivisible phenomenon of blue cloth, steel buttons, flesh resembling a face, and a helmet; "a stalwart guardian of the law"; to you little more human than an algebraic symbol: in a word—a policeman.

Only, that word actually conveys almost nothing to you of the reality which it stands for. You are satisfied with it as you are satisfied with the description of a disease. A friend tells you his eyesight is failing. You sympathise. "What is it?" you ask. "Glaucoma." "Ah! Glaucoma!" You don't know what glaucoma is. You are no wiser than you were before. But you are content. A name has contented you. Similarly the name of policeman contents you, seems to absolve you from further curiosity as to the phenomenon. You have looked at tens of thousands of policemen, and perhaps never seen the hundredth part of the reality of a single one. Your imagination has not truly worked on the phenomenon.

There may be some excuse for not seeing the reality of a policeman, because a uniform is always a thick veil. But you—I mean you,

I, any of us—are oddly dim-sighted also in regard to the civil population. For instance, we get into the empty motor-bus as it leaves the scene of the street accident, and examine the men and women who gradually fill it. Probably we vaunt ourselves as being interested in the spectacle of life. All the persons in the motor-bus have come out of a past and are moving towards a future. But how often does our imagination put itself to the trouble of realising this? We may observe with some care, yet owing to a fundamental defect of attitude we are observing not the human individuals, but a peculiar race of beings who pass their whole lives in motor-buses, who exist only in motor-buses and only in the present! No human phenomenon is adequately seen until the imagination has placed it back into its past and forward into its future. And this is the final process of observation of the individual.

VII

Seeing life, as I have tried to show, does not begin with seeing the individual. Neither does it end with seeing the individual. Particular and unsystematized observation cannot go on for ever, aimless, formless. Just as individuals are singled out from systems, in the earlier process of observation, so in the later processes individuals will be formed into new groups, which formation will depend upon the personal bent of the observer. The predominant interests of the observer will ultimately direct his observing activities to their own advantage. If he is excited by the phenomena of organisation—as I happen to be—he will see individuals in new groups that are the result of organisation, and will insist on the variations from type due to that grouping. If he is convinced—as numbers of people appear to be—that society is just now in an extremely critical pass, and that if something mysterious is not forthwith done the structure of it will crumble to atoms—he will see mankind grouped under the different reforms which, according to him, the human dilemma demands. And so on! These tendencies, while they should not be resisted too much, since they give character to observation and redeem it from the frigidity of mechanics, should be resisted to a certain extent. For, whatever they may be, they favour the growth of sentimentality, the protean and indescribably subtle enemy of common sense.

PART II

WRITING NOVELS

I

The novelist is he who, having seen life, and being so excited by it that he absolutely must transmit the vision to others, chooses narrative fiction as the liveliest vehicle for the relief of his feelings. He is like other artists—he cannot remain silent; he cannot keep himself to himself, he is bursting with the news; he is bound to tell— the affair is too thrilling! Only he differs from most artists in this— that what most chiefly strikes him is the indefinable humanness of human nature, the large general manner of existing. Of course, he is the result of evolution from the primitive. And you can see primitive novelists to this day transmitting to acquaintances their fragmentary and crude visions of life in the café or the club, or on the kerbstone. They belong to the lowest circle of artists; but they are artists; and the form that they adopt is the very basis of the novel. By innumerable entertaining steps from them you may ascend to the major artist whose vision of life, inclusive, intricate and intense, requires for its due transmission the great traditional form of the novel as perfected by the masters of a long age which has temporarily set the novel higher than any other art-form.

I would not argue that the novel should be counted supreme among the great traditional forms of art. Even if there is a greatest form, I do not much care which it is. I have in turn been convinced that Chartres Cathedral, certain Greek sculpture, Mozart's *Don Juan*, and the juggling of Paul Cinquevalli[1] was the finest thing in the world—not to mention the achievements of Shakespeare or Nijinsky. But there is something to be said for the real pre-eminence of prose fiction as a literary form. (Even the modern epic has learnt almost all it knows from prose-fiction.) The novel has, and always will have, the advantage of its comprehensive bigness. St Peter's at Rome is a trifle compared with Tolstoi's *War and*

1. Paul Cinquevalli (1859–1918), a famous juggler and music hall star. Bennett saw him in Paris at the Folies-Bergères in 1897.

Peace; and it is as certain as anything can be that, during the present geological epoch at any rate, no epic half as long as *War and Peace* will ever be read, even if written.

Notoriously the novelist (including the playwright, who is a sub-novelist) has been taking the bread out of the mouths of other artists. In the matter of poaching, the painter has done a lot, and the composer has done more, but what the painter and the composer have done is as naught compared to the grasping deeds of the novelist. And whereas the painter and the composer have got into difficulties with their audacious schemes, the novelist has poached, colonised, and annexed with a success that is not denied. There is scarcely any aspect of the interestingness of life which is not now rendered in prose fiction—from landscape-painting to sociology—and none which might not be. Unnecessary to go back to the ante-Scott age in order to perceive how the novel has aggrandised itself! It has conquered enormous territories even since *Germinal*. Within the last fifteen years it has gained. Were it to adopt the hue of the British Empire, the entire map of the universe would soon be coloured red. Wherever it ought to stand in the hierarchy of forms, it has, actually, no rival at the present day as a means for transmitting the impassioned vision of life. It is, and will be for some time to come, the form to which the artist with the most inclusive vision instinctively turns, because it is the most inclusive form, and the most adaptable. Indeed, before we are much older, if its present rate of progress continues, it will have reoccupied the dazzling position to which the mighty Balzac lifted it, and in which he left it in 1850. So much, by the way, for the rank of the novel.

II

In considering the equipment of the novelist there are two attributes which may always be taken for granted. The first is the sense of beauty—indispensable to the creative artist. Every creative artist has it, in his degree. He is an artist because he has it. An artist works under the stress of instinct. No man's instinct can draw him towards material which repels him—the fact is obvious. Obviously, whatever kind of life the novelist writes about, he has been charmed and seduced by it, he is under its spell—that is, he has seen beauty in it. He could have no other reason for writing about it. He may see a strange sort of beauty; he may—indeed he does—see a sort of beauty that nobody has quite seen before; he may see a sort of beauty that none save a few odd spirits ever will or can be made to see. But he does see beauty. To say, after reading a novel which has held you, that the author has no sense of beauty, is inept. (The mere fact that you turned over his pages with interest is an answer to the criticism—a criticism, indeed, which is not more sagacious than that of the reviewer who remarks: "Mr Blank has produced a thrilling novel, but unfortunately he cannot write." Mr Blank has written; and he could, anyhow, write enough to thrill the reviewer.) All that a wise person will assert is that an artist's sense of beauty is different for the time being from his own.

The reproach of the lack of a sense of beauty has been brought against nearly all original novelists; it is seldom brought against a mediocre novelist. Even in the extreme cases it is untrue; perhaps it is most untrue in the extreme cases. I do not mean such a case as that of Zola, who never went to extremes. I mean, for example, Gissing, a real extremist, who, it is now admitted, saw a clear and undiscovered beauty in forms of existence which hitherto no artist had deigned seriously to examine. And I mean Huysmans, a case even more extreme. Possibly no works have been more abused for ugliness than Huysmans' novel *En Ménage* and his book of descriptive essays *De Tout*. Both reproduce with exasperation what is generally regarded as the sordid ugliness of commonplace daily life. Yet both exercise a unique charm (and will surely be read when *La Cathédrale* is forgotten). And it is inconceivable that Huysmans—whatever he may have said—was not ravished by the secret beauty of his subjects and did not exult in it.

The other attribute which may be taken for granted in the novelist, as in every artist, is passionate intensity of vision. Unless the vision is passionately intense the artist will not be moved to transmit it. He will not be inconvenienced by it; and the motive to pass it on will thus not exist. Every fine emotion produced in the reader has been, and must have been, previously felt by the writer, but in a far greater degree. It is not altogether uncommon to hear a reader whose heart has been desolated by the poignancy of a narrative complain that the writer is unemotional. Such people have no notion at all of the processes of artistic creation.

III

A sense of beauty and a passionate intensity of vision being taken for granted, the one other important attribute in the equipment of the novelist—the attribute which indeed by itself practically suffices, and whose absence renders futile all the rest—is fineness of mind. A great novelist must have great qualities of mind. His mind must be sympathetic, quickly responsive, courageous, honest, humorous, tender, just, merciful. He must be able to conceive the ideal without losing sight of the fact that it is a human world we live in. Above all, his mind must be permeated and controlled by common sense. His mind, in a word, must have the quality of being noble. Unless his mind is all this, he will never, at the ultimate bar, be reckoned supreme. That which counts, on every page, and all the time, is the very texture of his mind—the glass through which he sees things. Every other attribute is secondary, and is dispensable. Fielding lives unequalled among English novelists because the broad nobility of his mind is unequalled. He is read with unreserved enthusiasm because the reader feels himself at each paragraph to be in close contact with a glorious personality. And no advance in technique among later novelists can possibly imperil his position. He will take second place when a more noble mind, a more superb common sense, happens to wield the narrative pen, and not before. What undermines the renown of Dickens is the growing conviction that the texture of his mind was common, that he fell short in courageous facing of the truth, and in certain delicacies of perception. As much may be said of Thackeray, whose mind was somewhat incomplete for so grandiose a figure, and not free from defects which are inimical to immortality.

It is a hard saying for me, and full of danger in any country whose artists have shown contempt for form, yet I am obliged to say that, as the years pass, I attach less and less importance to good technique in fiction. I love it, and I have fought for a better recognition of its importance in England, but I now have to admit that the modern history of fiction will not support me. With the single exception of Turgenev, the great novelists of the world, according to my own standards, have either ignored technique or have failed to understand it. What an error to suppose that the finest foreign novels show a better sense of form than the finest English novels! Balzac was a prodigious blunderer. He could not even manage a sentence, not to speak of the general form of a book. And as for a greater than Balzac—Stendhal—his scorn of technique was notorious. Stendhal was capable of writing, in a masterpiece: "By the way I ought to have told you earlier that the Duchess——!" And as for a greater than either Balzac or Stendhal—Dostoievsky— what a hasty, amorphous lump of gold is the sublime, the unapproachable *Brothers Karamazov*! Any tutor in a college for teaching the whole art of fiction by post in twelve lessons could show where Dostoievsky was clumsy and careless. What would have been Flaubert's detailed criticism of that book? And what would it matter? And, to take a minor example, witness the comically amateurish technique of the late "Mark Rutherford" [2]—nevertheless a novelist whom one can deeply admire.

And when we come to consider the great technicians, Guy de Maupassant and Flaubert, can we say that their technique will save them, or atone in the slightest degree for the defects of their minds? Exceptional artists both, they are both now inevitably falling in esteem to the level of the second-rate. Human nature being what it is, and de Maupassant being tinged with eroticism, his work is sure to be read with interest by mankind; but he is already classed. Nobody, now, despite all his brilliant excellences, would dream of putting de Maupassant with the first magnitudes. And the declension of Flaubert is one of the outstanding phenomena of modern French criticism. It is being discovered that Flaubert's mind was not quite noble enough—that, indeed, it was a cruel mind, and a little anaemic. *Bouvard et Pécuchet* was the crowning proof that Flaubert had lost sight of the humanness of the world,

2. "Mark Rutherford," pen name of William Hale White (1831–1913), author of novels about provincial nonconformity in nineteenth-century England. Bennett admired White's style—he described it in his journal as "almost the finest modern prose"—but found his constructions "extraordinarily amateurish." See *The Journal of Arnold Bennett* (New York, 1933), pp. 500 and 750.

and suffered from the delusion that he had been born on the wrong planet. The glitter of his technique is dulled now, and fools even count it against him. In regard to one section of human activity only did his mind seem noble—namely, literary technique. His correspondence, written, of course, currently, was largely occupied with the question of literary technique, and his correspondence stands forth to-day as his best work—a marvellous fount of inspiration to his fellow artists. So I return to the point that the novelist's one important attribute (beyond the two postulated) is fundamental quality of mind. It and nothing else makes both the friends and the enemies which he has; while the influence of technique is slight and transitory. And I repeat that it is a hard saying.

I begin to think that great writers of fiction are by the mysterious nature of their art ordained to be "amateurs." There may be something of the amateur in all great artists. I do not know why it should be so, unless because, in the exuberance of their sense of power, they are impatient of the exactitudes of systematic study and the mere bother of repeated attempts to arrive at a minor perfection. Assuredly no great artist was ever a profound scholar. The great artist has other ends to achieve. And every artist, major and minor, is aware in his conscience that art is full of artifice, and that the desire to proceed rapidly with the affair of creation, and an excusable dislike of re-creating anything twice, thrice, or ten times over—unnatural task!—are responsible for much of that artifice. We can all point in excuse to Shakespeare, who was a very rough-and-ready person, and whose methods would shock Flaubert. Indeed, the amateurishness of Shakespeare has been mightily exposed of late years. But nobody seems to care. If Flaubert had been a greater artist he might have been more of an amateur.

IV

Of this poor neglected matter of technique the more important branch is design—or construction. It is the branch of the art—of all arts—which comes next after "inspiration"—a capacious word meant to include everything that the artist must be born with and cannot acquire. The less important branch of technique—far less important—may be described as an ornamentation.

There are very few rules of design in the novel; but the few are capital. Nevertheless, great novelists have often flouted or ignored them—to the detriment of their work. In my opinion the first rule is that the interest must be centralised; it must not be diffused equally over various parts of the canvas. To compare one art with another may be perilous, but really the convenience of describing a novel as a canvas is extreme. In a well-designed picture the eye is drawn chiefly to one particular spot. If the eye is drawn with equal force to several different spots, then we reproach the painter for having "scattered" the interest of the picture. Similarly with the novel. A novel must have one, two, or three figures that easily overtop the rest. These figures must be in the fore-ground, and the rest in the middle-distance or in the back-ground.

Moreover, these figures—whether they are saints or sinners— must somehow be presented more sympathetically than the others. If this cannot be done, then the inspiration is at fault. The single motive that should govern the choice of a principal figure is the motive of love for that figure. What else could the motive be? The race of heroes is essential to art. But what makes a hero is less the deeds of the figure chosen than the understanding sympathy of the artist with the figure. To say that the hero has disappeared from modern fiction is absurd. All that has happened is that the characteristics of the hero have changed, naturally, with the times. When Thackeray wrote "a novel without a hero," he wrote a novel with a first-class hero, and nobody knew this better than Thackeray. What he meant was that he was sick of the conventional bundle of characteristics styled a hero in his day, and that he had changed the type. Since then we have grown sick of Dobbins, and the type has been changed again more than once. The fateful hour will arrive when we shall be sick of Ponderevos.

The temptation of the great novelist, overflowing with creative force, is to scatter the interest. In both his major works Tolstoi found the temptation too strong for him. *Anna Karenina* is not one novel, but two, and suffers accordingly. As for *War and Peace*, the reader wanders about in it as in a forest, for days, lost, deprived of a sense of direction, and with no vestige of a sign-post; at intervals encountering mysterious faces whose identity he in vain tries to recall. On a much smaller scale Meredith committed the same error. Who could assert positively which of the sisters Fleming is the heroine of *Rhoda Fleming*? For nearly two hundred pages at a stretch Rhoda scarcely appears. And more than once the author seems quite to forget that the little knave Algernon is not, after all, the hero of the story.

The second rule of design—perhaps in the main merely a different view of the first—is that the interest must be maintained. It may increase, but it must never diminish. Here is that special aspect of design which we call construction, or plot. By interest I mean the interest of the story itself, and not the interest of the continual play of the author's mind on his material. In proportion as the interest of the story is maintained, the plot is a good one. In so far as it lapses, the plot is a bad one. There is no other criterion of good construction. Readers of a certain class are apt to call good the plot of that story in which "you can't tell what is going to happen next." But in some of the most tedious novels ever written you can't tell what is going to happen next—and you don't care a fig what is going to happen next. It would be nearer the mark to say that the plot is good when "you want to make sure what will happen next"! Good plots set you anxiously guessing what will happen next.

When the reader is misled—not intentionally in order to get an effect, but clumsily through amateurishness—then the construction is bad. This calamity does not often occur in fine novels, but in really good work another calamity does occur with far too much frequency—namely, the tantalising of the reader at a critical point by a purposeless, wanton, or negligent shifting of the interest from the major to the minor theme. A sad example of this infantile trick is to be found in the thirty-first chapter of *Rhoda Fleming*, wherein, well knowing that the reader is tingling for the interview between Roberts and Rhoda, the author, unable to control his own capricious and monstrous fancy for Algernon, devotes some sixteen pages to the young knave's vagaries with an illicit thousand pounds. That the sixteen pages are excessively brilliant does not a bit excuse the wilful unshapeliness of the book's design.

The Edwardian and Georgian out-and-out defenders of Victorian fiction are wont to argue that though the event-plot in sundry great novels may be loose and casual (that is to say, simply careless), the "idea-plot" is usually close-knit, coherent, and logical. I have never yet been able to comprehend how an idea-plot can exist independently of an event-plot (any more than how spirit can be conceived apart from matter); but assuming that an idea-plot can exist independently, and that the mysterious thing is superior in form to its coarse fellow, the event-plot (which I positively do not believe), —even then I still hold that sloppiness in the fabrication of the event-plot amounts to a grave iniquity. In this connection I have in mind, among English novels, chiefly the work of "Mark Ruther-ford," George Eliot, the Brontës, and Anthony Trollope.

The one other important rule in construction is that the plot should be kept throughout within the same convention. All plots— even those of our most sacred naturalistic contemporaries—are and must be a conventionalisation of life. We imagine we have arrived at a convention which is nearer to the truth of life than that of our forerunners. Perhaps we have—but so little nearer that the difference is scarcely appreciable! An aviator at midday may be nearer the sun than the motorist, but regarded as a portion of the entire journey to the sun, the aviator's progress upward can safely be ignored. No novelist has yet, or ever will, come within a hundred million miles of life itself. It is impossible for us to see how far we still are from life. The defects of a new convention disclose themselves late in its career. The notion that "naturalists" have at last lighted on a final formula which ensures truth to life is ridiculous. "Naturalist" is merely an epithet expressing self-satisfaction.

Similarly, the habit of deriding as "conventional" plots con-structed in an earlier convention, is ridiculous. Under this head Dickens in particular has been assaulted; I have assaulted him my-self. But within their convention, the plots of Dickens are excellent, and show little trace of amateurishness, and every sign of skilled accomplishment. And Dickens did not blunder out of one convention into another, as certain of ourselves undeniably do. Thomas Hardy, too, has been arraigned for the conventionalism of his plots. And yet Hardy happens to be one of the rare novelists who have evolved a new convention to suit their idiosyncrasy. Hardy's idiosyncrasy is a deep conviction of the whimsicality of the divine power, and again and again he has expressed this with a virtuosity of skill which ought to have put humility into the hearts of naturalists, but which has not done so. The plot of *The Woodlanders* is one of the most exquisite examples of subtle symbolic illustration of an idea that a writer of fiction ever achieved; it makes the symbolism of Ibsen seem crude. You may say that *The Woodlanders* could not have occurred in real life. No novel could have occurred in real life. The balance of probabilities is incalculably against any novel whatsoever; and rightly so. A convention is essential, and the duty of a novelist is to be true within his chosen convention, and not further. Most novelists still fail in this duty. Is there any reason, indeed, why we should be so vastly cleverer than our fathers? I do not think we are.

V

Leaving the seductive minor question of ornamentation, I come lastly to the question of getting the semblance of life on to the page before the eyes of the reader—the daily and hourly texture of existence. The novelist has selected his subject; he has drenched himself in his subject. He has laid down the main features of the design. The living embryo is there, and waits to be developed into full organic structure. Whence and how does the novelist obtain the vital tissue which must be his material? The answer is that he digs it out of himself. First-class fiction is, and must be, in the final resort autobiographical. What else should it be? The novelist may take notes of phenomena likely to be of use to him. And he may acquire the skill to invent very apposite illustrative incident. But he cannot invent psychology. Upon occasion some human being may entrust him with confidences extremely precious for his craft. But such windfalls are so rare as to be negligible. From outward symptoms he can guess something of the psychology of others. He can use a real person as the unrecognisable but helpful basis for each of his characters. . . . And all that is nothing. And all special research is nothing. When the real intimate work of creation has to be done—and it has to be done on every page—the novelist can only look within for effective aid. Almost solely by arranging and modifying what he has felt and seen, and scarcely at all by inventing, can he accomplish his end.

An inquiry into the career of any first-class novelist invariably reveals that his novels are full of autobiography. But, as a fact, every good novel contains far more autobiography than any inquiry could reveal. Episodes, moods, characters of autobiography can be detected and traced to their origin by critical acumen, but the intimate autobiography that runs through each page, vitalising it, may not be detected. In dealing with each character in each episode the novelist must for a thousand convincing details interrogate that part of his own individuality which corresponds to the particular character. The foundation of his equipment is universal sympathy. And the result of this (or the cause—I don't know which) is that in his own individuality there is something of everybody. If he is a born novelist he is safe in asking himself, when in doubt as to the behaviour of a given personage at a given point: "Now, what should *I* have done?" And incorporating the answer! And this in practice is what he does. Good fiction is autobiography dressed in the colours of all mankind.

The necessarily autobiographical nature of fiction accounts for the creative repetition to which all novelists—including the most powerful—are reduced. They monotonously yield again and again to the strongest predilections of their own individuality. Again and again they think they are creating, by observation, a quite new character—and lo! when finished it is an old one—autobiographical psychology has triumphed! A novelist may achieve a reputation with only a single type, created and re-created in varying forms. And the very greatest do not contrive to create more than half a score genuine separate types. In Cerfberr and Christophe's biographical dictionary of the characters of Balzac, a tall volume of six hundred pages, there are some two thousand entries of different individuals, but probably fewer than a dozen genuine distinctive types. No creative artist ever repeated himself more brazenly or more successfully than Balzac. His miser, his vicious delightful actress, his vicious delightful duchess, his young man-about-town, his virtuous young man, his heroic weeping virgin, his angelic wife and mother, his poor relation, and his faithful stupid servant—each is continually popping up with a new name in the Human Comedy. A similar phenomenon, as Frank Harris has proved, is to be observed in Shakespeare.[3] Hamlet of Denmark was only the last and greatest of a series of Shakespearean Hamlets.

It may be asked, finally: What of the actual process of handling the raw material dug out of existence and of the artist's self—the process of transmuting life into art? There is no process. That is to say, there is no conscious process. The convention chosen by an artist is his illusion of the truth. Consciously, the artist only omits, selects, arranges. But let him beware of being false to his illusion, for then the process becomes conscious, and bad. This is sentimentality, which is the seed of death in his work. Every artist is tempted to sentimentalise, or to be cynical—practically the same thing. And when he falls to the temptation, the reader whispers in his heart, be it only for one instant: "That is not true to life." And in turn the reader's illusion of reality is impaired. Readers are divided into two classes—the enemies and the friends of the artist. The former, a legion, admire for a fortnight or a year. They hate an uncompromising struggle for the truth. They positively like the artist to fall to temptation. If he falls, they exclaim, "How sweet!" The latter are capable of savouring the fine unpleasantness of the struggle for truth. And when they whisper in their hearts: "That is not true to life," they are ashamed for the artist. They are few, very few; but a vigorous clan. It is they who confer immortality.

PART III

WRITING PLAYS

I

There is an idea abroad, assiduously fostered as a rule by critics who happen to have written neither novels nor plays, that it is more difficult to write a play than a novel. I do not think so. I have written or collaborated in about twenty novels and about

---

3. Bennett was much impressed by Frank Harris's *The Man Shakespeare and His Tragic Life Story* (London: Frank Palmer, 1909). He reviewed the book admiringly in the *New Age* (October 21, 1909), and described it in his journal as "masterful and masterly."

twenty plays, and I am convinced that it is easier to write a play than a novel. Personally, I would sooner *write* two plays than one novel; less expenditure of nervous force and mere brains would be required for two plays than for one novel. (I emphasise the word "write," because if the whole weariness between the first conception and the first performance of a play is compared with the whole weariness between the first conception and the first publication of a novel, then the play has it. I would sooner get seventy-and-seven novels produced than one play. But my immediate object is to compare only writing with writing.) It seems to me that the sole persons entitled to judge of the comparative difficulty of writing plays and writing novels are those authors who have succeeded or failed equally well in both departments. And in this limited band I imagine that the differences of opinion on the point could not be marked. I would like to note in passing, for the support of my proposition, that whereas established novelists not infrequently venture into the theatre with audacity, established dramatists are very cautious indeed about quitting the theatre. An established dramatist usually takes good care to write plays and naught else; he will not affront the risks of coming out into the open; and therein his instinct is quite properly that of self-preservation. Of many established dramatists all over the world it may be affirmed that if they were so indiscreet as to publish a novel, the result would be a great shattering and a great awakening.

II

An enormous amount of vague reverential nonsense is talked about the technique of the stage, the assumption being that in difficulty it far surpasses any other literary technique, and that until it is acquired a respectable play cannot be written. One hears also that it can only be acquired behind the scenes. A famous actor-manager once kindly gave me the benefit of his experience, and what he said was that a dramatist who wished to learn his business must live behind the scenes—and study the works of Dion Boucicault![4] The truth is that no technique is so crude and so simple as

4. Dion Boucicault (1822–1890), Irish-born actor and dramatist, author of many popular light plays, comedies, and melodramas.

the technique of the stage, and that the proper place to learn it is not behind the scenes but in the pit. Managers, being the most conservative people on earth, except compositors, will honestly try to convince the naïve dramatist that effects can only be obtained in the precise way in which effects have always been obtained, and that this and that rule must not be broken on pain of outraging the public.

And indeed it is natural that managers should talk thus, seeing the low state of the drama, because in any art rules and reaction always flourish when creative energy is sick. The mandarins have ever said and will ever say that a technique which does not correspond with their own is no technique, but simple clumsiness. There are some seven situations in the customary drama, and a play which does not contain at least one of those situations in each act will be condemned as "undramatic," or "thin," or as being "all talk." It may contain half a hundred other situations, but for the mandarin a situation which is not one of the seven is not a situation. Similarly there are some dozen character types in the customary drama, and all original—that is, truthful—characterisation will be dismissed as a total absence of characterisation because it does not reproduce any of these dozen types. Thus every truly original play is bound to be indicted for bad technique. The author is bound to be told that what he has written may be marvellously clever, but that it is not a play. I remember the day—and it is not long ago—when even so experienced and sincere a critic as William Archer[5] used to argue that if the "intellectual" drama did not succeed with the general public, it was because its technique was not up to the level of the technique of the commercial drama! Perhaps he has changed his opinion since then. Heaven knows that the so-called "intellectual" drama is amateurish enough, but nearly all literary art is amateurish, and assuredly no intellectual drama could hope to compete in clumsiness with some of the most successful commercial plays of modern times. I tremble to think what the mandarins and William Archer would say to the technique of *Hamlet*, could it by some miracle be brought forward as a new piece by a Mr Shakespeare.

5. William Archer (1856–1924), dramatist and critic. He was one of the first English critics to admire and support the works of Ibsen, and was a leader in movements to establish a national theater and to end censorship of the stage.

They would probably recommend Mr Shakespeare to consider the ways of Sardou, Henri Bernstein, and Sir Herbert Tree,[6] and be wise. Most positively they would assert that *Hamlet* was not a play. And their pupils of the daily press would point out—what surely Mr Shakespeare ought to have perceived for himself—that the second, third, or fourth act might be cut wholesale without the slightest loss to the piece.

In the sense in which mandarins understand the word technique, there is no technique special to the stage except that which concerns the moving of solid human bodies to and fro, and the limitations of the human senses. The dramatist must not expect his audience to be able to see or hear two things at once, nor to be incapable of fatigue. And he must not expect his interpreters to stroll round or come on or go off in a satisfactory manner unless he provides them with satisfactory reasons for strolling round, coming on, or going off. Lastly, he must not expect his interpreters to achieve physical impossibilities. The dramatist who sends a pretty woman off in street attire and seeks to bring her on again in thirty seconds fully dressed for a court ball may fail in stage technique, but he has not proved that stage technique is tremendously difficult; he has proved something quite else.

III

One reason why a play is easier to write than a novel is that a play is shorter than a novel. On the average, one may say that it takes six plays to make the matter of a novel. Other things being equal, a short work of art presents fewer difficulties than a longer one. The contrary is held true by the majority, but then the majority, having never attempted to produce a long work of art, are unqualified to offer an opinion. It is said that the most difficult form of poetry is the sonnet. But the most difficult form of poetry is the epic. The proof that the sonnet is the most difficult form is alleged to be in the fewness of perfect sonnets. There are, however, far more perfect sonnets than perfect epics. A perfect sonnet may be a

6. Victorien Sardou (1831–1908) and Henri Bernstein (1876–1953), French dramatists known for their stage effects. Sir Herbert Beerbohm Tree (1853–1917), the most successful of the Edwardian actor-managers, was a master of extravagant staging.

heavenly accident. But such accidents can never happen to writers of epics. Some years ago we had an enormous palaver about the "art of the short story," which numerous persons who had omitted to write novels pronounced to be more difficult than the novel. But the fact remains that there are scores of perfect short stories, whereas it is doubtful whether anybody but Turgenev ever did write a perfect novel. A short form is easier to manipulate than a long form, because its construction is less complicated, because the balance of its proportions can be more easily corrected by means of a rapid survey, because it is lawful and even necessary in it to leave undone many things which are very hard to do, and because the emotional strain is less prolonged. The most difficult thing in all art is to maintain the imaginative tension unslackened throughout a considerable period.

Then, not only does a play contain less matter than a novel— it is further simplified by the fact that it contains fewer kinds of matter, and less subtle kinds of matter. There are numerous delicate and difficult affairs of craft that the dramatist need not think about at all. If he attempts to go beyond a certain very mild degree of subtlety, he is merely wasting his time. What passes for subtle on the stage would have a very obvious air in a novel, as some dramatists have unhappily discovered. Thus whole continents of danger may be shunned by the dramatist, and instead of being scorned for his cowardice he will be very rightly applauded for his artistic discretion. Fortunate predicament! Again, he need not—indeed, he must not—save in a primitive and hinting manner, concern himself with "atmosphere." He may roughly suggest one, but if he begins on the feat of "creating" an atmosphere (as it is called), the last suburban train will have departed before he has reached the crisis of the play. The last suburban train is the best friend of the dramatist, though the fellow seldom has the sense to see it. Further, he is saved all descriptive work. See a novelist harassing himself into his grave over the description of a landscape, a room, a gesture—while the dramatist grins. The dramatist may have to imagine a landscape, a room, or a gesture; but he has not got to write it—and it is the writing which hastens death. If a dramatist and a novelist set out to portray a clever woman, they are almost equally matched, because each has to make the creature say things and do things. But if they set out to portray a charming woman, the dramatist can recline in an easy chair and smoke while the novelist is ruining temper, digestion and eyesight, and spreading terror in his household by his moodiness and unapproachability. The electric light burns in the novelist's study at three a.m.,—the novelist is still endeavouring to convey by means of words the extraordinary fascination that his heroine could exercise over mankind by the mere act of walking into a room; and he never has really succeeded and never will. The dramatist writes curtly, "Enter Millicent." All are anxious to do the dramatist's job for him. Is the play being read at home—the reader eagerly and with brilliant success puts his imagination to work and completes a charming Millicent after his own secret desires. (Whereas he would coldly decline to add one touch to Millicent were she the heroine of a novel.) Is the play being performed on the stage—an experienced, conscientious, and perhaps lovely actress will strive her hardest to prove that the dramatist was right about Millicent's astounding fascination. And if she fails, nobody will blame the dramatist; the dramatist will receive naught but sympathy.

And there is still another region of superlative difficulty which is narrowly circumscribed for the spoilt dramatist: I mean the whole business of persuading the public that the improbable is probable. Every work of art is and must be crammed with improbabilities and artifice; and the greater portion of the artifice is employed in just this trickery of persuasion. Only, the public of the dramatist needs far less persuading than the public of the novelist. The novelist announces that Millicent accepted the hand of the wrong man, and in spite of all the novelist's corroborative and exegetical detail the insulted reader declines to credit the statement and condemns the incident as unconvincing. The dramatist decides that Millicent must accept the hand of the wrong man, and there she is on the stage in flesh and blood, veritably doing it! Not easy for even the critical beholder to maintain that Millicent could not and did not do such a silly thing when he has actually with his eyes seen her in the very act! The dramatist, as usual, having done less, is more richly rewarded by results.

Of course it will be argued, as it has always been argued, by those who have not written novels, that it is precisely the "doing less"—the leaving out—that constitutes the unique and fearful difficulty of dramatic art. "The skill to leave out"—lo! the master faculty of the dramatist! But, in the first place, I do not believe that, having regard to the relative scope of the play and of the novel, the necessity for leaving out is more acute in the one than in the other. The adjective "photographic" is as absurd applied to the novel as to the play. And, in the second place, other factors being equal, it is less exhausting, and it requires less skill, to refrain from doing than to do. To know when to refrain from doing may be hard, but positively to do is even harder. Sometimes, listening to partisans of the drama, I have been moved to suggest that, if the art of omission is so wondrously difficult, a dramatist who practised the habit of omitting to write anything whatever ought to be hailed as the supreme craftsman.

IV

The more closely one examines the subject, the more clear and certain becomes the fact that there is only one fundamental artistic difference between the novel and the play, and that difference (to which I shall come later) is not the difference which would be generally named as distinguishing the play from the novel. The apparent differences are superficial, and are due chiefly to considerations of convenience.

Whether in a play or in a novel the creative artist has to tell a story—using the word story in a very wide sense. Just as a novel is divided into chapters, and for a similar reason, a play is divided into acts. But neither chapters nor acts are necessary. Some of Balzac's chief novels have no chapter-divisions, and it has been proved that a theatre audience can and will listen for two hours to "talk," and even recitative singing, on the stage, without a pause. Indeed, audiences, under the compulsion of an artist strong and imperious enough, could, I am sure, be trained to marvellous feats of prolonged receptivity. However, chapters and acts are usual, and they involve the same constructional processes on the part of the artist. The entire play or novel must tell a complete story—

that is, arouse a curiosity and reasonably satisfy it, raise a main question and then settle it. And each act or other chief division must tell a definite portion of the story, satisfy part of the curiosity, settle part of the question. And each scene or other minor division must do the same according to its scale. Everything basic that applies to the technique of the novel applies equally to the technique of the play.

In particular, I would urge that a play, any more than a novel, need not be dramatic, employing the term as it is usually employed. In so far as it suspends the listener's interest, every tale, however told, may be said to be dramatic. In this sense *The Golden Bowl* is dramatic; so are *Dominique*[7] and *Persuasion*. A play need not be more dramatic than that. Very emphatically a play need not be dramatic in the stage sense. It need never induce interest to the degree of excitement. It need have nothing that resembles what would be recognisable in the theatre as a situation. It may amble on—and it will still be a play, and it may succeed in pleasing either the fastidious hundreds or the unfastidious hundreds of thousands, according to the talent of the author. Without doubt mandarins will continue for about a century yet to excommunicate certain plays from the category of plays. But nobody will be any the worse. And dramatists will go on proving that whatever else divides a play from a book, "dramatic quality" does not. Some arch-Mandarin may launch at me one of those mandarinic epigrammatic questions which are supposed to overthrow the adversary at one dart. "Do you seriously mean to argue, sir, that drama need not be dramatic?" I do, if the word dramatic is to be used in the mandarinic signification. I mean to state that some of the finest plays of the modern age differ from a psychological novel in nothing but the superficial form of telling. Example, Henri Becque's *La Parisienne*, than which there is no better. If I am asked to give my own definition of the adjective "dramatic," I would say that that story is dramatic which is told in dialogue imagined to be spoken by actors and actresses on the stage, and that any narrower definition is bound

7. *Dominique*, by Eugene Fromentin (1820–1876), a novel of psychological analysis rather than of action, and thus "dramatic" only in Bennett's special sense.

to exclude some genuine plays universally accepted as such—
even by mandarins. For be it noted that the mandarin is never
consistent.

My definition brings me to the sole technical difference between
a play and a novel—in the play the story is told by means of a
dialogue. It is a difference less important than it seems, and not
invariably even a sure point of distinction between the two kinds
of narrative. For a novel may consist exclusively of dialogue. And
plays may contain other matter than dialogue. The classic chorus is
not dialogue. But nowadays we should consider the device of the
chorus to be clumsy, as, nowadays, it indeed would be. We have
grown very ingenious and clever at the trickery of making characters
talk to the audience and explain themselves and their past history
while seemingly innocent of any such intention. And here, I admit,
the dramatist has to face a difficulty special to himself, which the
novelist can avoid. I believe it to be the sole difficulty which is
peculiar to the drama, and that it is not acute is proved by the ease
with which third-rate dramatists have generally vanquished it.
Mandarins are wont to assert that the dramatist is also handi-
capped by the necessity for rigid economy in the use of material.
This is not so. Rigid economy in the use of material is equally
advisable in every form of art. If it is a necessity, it is a necessity
which all artists flout from time to time, and occasionally with
gorgeous results, and the successful dramatist has hitherto not been
less guilty of flouting it than the novelist or any other artist.

V

And now, having shown that some alleged differences between the
play and the novel are illusory, and that a certain technical difference, though possibly real, is superficial and slight, I come to the
fundamental difference between them—a difference which the
laity does not suspect, which is seldom insisted upon and never
sufficiently, but which nobody who is well versed in the making of
both plays and novels can fail to feel profoundly. The emotional
strain of writing a play is not merely less prolonged than that of
writing a novel, it is less severe even while it lasts, lower in degree

and of a less purely creative character. And herein is the chief of all the reasons why a play is easier to write than a novel. The drama does not belong exclusively to literature, because its effect depends on something more than the composition of words. The dramatist is the sole author of a play, but he is not the sole creator of it. Without him nothing can be done, but, on the other hand, he cannot do everything himself. He begins the work of creation, which is finished either by creative interpreters on the stage, or by the creative imagination of the reader in the study. It is as if he carried an immense weight to the landing at the turn of a flight of stairs, and that thence upward the lifting had to be done by other people. Consider the affair as a pyramidal structure, and the dramatist is the base—but he is not the apex. A play is a collaboration of creative faculties. The egotism of the dramatist resents this uncomfortable fact, but the fact exists. And further, the creative faculties are not only those of the author, the stage-director ("producer") and the actors—the audience itself is unconsciously part of the collaboration.

Hence a dramatist who attempts to do the whole work of creation before the acting begins is an inartistic usurper of the functions of others, and will fail of proper accomplishment at the end. The dramatist must deliberately, in performing his share of the work, leave scope for a multitude of alien faculties whose operations he can neither precisely foresee nor completely control. The point is not that in the writing of a play there are various sorts of matters— as we have already seen—which the dramatist must ignore; the point is that even in the region proper to him he must not push the creative act to its final limit. He must ever remember those who are to come after him. For instance, though he must visualise a scene as he writes it, he should not visualise it completely, as a novelist should. The novelist may perceive vividly the faces of his personages, but if the playwright insists on seeing faces, either he will see the faces of real actors and hamper himself by moulding the scene to suit such real actors, or he will perceive imaginary faces, and the ultimate interpretation will perforce falsify his work and nullify his intentions. This aspect of the subject might well be much amplified, but only for a public of practising dramatists.

VI

When the play is "finished," the processes of collaboration have yet to begin. The serious work of the dramatist is over, but the most desolating part of his toil awaits him. I do not refer to the business of arranging with a theatrical manager for the production of the play. For, though that generally partakes of the nature of tragedy, it also partakes of the nature of amusing burlesque, owing to the fact that theatrical managers are—no doubt inevitably—theatrical. Nevertheless, even the theatrical manager, while disclaiming the slightest interest in anything more vital to the stage than the box-office, is himself in some degree a collaborator, and is the first to show to the dramatist that a play is not a play till it is performed. The manager reads the play, and, to the dramatist's astonishment, reads quite a different play from that which the dramatist imagines he wrote. In particular the manager reads a play which can scarcely hope to succeed—indeed, a play against whose chances of success ten thousand powerful reasons can be adduced. It is remarkable that a manager nearly always foresees failure in a manuscript, and very seldom success. The manager's profoundest instinct—self-preservation again!—is to refuse a play; if he accepts, it is against the grain, against his judgment—and out of a mad spirit of adventure. Some of the most glittering successes have been rehearsed in an atmosphere of settled despair. The dramatist naturally feels an immense contempt for the opinions artistic and otherwise of the manager, and he is therein justified. The manager's vocation is not to write plays, nor (let us hope) to act in them, nor to direct the rehearsals of them, and even his knowledge of the vagaries of his own box-office has often proved to be pitiably delusive. The manager's true and only vocation is to refrain from producing plays. Despite all this, however, the manager has already collaborated in the play. The dramatist sees it differently now. All sorts of new considerations have been presented to him. Not a word has been altered; but it is noticeably another play. Which is merely to say that the creative work on it which still remains to be done has been more accurately envisaged. This strange experience could not happen to a novel, because when a novel is written it is finished.

And when the director of rehearsals, or producer, has been chosen, and this priceless and mysterious person has his first serious confabulation with the author, then at once the play begins to assume new shapes—contours undreamt of by the author till that startling moment. And even if the author has the temerity to conduct his own rehearsals, similar disconcerting phenomena will occur; for the author as a producer is a different fellow from the author as author. The producer is up against realities. He, first, renders the play concrete, gradually condenses its filmy vapours into a solid element. . . . He suggests the casting. "What do you think of X. for the old man?" asks the producer. The author is staggered. Is it conceivable that so renowned a producer can have so misread and misunderstood the play? X. would be preposterous as the old man. But the producer goes on talking. And suddenly the author sees possibilites in X. But at the same time he sees a different play from what he wrote. And quite probably he sees a more glorious play. Quite probably he had not suspected how great a dramatist he is. . . . Before the first rehearsal is called, the play, still without a word altered, has gone through astounding creative transmutations; the author recognises in it some likeness to his beloved child, but it is the likeness of a first cousin.

At the first rehearsal, and for many rehearsals, to an extent perhaps increasing, perhaps decreasing, the dramatist is forced into an apologetic and self-conscious mood; and his mien is something between that of a criminal who has committed a horrid offence and that of father over the crude body of a new-born child. Now in truth he deeply realises that the play is a collaboration. In extreme cases he may be brought to see that he himself is one of the less important factors in the collaboration. The first preoccupation of the interpreters is not with his play at all, but—quite rightly— with their own careers; if they were not honestly convinced that their own careers were the chief genuine excuse for the existence of the theatre and the play they would not act very well. But, more than that, they do not regard his play as a sufficient vehicle for the furtherance of their careers. At the most favourable, what they secretly think is that if they are permitted to exercise their talents on his play there is a chance that they may be able to turn it into a sufficient vehicle for the furtherance of their careers. The attitude of every actor towards his part is: "My part is not much of a part as it stands, but if my individuality is allowed to get into free contact with it, I may make something brilliant out of it." Which attitude is a proper attitude, and an attitude in my opinion justified by the facts of the case. The actor's phrase is that he *creates* a part, and he is right. He completes the labour of creation begun by the author and continued by the producer, and if reasonable liberty is not accorded to him—if either the author or the producer attempts to do too much of the creative work—the result cannot be satisfactory.

As the rehearsals proceed the play changes from day to day. However autocratic the producer, however obstinate the dramatist, the play will vary at each rehearsal like a large cloud in a gentle wind. It is never the same play for two days together. Nor is this surprising, seeing that every day and night a dozen, or it may be two dozen, human beings endowed with the creative gift are creatively working on it. Every dramatist who is candid with himself—I do not suggest that he should be candid to the theatrical world—well knows that though his play is often worsened by his collaborators it is also often improved,—and improved in the most mysterious and dazzling manner—without a word being altered. Producer and actors do not merely suggest possibilities, they execute them. And the author is confronted by artistic phenomena for which lawfully he may not claim credit. On the other hand, he may be confronted by inartistic phenomena in respect to which lawfully he is blameless, but which he cannot prevent; a rehearsal is like a battle,—certain persons are theoretically in control, but in fact the thing principally fights itself. And thus the creation goes on until the dress-rehearsal, when it seems to have come to a stop. And the dramatist lying awake in the night reflects, stoically, fatalistically: "Well, that is the play that they have made of *my* play!" And he may be pleased or he may be disgusted. But if he attends the first performance he cannot fail to notice, after the first few minutes of it, that he was quite mistaken, and that what the actors are performing is still another play. The audience is collaborating.

PART IV

THE ARTIST AND THE PUBLIC

I

I can divide all the imaginative writers I have ever met into two classes—those who admitted and sometimes proclaimed loudly that they desired popularity; and those who expressed a noble scorn or a gentle contempt for popularity. The latter, however, always failed to conceal their envy of popular authors, and this envy was a phenomenon whose truculent bitterness could not be surpassed even in political or religious life. And indeed, since (as I have held in a previous chapter) the object of the artist is to share his emotions with others, it would be strange if the normal artist spurned popularity in order to keep his emotions as much as possible to himself. An enormous amount of dishonest nonsense has been and will be written by uncreative critics, of course in the higher interests of creative authors, about popularity and the proper attitude of the artist thereto. But possibly the attitude of a first-class artist himself may prove a more valuable guide.

The *Letters of George Meredith* (of which the first volume is a magnificent unfolding of the character of a great man) are full of references to popularity, references overt and covert. Meredith could never—and quite naturally—get away from the idea of popularity. He was a student of the English public, and could occasionally be unjust to it. Writing to M. André Raffalovich (who had sent him a letter of appreciation) in November, 1881, he said: "I venture to judge by your name that you are at most but half English. I can consequently believe in the feeling you express for the work of an unpopular writer. Otherwise one would incline to be sceptical, for the English are given to practical jokes, and to stir up the vanity of authors who are supposed to languish in the shade amuses them." A remark curiously unfair to the small, faithful band of admirers which Meredith then had. The whole letter, while warmly and touchingly grateful, is gloomy. Further on in it he says: "Good work has a fair chance to be recognised in the end, and if not, what does it matter?" But there is constant proof that it did matter very much. In a letter to William Hardman, written when he was well and hopeful, he says: "Never mind: if we do but get the public ear, oh, my dear old boy!" To Captain Maxse, in reference to a vast sum of £8,000 paid by the *Cornhill* people to George Eliot (for an unreadable novel), he exclaims: "Bon Dieu! Will aught like this ever happen to me?"

And to his son he was very explicit about the extent to which unpopularity "mattered": "As I am unpopular I am ill-paid, and therefore bound to work double tides, hardly ever able to lay down the pen. This affects my weakened stomach, and so the round of the vicious circle is looped." (Vol. I., p. 322.) And in another letter to Arthur Meredith about the same time he sums up his career thus: "As for me, I have failed, and I find little to make the end undesirable." (Vol. I., p. 318.) This letter is dated June 23rd, 1881. Meredith was then fifty-three years of age. He had written *Modern Love, The Shaving of Shagpat, The Ordeal of Richard Feverel, Rhoda Fleming, The Egoist* and other masterpieces. He knew that he had done his best and that his best was very fine. It would be difficult to credit that he did not privately deem himself one of the masters of English literature and destined to what we call immortality. He had the enthusiastic appreciation of some of the finest minds of the epoch. And yet, "As for me, I have failed, and I find little to make the end undesirable." But he had not failed in his industry, nor in the quality of his work, nor in achieving self-respect and the respect of his friends. He had failed only in one thing— immediate popularity.

II

Assuming then that an author is justified in desiring immediate popularity, instead of being content with poverty and the unheard plaudits of posterity, another point presents itself. Ought he to limit himself to a mere desire for popularity, or ought he actually to do something, or to refrain from doing something, to the special end of obtaining popularity? Ought he to say: "I shall write exactly what and how I like, without any regard for the public; I shall consider nothing but my own individuality and powers; I shall be guided solely by my own personal conception of what the public ought to like"? Or ought he to say: "Let me examine this public, and let me see whether some compromise between us is not possible"?

Certain authors are never under the necessity of facing the alternative. Occasionally, by chance, a genius may be so fortunately constituted and so brilliantly endowed that he captures the public at once, prestige being established, and the question of compromise never arises. But this is exceedingly rare. On the other hand, many mediocre authors, exercising the most complete sincerity, find ample appreciation in the vast mediocrity of the public, and are never troubled by any problem worse than the vagaries of their fountain-pens. Such authors enjoy in plenty the gewgaw known as happiness. Of nearly all really original artists, however, it may be said that they are at loggerheads with the public—as an almost inevitable consequence of their originality; and for them the problem of compromise or no-compromise acutely exists.

George Meredith was such an artist. George Meredith before anything else was a poet. He would have been a better poet than a novelist, and I believe that he thought so. The public did not care for his poetry. If he had belonged to the no-compromise school, whose adherents usually have the effrontery to claim him, he would have said: "I shall keep on writing poetry, even if I have to become a stockbroker in order to do it." But when he was only thirty-three— a boy, as authors go—he had already tired of no-compromise. He wrote to Augustus Jessopp: "It may be that in a year or two I shall find time for a full sustained Song. . . . The worst is that having taken to prose delineations of character and life, one's affections are divided. . . . And in truth, being a servant of the public, *I must wait till my master commands before I take seriously to singing.*" (Vol. I., p. 45.) Here is as good an example as one is likely to find of a first-class artist openly admitting the futility of writing what will not be immediately read, when he can write something else, less to his taste, that will be read. The same sentiment has actuated an immense number of first-class creative artists, including Shakespeare, who would have been a rare client for a literary agent. . . . So much for refraining from doing the precise sort of work one would prefer to do because it is not appreciated by the public.

There remains the doing of a sort of work against the grain because the public appreciates it—otherwise the pot-boiler. In 1861 Meredith wrote to Mrs Ross: "I am engaged in extra potboiling work which enables me to do this," *i.e.*, to write an occasional long poem. (Vol. I., p. 52.) Oh, base compromise! Seventeen years later he wrote to R. L. Stevenson: "Of potboilers let none speak. Jove hangs them upon necks that could soar above his heights but for the accursed weight." (Vol. I., p. 291.) It may be said that Meredith was forced to write potboilers. He was no more forced to write potboilers than any other author. Sooner than wallow in that shame, he might have earned money in more difficult ways. Or he might have indulged in that starvation so heartily prescribed for authors by a plutocratic noble who occasionally deigns to employ the English tongue in prose. Meredith subdued his muse, and Meredith wrote potboilers, because he was a first-class artist and a man of profound common sense. Being extremely creative, he had to arrive somehow, and he remembered that the earth is the earth, and the world the world, and men men, and he arrived as best he could. The great majority of his peers have acted similarly.

The truth is that an artist who demands appreciation from the public on his own terms, and on none but his own terms, is either a god or a conceited and impractical fool. And he is somewhat more likely to be the latter than the former. He wants too much. There are two sides to every bargain, including the artistic. The most fertile and the most powerful artists are the readiest to recognise this, because their sense of proportion, which is the sense of order, is well developed. The lack of the sense of proportion is the mark of the *petit maître*. The sagacious artist, while respecting himself, will respect the idiosyncrasies of his public. To do both simultaneously is quite possible. In particular, the sagacious artist will respect basic national prejudices. For example, no first-class English novelist or dramatist would dream of allowing to his pen the freedom in treating sexual phenomena which Continental writers enjoy as a matter of course. The British public is admittedly wrong on this important point—hypocritical, illogical and absurd. But what would you? You cannot defy it; you literally cannot. If you tried, you would not even get as far as print, to say nothing of library counters. You can only get round it by ingenuity and guile. You can only go a very little further than is quite safe. You can only do one man's modest share in the education of the public.

In Valery Larbaud's latest novel, *A. O. Barnabooth*, occurs a phrase of deep wisdom about women: *"La femme est une grande réalité, comme la guerre."* It might be applied to the public. The public is a great actuality, like war. If you are a creative and creating artist, you cannot ignore it, though it can ignore you. There it is! You can do something with it, but not much. And what you do not do with it, it must do with you, if there is to be the contact which is essential to the artistic function. This contact may be closened and completed by the artist's cleverness—the mere cleverness of adaptability which most first-class artists have exhibited. You can wear the fashions of the day. You can tickle the ingenuous beast's ear in order to distract his attention while you stab him in the chest. You can cajole money out of him by one kind of work in order to gain leisure in which to force him to accept later on something that he would prefer to refuse. You can use a thousand devices on the excellent simpleton. . . . And in the process you may degrade yourself to a mere popularity-hunter! Of course you may; as you may become a drunkard through drinking a glass of beer. Only, if you have anything to say worth saying, you usually don't succumb to this danger. If you have anything to say worth saying, you usually manage somehow to get it said, and read. The artist of genuine vocation is apt to be a wily person. He knows how to sacrifice inessentials so that he may retain essentials. And he can mysteriously put himself even into a potboiler. *Clarissa Harlowe*, which influenced fiction throughout Europe, was the direct result of potboiling. If the artist has not the wit and the strength of mind to keep his own soul amid the collisions of life, he is the inferior of a plain, honest merchant in stamina, and ought to retire to the upper branches of the Civil Service.

III

When the author has finished the composition of a work, when he has put into the trappings of the time as much of his eternal self as they will safely hold, having regard to the best welfare of his creative career as a whole, when, in short, he has done all that he can to ensure the fullest public appreciation of the essential in him— there still remains to be accomplished something which is not un- important in the entire affair of obtaining contact with the public. He has to see that the work is placed before the public as advan- tageously as possible In other words, he has to dispose of the work as advantageously as possible. In other words, when he lays down the pen he ought to become a merchant, for the mere reason that he has an article to sell, and the more skilfully he sells it the better will be the result, not only for the public appreciation of his message, but for himself as a private individual and as an artist with further activities in front of him.

Now this absolutely logical attitude of a merchant towards one's finished work infuriates the dilettanti of the literary world, to whom the very word "royalties" is anathema. They apparently would prefer to treat literature as they imagine Byron treated it, although as a fact no poet in a short life ever contrived to make as many pounds sterling out of verse as Byron made. Or perhaps they would like to return to the golden days when the author had to be "patro- nised" in order to exist; or even to the mid-nineteenth century, when practically all authors save the most successful—and not a few of the successful also—failed to obtain the fair reward of their work. The dilettanti's snobbishness and sentimentality prevent them from admitting that, in a democratic age, when an author is genu- inely appreciated, either he makes money or he is the foolish victim of a scoundrel. They are fond of saying that agreements and royal- ties have nothing to do with literature. But agreements and royalties have a very great deal to do with literature. Full contact between artist and public depends largely upon publisher or manager being compelled to be efficient and just. And upon the publisher's or manager's efficiency and justice depend also the dignity, the leisure, the easy flow of coin, the freedom, and the pride which are helpful to the full fruition of any artist. No artist was ever assisted in his career by the yoke, by servitude, by enforced monotony, by over- work, by economic inferiority. See Meredith's correspondence everywhere.

Nor can there be any satisfaction in doing badly that which might be done well. If an artist writes a fine poem, shows it to his dearest friend, and burns it—I can respect him. But if an artist writes a fine poem, and then by sloppiness and snobbishness allows it to be inefficiently published, and fails to secure his own interests in the transaction, on the plea that he is an artist and not a merchant, then I refuse to respect him. A man cannot fulfil, and has no right to fulfil, one function only in this complex world. Some, indeed many, of the greatest creative artists have managed to be very good merchants also, and have not been ashamed of the double *rôle*. To read the correspondence and memoirs of certain supreme artists one might be excused for thinking, indeed, that they were more interested in the *rôle* of merchant than in the other *rôle*; and yet their work in no wise suffered. In the distribution of energy between the two *rôles* common sense is naturally needed. But the artist who has enough common sense—or, otherwise expressed, enough sense of reality—not to disdain the *rôle* of merchant will probably have enough not to exaggerate it. He may be reassured on one point—namely, that success in the *rôle* of merchant will never impair any self-satisfaction he may feel in the *rôle* of artist. The late discovery of a large public in America delighted Meredith and had a tonic effect on his whole system. It is often hinted, even if it is not often said, that great popularity ought to disturb the conscience of the artist. I do not believe it. If the conscience of the artist is not disturbed during the actual work itself, no subsequent phenomenon will or should disturb it. Once the artist is convinced of his artistic honesty, no public can be too large for his peace of mind. On the other hand, failure in the *rôle* of merchant will emphatically impair his self-satisfaction in the *rôle* of artist and his courage in the further pursuance of that *rôle*.

But many artists have admittedly no aptitude for merchantry. Not only is their sense of the bindingness of a bargain imperfect, but they are apt in business to behave in a puerile manner, to close an arrangement out of mere impatience, to be grossly undiplomatic, to be victimised by their vanity, to believe what they ought not to believe, to discredit what is patently true, to worry over negligible trifles, and generally to make a clumsy mess of their affairs. An artist may say: "I cannot work unless I have a free mind, and I cannot have a free mind if I am to be bothered all the time by details of business."

Apart from the fact that no artist who pretends also to be a man can in this world hope for a free mind, and that if he seeks it by neglecting his debtors he will be deprived of it by his creditors—apart from that, the artist's demand for a free mind is reasonable. Moreover, it is always a distressing sight to see a man trying to do what nature has not fitted him to do, and so doing it ill. Such artists, however—and they form possibly the majority—can always employ an expert to do their business for them, to cope on their behalf with the necessary middleman. Not that I deem the publisher or the theatrical manager to be by nature less upright than any other class of merchant. But the publisher and the theatrical manager have been subjected for centuries to a special and grave temptation. The ordinary merchant deals with other merchants—his equals in business skill. The publisher and the theatrical manager deal with what amounts to a race of children, of whom even arch-angels could not refrain from taking advantage.

When the democratisation of literature seriously set in, it inevitably grew plain that the publisher and the theatrical manager had very humanly been giving way to the temptation with which heaven in her infinite wisdom had pleased to afflict them,—and the Society of Authors came into being. A natural consequence of the general awakening was the self-invention of the literary agent. The Society of Authors, against immense obstacles, has performed wonders in the economic education of the creative artist, and therefore in the improvement of letters. The literary agent, against obstacles still more immense, has carried out the details of the revolution. The outcry—partly sentimental, partly snobbish, but mainly interested —was at first tremendous against these meddlers who would destroy the charming personal relations that used to exist between, for example, the author and the publisher. (The less said about those charming personal relations the better. Documents exist.) But the main battle is now over, and everyone concerned is beautifully aware who holds the field. Though much remains to be done, much has been done; and to-day the creative artist who, conscious of inability to transact his own affairs efficiently, does not obtain efficient advice and help therein, stands in his own light both as an artist and as a man, and is a reactionary force. He owes the practice of elementary common sense to himself, to his work, and to his profession at large.

IV

The same dilettante spirit which refuses to see the connection between art and money has also a tendency to repudiate the world of men at large, as being unfit for the habitation of artists. This is a still more serious error of attitude—especially in a storyteller. No artist is likely to be entirely admirable who is not a man before he is an artist. The notion that art is first and the rest of the universe nowhere is bound to lead to preciosity and futility in art. The artist who is too sensitive for contacts with the non-artistic world is thereby too sensitive for his vocation, and fit only to fall into gentle ecstasies over the work of artists less sensitive than himself.

The classic modern example of the tragedy of the artist who repudiates the world is Flaubert. At an early age Flaubert convinced himself that he had no use for the world of men. He demanded to be left in solitude and tranquillity. The morbid streak in his constitution grew rapidly under the fostering influences of peace and tranquillity. He was brilliantly peculiar as a schoolboy. As an old man of twenty-two, mourning over the vanished brio of youth, he carried morbidity to perfection. Only when he was travelling (as, for example, in Egypt) do his letters lose for a time their distemper. His love-letters are often ignobly inept, and nearly always spoilt by the crass provincialism of the refined and cultivated hermit. His mistress was a woman difficult to handle and indeed a Tartar in egotism, but as the recipient of Flaubert's love-letters she must win universal sympathy.

Full of a grievance against the whole modern planet, Flaubert turned passionately to ancient times (in which he would have been equally unhappy had he lived in them), and hoped to resurrect beauty when he had failed to see it round about him. Whether or not he did resurrect beauty is a point which the present age is now deciding. His fictions of modern life undoubtedly suffer from his detestation of the material; but considering his manner of existence it is marvellous that he should have been able to accomplish any of them, except *Un Coeur Simple*. The final one, *Bouvard et Pécuchet*, shows the lack of the sense of reality which must be the inevitable sequel of divorce from mankind. It is realism without conviction. No such characters as Bouvard and Pecuchet could ever have existed outside Flaubert's brain, and the reader's resultant impression is that the author has ruined a central idea which was well suited for a grand larkish extravaganza in the hands of a French Swift. But the spectacle of Flaubert writing in *mots justes* a grand larkish extravaganza cannot be conjured up by fancy.

There are many sub-Flauberts rife in London. They are usually more critical than creative, but their influence upon creators, and especially the younger creators, is not negligible. Their aim in preciosity would seem to be to keep themselves unspotted from the world. They are for ever being surprised and hurt by the crudity and coarseness of human nature, and for ever bracing themselves to be not as others are. They would have incurred the anger of Dr Johnson, and a just discipline for them would be that they should be cross-examined by the great bully in presence of a jury of butchers and sentenced accordingly. The morbid Flaubertian shrinking from reality is to be found to-day even in relatively robust minds. I was recently at a provincial cinema, and witnessed on the screen with a friend a wondrously ingenuous drama entitled "Gold is not All." My friend, who combines the callings of engineer and general adventurer with that of serving his country, leaned over to me in the darkness amid the violent applause, and said: "You know, this kind of thing always makes me ashamed of human nature." I answered him as Johnsonially as the circumstances would allow. Had he lived to the age of fifty so blind that it needed a cinema audience to show him what the general level of human nature really is? Nobody has any right to be ashamed of human nature. Is one ashamed of one's mother? Is one ashamed of the cosmic process of evolution? Human nature *is*. And the more deeply the creative artist, by frank contacts, absorbs that supreme fact into his brain, the better for his work.

There is a numerous band of persons in London—and the novelist and dramatist are not infrequently drawn into their circle—who spend so much time and emotion in practising the rites of the religion of art that they become incapable of real existence. Each is a Stylites on a pillar. Their opinion on Leon Bakst, Francis Thompson, Augustus John, Cyril Scott, Maurice Ravel, Vuillard, James Stephens, E. A. Rickards, Richard Strauss, Eugen D'Albert,[8] etc., may not be without value, and their genuine feverish morbid interest in art has its usefulness; but they know no more about reality than a Pekinese dog on a cushion. They never approach normal life. They scorn it. They have a horror of it. They class politics with the differential calculus. They have heard of Lloyd George, the rise in the price of commodities, and the eternal enigma, what is a sardine; but only because they must open a newspaper to look at the advertisements and announcements relating to the arts. The occasional frequenting of this circle may not be disadvantageous to the creative artist. But let him keep himself inoculated against its disease by constant steady plunges into the cold sea of the general national life. Let him mingle with the public, for God's sake! No phenomenon on this wretched planet, which after all is ours, is meet for the artist's shrinking scorn. And the average

8. This list of names shows Bennett's familiarity with the Edwardian *avant-garde* (and perhaps also his desire to demonstrate that familiarity). Leon Bakst was a set designer for Diaghilev's Russian Ballet, which had just finished a brilliant season in London, including the English premiere of *Le Sacre du Printemps*, with Nijinsky. Francis Thompson's *Works*, and a standard life, by Everard Meynell, were published in, 1913. Augustus John was gaining recognition as a painter. Cyril Scott, a young composer then in his early thirties, had been invited by the widow of Gustave Mahler to direct a performance of his own work in Vienna. Maurice Ravel, a friend of Bennett's from 1908 until Bennett's death, had recently finished *Daphnis et Chloe* for Diaghilev. Bennett bought a small painting by Vuillard in the month that this part of *The Story Teller's Craft* was published. James Stephens's *The Crock of Gold* was published in 1912. E. A. Rickards, a lifelong friend of Bennett's, was an architect; he designed the Central Hall, Westminster, which had just been completed. Three of Strauss's operas had been performed at Covent Garden—*Elektra* and *Salomé* in 1910, and *Rosenkavalier* in 1913; Bennett attended the premiere of the latter. Eugen D'Albert was an English-born pianist and composer.

man, as to whom the artist's ignorance is often astounding, must for ever constitute the main part of the material in which he works.

Above all, let not the creative artist suppose that the antidote to the circle of dilettantism is the circle of social reform. It is not. I referred in the first chapter to the prevalent illusion that the republic has just now arrived at a crisis, and that if something is not immediately done disaster will soon be upon us. This is the illusion to which the circle of social reforms is naturally prone, and it is an illusion against which the common sense of the creative artist must mightily protest. The world is, without doubt, a very bad world; but it is also a very good world. The function of the artist is certainly concerned more with what is than with what ought to be. When all necessary reform has been accomplished our perfected planet will be stone-cold. Until then the artist's affair is to keep his balance amid warring points of view, and in the main to record and enjoy what is. . . . But is not the Minimum Wage Bill urgent? But when the minimum wage is as trite as the jury system, the urgency of reform will still be tempting the artist too far out of his true path. And the artist who yields is lost.

First published as "The Story Teller's Craft," *English Review*, XIV (April, June, and July, 1913), 17–29, 349–360, 556–568, and XV (October, 1913), 331–342. Reprinted as *The Author's Craft* (New York: George H. Doran Co., 1914).

The "Average Reader" and the Recipe for Popularity (1901)

Not only is art a factor in life; it is a factor in all lives. The division of the world into two classes, one of which has a monopoly of what is called "artistic feeling," is arbitrary and false. Everyone is an artist, more or less; that is to say, there is no person quite without that faculty of poetising, which by seeing beauty creates beauty, and which, when it is sufficiently powerful and articulate, constitutes the musical composer, the architect, the imaginative writer, the sculptor and the painter. To the persistent ignoring of this obvious truth is due much misunderstanding and some bitterness. The fault lies originally with the minority, the more artistic, which has imposed an artificial distinction upon the majority, the less artistic. The majority, having accepted the distinction, naturally takes care to find in it a source of pride, and the result is two camps which vituperate and scorn each other: the minority despises the majority for being "inartistic," and the resentful majority accuses the minority of arrogance and affectation.

In the field of fiction—the art with which this book is concerned, and which, perhaps, most closely touches the world at large—the two camps seldom communicate save in terms of sarcasm. Certainly they make no attempt towards understanding one another. That the majority could understand the minority is perhaps impossible; but the minority might and should understand the majority, and not until it begins to do so will the best forms of art begin to take hold of the race. Now the appearance of an extremely popular novel, which, used with pacific intelligence, might form a basis of mutual comprehension, is invariably turned into a fresh *casus belli*. The champions of the minority fall on the book with all arms of satiric analysis and contempt; the champions of the majority defend it with what skill they can muster, making up in brute

51

force what they lack in adroitness. The minority says curtly, "This is not art"; the majority answers, "Never mind, it is what we like. Besides, it *is* art. Who are you that you should define art? Anyhow it is popular." The minority sneers; the majority retorts a single word, "Envy." The breach is widened. Why should these things occur? Why should not the minority abandon the rôle of the superior person, and reason together—if not with the enemy? To admire the less admirable in art is not a crime, nor the fruit of a mischievous intention to overthrow the august verdict of the centuries: nor is it a mere vagary. If 50,000 people buy a novel whose shortcomings render it tenth-rate, we may be sure that they have not conspired to do so, and also that their apparently strange unanimity is not due to chance. There must be another explanation of the phenomenon, and when this explanation is discovered some real progress will have been made towards that democratisation of art which it is surely the duty of the minority to undertake, and to undertake in a religious spirit. The missionary does not make converts by a process of jeers; he minimises the difference between himself and the heathen, assumes a brotherhood, and sympathetically leads forward from one point of view to another; and in order thus to lead forward he finds out what the first point of view is. I am aware that a few of the minority regard the democratisation of art as both undesirable and impossible, but even they will admit that this particular problem in the "psychology of crowds"—the secret of popularity in an art— has sufficient intrinsic interest to be attacked for its own sake, apart from any end which the solving might or might not serve.

My chief aim in most of the following chapters is to explain to the minority why the majority likes or dislikes certain modern novelists. In approaching matters so inflammatory to the wicked passions of the artistic, my aim has been to keep a friendly attitude, to avoid spleen, heat, and, above all, arrogance. I came neither to scoff nor to patronise, but to comprehend. I am conscious that there have been moments—especially when dealing with fashionable, as distinguished from popular, authors—at which, despite the most honest endeavour, I somewhat fell away from this counsel of perfection; but such occasional lapses were perhaps inevitable. In every case of a popular author firmly established I have found qualities which demand respect, and which few except those who are wholly preoccupied with the dandyism of technique could fail to admire. That these qualities are sometimes rather moral than artistic was to be expected. Within the last fifty years there have been many attempts to delimit a frontier between art and morals, but none has yet succeeded; and it may perhaps be said that in the wide kingdom of popularity the two provinces of art and morals overlap each other more confusingly than in the narrower domain where reason has refined the crude operations of instinct.

The subjects whom I have chosen group themselves under five heads: "Classics of a period," like Mr J. M. Barrie, Miss Braddon, and Charlotte M. Yonge;[1] fashionable novelists of the moment, like Miss Marie Corelli and Miss Ellen Thorneycroft Fowler;[2] *very* popular writers, like Mr Silas Hocking[3] and the magazine-furnishers; American writers who have been responsible for what amounts to a national craze, like the authors of *The Choir Invisible*, *David Harum*, and *Richard Carvel*;[4] and lastly a small nondescript class of the non-popular or misunderstood—Ivan Turgenev, Mr George Gissing, and Mr George Moore. I included Turgenev in my list partly because the recent issue of a complete translation of his works renders him now, for the first time, properly accessible to English readers, and partly because the enthusiasm of Eastern Europe and the apathy of Western Europe in his regard, constitute

1. J. M. Barrie (1860–1937), author of *Peter Pan* (1904). His fiction included *Auld Licht Idylls* (1888), *A Window in Thrums* (1889), and *Sentimental Tommy* (1895). Mary Elizabeth Braddon (1837–1915) wrote some 70 thrillers, including the popular *Lady Audley's Secret* (1862). Charlotte M. Yonge (1823–1901) had her greatest success with *The Heir of Redclyffe* (1853); she wrote in all 160 books.

2. Marie Corelli (1855–1924) wrote sensational, very popular, very bad novels; the most notorious was *The Sorrows of Satan* (1895). Ellen Thorneycroft Fowler (1860–1929), author of 12 novels, including *The Farringdons* (1900), which Bennett discussed in his chapter on Miss Fowler in *Fame and Fiction*.

3. Silas Hocking (1850–1935), author of some 90 novels, pious in character and Cornish in setting.

4. *The Choir Invisible* (1899), by James Lane Allen (1849–1925), an American writer of romances of the Old South. *David Harum* (1898), by Edward Noyes Wescott (1846–1898), one of the first American best sellers (400,000 copies in two years). *Richard Carvel* (1899), by the American historical novelist Winston Churchill (1871–1947).

together a problem of popularity very wide in its scope, and of a curious fascination. The case of Mr George Moore stands quite by itself. Mr Moore is indeed a singular and solitary figure in modern literature. In his best books he has never swerved from an artistic ideal positively distasteful to the English temperament, and yet his best books have had a large and steady sale. The majority have read him without in the least comprehending his aims; the minority have decidedly given him less than his due. His reputation has, in fact, always been somewhat under a cloud. Believing him to be one of the most sincere and one of the most distinguished novelists of the latter half of the nineteenth century, I have thought it more useful to make a general explanatory survey of his methods and his work than to offer any precise conclusions as to the causes of his strange position.

If it be charged against me that certain renowned or notorious names are missing from this book, I have to answer that I was compelled to select, and that I selected those cases which seemed to be the most interesting. The vogue of some writers, and the neglect of some others, call for no explanation.

Although it is a very long time now since I began my researches into the true nature of what is called "the popular taste in fiction," and although I have pursued the inquiry not only in the pages of books and the houses of the uncritical, but also in the *sancta* of publishers and all the marts where fiction is appraised and bought and sold, I cannot assert that I have arrived at any definition of that taste, either by inclusion or exclusion. The great public is so various, and its predilections so subtly and mysteriously instinctive—so personal and intimate, that it may not be said to have a secret; it has a thousand secrets, all interwoven, and none to be fully interpreted till the last of all is found. If, however, balancing one variety of the uncultured against another, we assume the existence of an "average reader," certain good qualities and defects may be positively attributed to this individual's literary taste. The catalogue is far from a complete one, more than probably it omits the items most essential to a full definition, but such as it is I will give it.

The average reader is unaffected. He has no pose. In social converse he may—though even this is rare—faintly assent to propositions which he feels to be untrue; but he will never carry dissimulation so far as to read, still less to buy, any novel that he dislikes or thinks he would dislike. *Qua* reader and buyer he is honest as the day. Literature in his eyes is too trivial an affair to be worthy of serious and sustained lying. In this particular he differs from many members of the minority who have a passion and a true though limited taste for books.

The average reader is an intelligent and reasonable being. He is neither an idiot nor perverse. The attitude of the literary superior person usually implies that the literary proletariat patronises what it ought to ignore and ignores what it ought to patronise, out of sheer irrational contumacy. This is not so. The average reader (like Goethe and Ste Beuve) has his worse and his better self, and there are times when he will yield to the former; but on the whole his impulses are good. In every writer who earns his respect and enduring love there is some central righteousness, which is capable of being traced and explained, and at which it is impossible to sneer. I do not say that the average reader likes a bad novel purely for the goodness in it, but I do say that he is never hoodwinked for long by an unredeemed fraud.

The average reader likes an imposing plot, heroical characters, and fine actions. Grandeur of subject will always be his first demand. This is of course notorious. A fact less notorious is that this preference of the average reader's is a classic preference, that all the finest art conforms to it, and that during the last fifty years it has exercised a valuable corrective influence against the theories of the brilliant decadents who have flourished (and in some ways have done so much for the novel) since Balzac died and the grand manner died with him. There can be no doubt that in putting subject before treatment, the majority has held to the straight path at a point where the minority has shown an inclination to wander. "The individual writer," says Matthew Arnold in the masterly essay on certain principles of art prefixed to the 1853 edition of his *Poems*, "may certainly learn of the ancients . . . three things which it is vitally important for him to know:—the all-importance of the choice of a subject; the necessity of accurate construction; and the subordinate character of expression." And again: "It is a pity that

power should be wasted; and that the poet should be compelled
to impart interest and force to his subject, instead of receiving them
from it, and thereby doubling his impressiveness." Thus Matthew
Arnold reinforcing the subscriber to Mudie's![5] And here it may be
remarked that the grandeur of subject which Matthew Arnold and
the average reader insist upon can be only a moral grandeur.
Events have no significance except by virtue of the ideas from which
they spring; the clash of events is the clash of ideas, and out of this
clash the moral lesson inevitably emerges, whether we ask for it or
no. Hence every great book is a great moral book, and there is a
true and fine sense in which the average reader is justified in regard-
ing art as the handmaid of morality.

The average reader appreciates sincerity and painstaking. He
admires these qualities for themselves, apart from results. No
novelist, however ingenious, who does not write what he feels, and
what, by its careful finish, approximately pleases himself, can continue to satisfy the average reader. He may hang for years precariously on the skirts of popularity, but in the end he will fall;
he will be found out.

Coming to the defects of our reader's taste, the first and worst is
that he has no sense of beauty—that is, the beauty of form. He
ignores it, not only in imaginative literature, but in every art,
and in life. The most atrocious ugliness does not annoy him, and
he has a blind spot in his eye for beauty. Perhaps the utter collapse
of architecture, the most influential of all the arts, has something to
do with this condition of things; perhaps it is only an effect. But
whatever the cause, the result is desolating for fiction. It means
that style is degraded, and that the supreme function of art, that of
creatively interpreting beauty, is rendered null and inefficacious.
Another limitation, scarcely less serious, is the inability to retire from
an art-work and perceive it as a whole. Our reader's attention is always
diverted from the main contour by trivial accessories. If the accessories amuse or impress him, then all is well; if the accessories are
not striking, that is to say, if he is not titillated with reasonable
frequency, then nothing is well. Make him laugh or cry, or shudder
or think, sufficiently often, and you need trouble about nothing

5. Mudie's Select Library, the largest of the Victorian lending libraries.

else. Omit to attend to these matters, and you may have written the *Antigone*, but it will not be read. "What distinguishes the artist from the mere amateur," says Goethe, "is *Architectonicé* in the highest sense: that power of execution, which creates, forms and constitutes; not the profoundness of single thoughts, not the richness of imagery, not the abundance of illustration." [6] Behold a primal truth which the average reader has not even guessed at—that there is a whole beauty, surpassing the beauty of parts. From his lack of perception arises the prosperity of the amateur novelist, with her following of fifty thousand souls; and to the same source may be traced that extravagance of mere illustrative decoration which mars all popular English fiction, making it ungainly, unsightly and vulgar.

Further, the average reader has some of the instincts of the untutored savage. To employ the terminology of other arts, he likes glaring tints; he prefers the chromograph to the oil painting. Drums and trumpets will please his ear better than any orchestra of strings. He wants crudity, and he does not want fine shades. Unless he is knocked down, or blinded, or deafened, he does not consider that he has been impressed. And in particular he desires and will have crudity of sentiment. For him sentiment cannot be too gross, too cloying in its sweetness, too sickly in its pathos. All popular writers are highly sentimental, even those who most industriously pretend to be otherwise. Nothing has contributed more surely to the vogue of Mr Rudyard Kipling among the majority than his constant abuse and falsification of sentiment.

Lastly, the average reader does not care to have the basic ideas of his existence disturbed. He may be emotionally aroused, but mentally he must be soothed, lulled, drugged. He is capable of a personal *animus* against the novelist who with too much suddenness invites him to readjust his scheme of things. A book of revolutionary ideas sometimes succeeds enormously, but it is a success of scandal. If you wish to tell the average reader that the earth is round, you must begin by hinting that it has occurred to you that perhaps there is the

6. The quotation is from Goethe's "Über den sogennanten Dilettantismus," but Bennett undoubtedly found it in Arnold's preface to *Poems* (1853), from which he quotes earlier in this essay.

slightest conceivable curvature in the flatness of it; but no violence, no haste, no directness! On the other hand, though he resents a shock, he does not resent dulness. I am convinced that the average reader is seldom bored except by what is beyond his comprehension. In order to be bored, one must be sufficiently alert to know when one is bored; but the average reader is too somnolent to be self-analytic. From the relatively exciting portions of a book he acquires a momentum of interest which will carry him without fatigue through illimitable expanses of dulness. This strange phenomenon explains why some of the most prodigiously dull novels ever penned have achieved a firm and honourable popularity.

There is a theory that the great public can appreciate a great novel, that the highest modern expression of literary art need not appeal in vain to the average reader. And I believe this to be true—provided that such a novel is written with intent, and with a full knowledge of the peculiar conditions to be satisfied; I believe that a novel could be written which would unite in a mild ecstasy of praise the two extremes—the most inclusive majority and the most exclusive minority. To capture the latter, the author of this novel must have first-rate imaginative power, in consideration of which the minority will, rightly, condone every fault. The majority is indifferent to sheer power, not desirous, indeed not capable, of being deeply stirred. The author's principal care must be, while ministering to the higher, not to offend the lower, instincts of the average reader. Thus he should choose a grandiose subject, rooting the whole story in one superb moral idea; but his treatment must not be too austere; he must employ that profoundness of single thoughts, that richness of imagery, and that abundance of illustration, which Goethe said were *not* the distinguishing mark of the artist, but which Goethe did not say the artist might not use. This overlaid decoration, however, must not be too uniformly brilliant, lest the average reader grow weary in the continual effort to grasp it; there must be intervals—spaces of plainness. With regard to subject, a religious or quasi-religious subject is to be preferred, because it will make the widest appeal. In the popular mind *Robert Elsmere* and *The Sorrows of Satan*[7] are the most striking novels of the

7. Two novels of religious doubt: *Robert Elsmere* (1888) by Mrs. Humphry Ward (1851–1920), and *Sorrows of Satan* by Marie Corelli.

last decade. The subject must afford abundant natural opportunities for sentiment of the simplest, lucidest, least subtle kind, and this sentiment must be produced by the machinery of physical event. The average reader has not yet perceived that a soul may have its history apart from the body; he can only see the one in the other, and if you offer him the one without the other, he will be mystified, and therefore aggrieved. It is not quite essential that the dominant interest of the novel should be a love-interest; I have shown in the chapter on Magazine Fiction that the great fiction-consuming public does not always demand its dish of Love; but a dominant love-interest would be advisable, because any taint of eccentricity is to be avoided, and because nothing can compare with a love-interest as a continual fount of sentiment. As to the plot, its march must not be too rapid or too thrilling; a headlong gallop, or any excess of sensationalism, is very likely to estrange the average reader. It should move obviously and leisurely, amid various and contrasted scenes, and of these scenes a proportion should be arranged to display the luxury of wealth and the most elaborate forms of social ritual. The principal characters must be devised to catch both the sympathy and the admiration of the reader, and for this purpose they should have exceptional nobility; they must not be ordinary people, astoundingly revealed by art in an extraordinary light; that is not enough; they must be heroes and heroines. The tale must end happily—not because the reader cannot bear to be agonised—he likes to be mildly agonised, just before the climax—but because only by a happy ending can virtue meet with what the average man considers to be its deserts. The profoundest belief of the average man is that virtue ought never to be its own reward. Shake that belief and you commit the cardinal sin; you disturb his mental quietude. The "tone" of the book should be serious and even staid, but not pessimistic; pessimism connotes lack of faith; it also saddens. "Is not life sad enough already?" This protesting query, so often heard, means that our novel must not embrace the whole of life; and indeed it must not. The novelist who gives too bold a prominence to that side of things which is not "the bright side" will never write our novel. Concerning style, the average reader will tolerate the highest excellence, provided that it involves him in no fatigue; he does not care to have to translate a fine style into what he calls plain English. Therefore the style must be neither subtle nor complicated nor of an original technique. Similarly, the mental and moral attitude of the historian must conform, broadly, to current ideas. There must be nothing in it really subversive of that vast fabric of prejudices and misconceptions which the worthy reader would call his philosophy. As for humour, as for wit, our novel need possess neither quality, but if either should happen to be present in it, the humour must not be deep, nor the wit subtle. Finally, and most important, our novel must, as I have already pointed out, be an absolutely sincere expression of the author's mind; but it need not be an expression of the whole of his mind.

Given the heaven-sent author, is there any reason why such a novel as I have circumscribed should not be a distinguished work of art?

Fame and Fiction (London: Grant Richards, 1901), pp. 3–20.

The Fallow Fields of Fiction (1901)

I

Those who make it their business to examine the whole output of modern fiction must necessarily be depressed and wearied by the heavy sensation of its sameness, its futility, its lack of enterprise. We say modern fiction, not because we think that the fiction of the past was better—it was certainly worse—but in order to limit and simplify the subject. The continual reading of new novels devastates, desolates, and sears the soul. It is like living at the Royal Academy; but the Royal Academy is only open for three months in the year. And just as in that palace of sentimentality the damnable iteration of Sunshines after Rains, Evening Glows, Last Furrows, Guineveres, Ionian Weathers, Portraits of a Lady and of a Gentleman, and Baby's Tubs, drives the exhausted visitor into Piccadilly with a protest almost hysteric, so the eternal and tedious monotony of British fiction extorts at last a cry for mercy and a passionate demand for some means of escape. Why will people persist in saying over again what cannot be said over again? Why do our novelists follow each other through the wide world in Indian file, looking neither to the right nor to the left? Why do our best novelists, the men whose talents compel us, angry, to admire, exhibit all the magnificence and pageant of England as a theatre for the permutations and combinations of two men and a maid, or two maids and a man? The late William Black[1] exclaimed grandly: "So long as there are two men and a maid, the novel . . .," &c. What rubbish! Why is Love the Lord of all? *Is* Love the Lord of all? Well, it is not, and that is the point. Ask yourself, you the lawyer, you the stockbroker, you the pedagogue, you the doctor, you the soldier, you the housemistress, you the professional beauty, you the typist, you the clerk

---

1. William Black (1841–1898), a Scottish novelist, member of the "kailyard" school. His rather sentimental romances were set in the Hebrides.

with the cigarette, the *Daily Mail,* and the second-class season ticket, how often you think of Love. Are you worshipping the god all day? Would you, straight, give a thousand a year for Love if you had to buy that archer in the market? Not one in ten of you! You say you could not do without him. You could less easily dispense with money; yet your tame novelists are afraid to offer you a novel about the Kaffir Circus[2] lest you should call it sordid and dull. You ask of your tame novelists a dish of love, because you like to pretend that love is the one thing you love, but you seldom get it; what you get is a syrup of sentimentality. If they gave you love, if they could give it, the probability is that you would not enjoy it, would call it either impure or high-flown. At the present there are being produced five sorts of novels: the domestic, the historical, the criminal, the theological, and the bellicose. Of these the first sort far outnumbers the rest; the second is moribund, and survives solely by the assistance of the aforesaid syrup; the third, while often ignoring love itself, is always as sentimental as a ballad; the fourth merely shows the influence of theology on love and of love on theology; the fifth is usually a love story against a background of England beating the universe. Not ten novels in a year fall outside these classes (we admit a few admirable exceptions). Not ten novels in a year but ignore every human activity save love (or, rather, its counterfeit), crime, and war; conjecture concerning the future life can hardly be termed an activity.

Why is this? We do not propose to reply to that question, but to put another one: Need it be so? And to answer dogmatically: It need not. Readers may expostulate, "But we desire no change"; and writers may complain, "If we give them anything different, they won't have it." No matter! Both are wrong. The change, the enlargement, will assuredly come. Nothing can stop it. When Ibsen, in *An Enemy of the People,* made his third act out of a rate-payers' meeting, the mandarins with one accord said, "This will never do." But it has done. Where are the mandarins now? Those particular mandarins are simply dead and buried, extinguished by an imaginative Force. Other mandarins live patriarchally on, who,

2. A slang term for that part of the British Stock Exchange that dealt in South African gold shares.

when someone writes a great novel about a municipal struggle, will say again, "This will never do." And they, too, in their turn will suffer extinction. You may have noticed that art progresses only over the dead bodies of mandarins. Balzac, who did more to emancipate the novel than even Richardson or Scott, killed dozens of mandarins, and to the untimely end of his career he never troubled to hide his murderous scorn of them. We have mentioned Balzac purposely, for it is a strange fact that, though English novelists have more to learn from him than from any other author, he has been practically without influence in England, despite many, and some excellent, translations. People talk easily here of the Scope of the Modern Novel (since *Robert Elsmere*, presumably) ; but before uttering that foolish phrase again it would be well for them to read the whole of the *Comédie Humaine*. We have no intention of discovering Balzac for the benefit of the Authors' Society; nor do we think it possible to say anything new about Balzac. Our idea is that Balzac, like most classics, is more taken for granted than read; and that his work, if authors and public could be got to swallow it, would form a valuable stimulant and corrective medicine. It would correct the current notions about the all-embracing quality of the English novel, and it might stimulate the English novelist to invent a new pattern of plot. What separates Balzac from nearly all other novelists is not his width of range in the portrayal of individuals, but his faculty for portraying communities, and for describing large co-operative activities. The world is made up of individuals, but it is also made up of communities, and the community is surely as interesting as the individual. Why, then, should the novelist confine himself to one or the few? A hundred sheep are more interesting than one, or than five. Note that the deification of love in fiction involves the sacrifice of the community as a subject. Men and women make love, not as members of a community, but as individuals; but when they proceed to other affairs, they at once resume their position in the community. Much of Balzac's best work was miles away from the *pays du tendre*.[3] Take *The Country Doctor*, which is the history of the

3. Literally, "the country of tender sentiments." An allusion to the allegorical map of love composed by Mlle de Scudéry (1607–1701) and her salon; hence any highly artificial treatment of love.

regeneration of a country-side. Till nearly the close there is no hint of love, and there is no hint of a plot in our restricted sense of the term. Yet *The Country Doctor* is of Balzac's very finest. No one can read it without feeling the pettiness of the modern novel. Another similar example, by a curious coincidence of title, is *The Country Parson* (we give the names for convenience from Dent's uniform edition). Still another example, and the most striking of all, though not the most successful, is *Bureaucracy*, in which the microcosm of a Government office is used as the sole material for an absorbing drama. Even where Balzac centred the light of imagination on an individual, ignoring partially the individual's relation to any community, he seldom made love the predominant theme. *Old Goriot*, *The Wild Ass's Skin*, *The Quest of the Absolute*, and *The Commission in Lunacy* show what he could do without the enkindling spark of love. We do not at all mean to infer that Balzac despised love. He was a great lover, and a great writer of love-letters—one of the greatest; his finest work, in the opinion of most persons, is a love-story. We mean only that he was not obsessed by love, and that he found his material everywhere; he had no prejudices in favour of this or against that kind of material. With him it was an axiom that no aspect of human life and activity is lacking in interest; his net was cast with an inclusive sweep. He sought to hold the mirror up, not to two men trying to kiss one maid, but to the whole of human nature. Further, he never tried to divert his readers, but rather to enthral them; he could not stoop to the trickeries by which the practised writer keeps the reader from being bored. He gave his readers credit for the same seriousness as himself—and the astonishing thing is that they justified his belief in them. They listened eagerly while he told them of matters of which they had not heard before and have never heard since.

The fields which Balzac tilled lie fallow now, and more also, for even he could not plough the entire domain. Meantime, we continue blandly the raising of our five varieties of novel. In a world more complex than that of Balzac, a world where mutual comprehension and imaginative sympathy are the conditions precedent to any real social progress, our novelists, whose supreme function it is to promote by their imagination such imaginative sympathy, go on with their endless repetition of an erotic pattern. Love will survive the neglect of novelists: have no fear. The poets can safely be left to attend to love for a while, thus allowing the novelists to study concerns less sublime, but scarcely less vital. Novelists have work to do (you may call it humdrum work, if you like), and they are not doing it. All the great novelists, from Cervantes to Tolstoi, have felt the consciousness of a mission to humanity, an impulse equal with the impulse of pure art. All of them have accomplished more than art. What are our novelists doing? If they are not fiddling while Rome burns, they are certainly flirting pre-occupied on lawns while the Parish Council outside is manufacturing raw drama by the ton.

In our next article we propose to refer to some aspects of modern life which seem to us to offer material for novels that should appeal to intelligent people.

II

In our first article we tried to show that the scope of the modern novel, despite vague talk about its enlargement, is a very limited one. We pointed out that it seldom attempted to deal with the organic life of communities, and that even in dealing with individual lives it ignored all activities save those of love, war, and theological speculation, utilising the whole world-spectacle merely as a background for a love-affair. We gave Balzac as almost the solitary instance of a novelist who had reduced love to its proper level in the scheme of things, and had wrought the material of his novels with equal impartiality from all human activities, individual and communal, recognising all as equally fit—love among the rest. We promised to refer to some aspects of modern life which should yield the stuff of novels that might appeal to intelligent people.

We must now be allowed to proceed from abstract generalisation to the concrete and the personal, since it is only by so doing that we can usefully enforce our argument. Some weeks ago the present writer dined at an Italian restaurant in Victoria-street—a long and ornate refectory frequented by engineers, shopkeepers, travellers, demi-mondaines, and the indefinable: all London either dines or starves every day, and there are a dozen epical novels in any large restaurant—but that is an aside. We dined early, and the sun was still above the sky-affronting roofs of the thoroughfare when we passed into Victoria-street with the intention of perceiving London as though it were a foreign city. We had not gone a hundred yards before we descried a red campanile overtopping the houses on the South side. The original and striking beauty of this tower drew us at once, and we were soon in front of a prodigious edifice which has lately risen like an island out of the sea of flats stretching between Victoria-street and the river. Now we were intellectually aware that a Roman Catholic cathedral was being erected in London, but we had till that moment no idea of its size, its beauty, or its significance.[4] During the nineteenth century only one cathedral came into existence in England, that of Truro. In an epoch of steam, cathedrals do not spring up like mushrooms. This cathedral in Victoria-street, we were informed and believe, is larger than St. Paul's; you could put Truro inside it. Indeed, it is colossal; and it is probably dissimilar from any other cathedral in the world. Its beauty, an indisputable beauty, is attained upon a new plan, which we are not sufficiently expert to describe, but which we may say is an abrupt departure from the Gothic in the direction of a Byzantine style. It impressed us as an art-work of genuine inspiration, as the disclosure of the individuality of a powerful artist. We stood in front of it a long time, as it were nonplussed by this phenomenon of splendid art asserting itself so mildly yet so irresistibly amid the heaped-up ugliness of the West End, a superb refutation of the theory that an inartistic age can produce nothing artistic. The lower part of the main front was hidden by scaffolding and enclosed by the same wooden palings that enclose an inchoate hotel; in the palings was a door, and at the door stood a watchman.

"Have you realised the grandeur of the activity of which you are a necessary part?" we almost demanded of the watchman, but happily refrained from the absurdity. Instead, we gave him a shilling and asked leave to inspect the works. He consented, like a humane watchman, and told us that the architect himself was within. The interior of the cathedral proved to be even superior to the exterior. The building has evidently been designed, as it

4. Westminster Roman Catholic Cathedral was begun in 1895 and completed in 1903.

should be, from within outwards, and not from without inwards. The sense of spaciousness, already great, is greatly increased as you stand inside the vast portals and behold the interior perspective. Everywhere are large flat surfaces, broken only by other flat surfaces. No matter where the eye turns, it is met by arched perspectives. The roof is a succession of domes. The floor rises in a series of planes to the apse. With a huge traction-engine to the left, a sort of mortar-mill to the right, and the wild litter of construction before and behind, we gazed about us on the bare and glorious walls. The rays of the setting sun slanted in through the fretted stone *grilles* of the western windows: a ballad-like detail, but we record it. We gazed at the distant apse. Under the apse, looking round, stood a figure in a frock-coat and a silk hat. That figure was the architect—the artist surveying the art-work at the close of the day's labour; a few artisans—carvers, and the like—engaged on sub-contracts, alone remained of the army of labourers, industrious ants dotted here and there in the immense nave. The scene, though almost static at that juncture, was intensely dramatic; it might have been arranged for us. And we are eager to admit that it appealed with tremendous force to our imagination. We registered as a noble day that day on which we had been privileged—yes, privileged—to see the artist beneath his own domes, yet unfinished, yet untidy and unkempt, but whose massive grandeur no planks and poles, no refuse of brick-ends, no cranes and traction-engines could for an instant disguise. Well might the artist say, to future ages as to this unheeding age: "*Si monumentum requiris, circumspice.*" 5

Huysmans has written a finicking and egotistic novel, *La Cathé-drale*, in which the unsurpassed beauty of Chartres is degraded to the uses of an arena for the antics of a diseased soul. Why should we not have a novel entitled *The Cathedral* of which the cathedral is not the theatre but the theme? Take this cathedral at Westminster, and follow backwards the two wonderful streams of creative force of which it is the confluence. First, there is the desire, vaguely stirring in the Roman Catholic community in England, for a Sign,

5. "If you would see his monument, look around you." An epitaph for Sir Christopher Wren, inscribed over the north door of Saint Paul's Cathedral, London.

a supreme outward demonstration that Catholicism authentically lives on. You can judge every religion by its fanes, and the sign must be a fane; a fane splendid among fanes, one that shall silence argument and compel an awful respect. Consider the courage of the first man of them that said: "Let us build the greatest cathedral in London, perhaps in England." Think of the tremors of exquisite excitement and anticipation that thrilled the small assembly—it must have been a small one—where the audacious proposal was mooted. Think how the idea spread abroad through England went over to Rome, and came back sealed with the seal of Papal consent. Think of the thousand intrigues, base and otherwise, which always precede the practical inception of a co-operative enterprise such as this, and which are buried beneath its foundations as the Orientals bury human victims beneath their still more splendid *basilicae*; the intrigues of the site, of the money, of the builder, of the architect. Before a stone is laid, or even a sketch drawn, probably hundreds of people have been potentially unhoused: think of that simple detail. Such a mighty business embraces the whole human comedy.

And then tremble before the indubitable fact that all this complex and passionate preliminary effort will be rendered futile and nugatory unless the Artist can be found. Belgium spent sixty millions of francs on a Palace of Justice, and got, not a work of art, but merely the biggest building of the century. The Catholics of England might have fared as badly, or even worse. Now pass to the second stream of creative force—the career of the destined artist. We shall be pardoned for mentioning here a picturesque but not essential rumour—namely, that the architect of the Westminster Cathedral began life humbly, as a worker with his hands. It matters not a whit, since in any event he must have begun humbly; if he had been a duke's son, his beginning would still have been humble in comparison with the fine climax as he stands under his own dome. Watch the genius of this man unfolding, conquering obstacle after obstacle, and gradually emerging into the light of due appreciation. At length he has matured; he exists as the artist competent to perform the work. Now comes the dramatic moment—will he be chosen? The chances are a hundred to one against it, for it is notorious that opportunity, especially in architecture, almost always knocks at the wrong door;

fails often indeed, to get into the right street. An hour's walk through the heart of London will amply prove this. But by some amazing chance the artist and the opportunity for once meet. The artist receives the majestic order: "Build us a great cathedral. There shall be no contract. Ask for money and you will get it."

It was not business, but it was magnificent.

When the Cathedral is consecrated, and that overwhelming result of an aspiration fundamentally religious bursts on the world in a scenic display ordained to the last detail by centuries of immutable precedent, who will think of these things? Who will have the historic imagination to perceive the strange and lovely significance of that ritualised act so belated in the twentieth century? Who will follow the two streams of force to their origins? Not twenty, not ten people, in the ten thousand who will sniff the incense of a great occasion. Here, then, is the chance for the novelist, and his duty is to seize it. We are not, of course, so indiscreet as to say that the novelist should weave his fiction out of *that* cathedral-raising, or out of any cathedral-raising. His use of actuality may be less crude, without losing a particle of its effectiveness. We have merely indicated a general direction in which the novelist might proceed. We have adumbrated a sort of novel which would be utterly different from any modern novel. If it be urged that *The Cathedral* would of necessity be a dull novel, we ask: Why should it be dull? It would comprise a large segment of the circle of life; it might include all passions, and many various activities both artistic and commercial. It would be dramatic, and certainly it would be realistic. Finally, it would be grandiose, and would culminate in a spectacle of sheer beauty.

"But," says the literal person, the person who reads only what is written and hears only what is said, "a cathedral is not built every day." In a third article we will try to discover subjects more workaday and practicable which are crying aloud to be dealt with.

III

In previous articles we have attempted to show that much of modern life is ignored by the novelist, who, pre-occupied with love-affairs, persists in wholly disregarding the organic existence of communities, and we have given an illustration, in the shape of a brief description of an imaginary story, called *The Cathedral*, of the sort of novel, dealing with life in the communal mass, which might be written, but is not written—at any rate in England. Lest that illustration may be considered too grandiose and exceptional to rank as a fair average example (we admit that it is almost unique), we propose now to give one or two other instances of rich life-ore from which a new fiction might be "got" by any novelist who does not deem himself bound to do nothing that has not been done before.

We were going through a famous park a few weeks since, and the road, leaving the park, ascended to a high bridge, and gave a surprisingly sudden view of the London and North Western main line. To the right, the quadruple "way," proudly styled "permanent," stretched for a thousand yards in an absolutely straight line to the next bridge, where it vanished on a curve: and the thousand yards looked like a hundred. To the left lay the station, a countryside station, but spacious and commanding, like everything on the North Western, specklessly clean, painfully in order—not a truck or a fire-bucket out of place. Four enamelled signs, white on a profound blue, proclaimed the legend, "Cheddington," at distances mathematically calculated. As we looked on the complex and immense apparatus of rails and wires and posts and levers and platforms and granite chippings, lifeless, and apparently deserted in the fierce sunshine of the summer afternoon, the romance, the humanity, and the passions of a great railway system seemed to rise up and overwhelm us. We thought of Kipling's line, as essential truth:

Romance brought up the nine-fifteen. [6]

We thought, too, of a little German *frau* whom we had once known, whose chief pride was that her husband, an Englishman, was a booking-clerk at Paddington. No one ever saw that husband, because he was always giving out tickets for the Thames Valley, Devonshire, and Wales. Imprisoned in a cabinet from morn till night, he selected with unerring precision magic bits of cardboard from hundreds of square holes, so that people, labelled with these, might be carried, like parcels, from one spot on the earth's surface

6. From "The King" (1894).

to another. At night he went home to his loving wife, and during the day his wife walked about in the radiance reflected from his singular calling. And the curious, the interesting, thing is, that her acquaintances accepted her pride in this clerkship as justifiable and proper. It *did* give her a distinction lacking to other *fraus* of her status, and no one mentioned her without mentioning that her husband was a booking-clerk at Paddington. Here was another aspect of a great railway system. We thought, also, of the departures of the Scotch expresses from Euston in the last race to the north: twenty thousand pounds' worth of rolling-stock upstanding motionless till the seconds'-hand of the stationmaster's chronometer showed precisely, to the least infinitesimal fraction, ten o'clock; the calm and yet self-conscious step of the young engineer, in blue, with a bowler-hat, as he made his way to the engine and assumed command for those breathless journeys over the wise greybeard who had driven engines before he was born; the expectant hush, the final slam, whistle, and flag-waving, and then the slow and stately withdrawal from the precincts of the station. So that was the Scotch express! It was nothing after all! And yet what could be more impressive, romantic? Can one wonder that Reuter and the Central News followed it mile by mile, and as July advanced to August the record of its feats got nearer to the middle page of the newspaper, and the top of the column in that page? We thought, too, of a conversation we had had with a porter on a tiny branch line about the grand altercation between directors and men at Stockport, and with what a sad, shrewd air he gave up the men for lost. "The directors won't stand no nonsense." *The directors*—his accent as he spoke that word, with a kind of fearful pride in those terrible autocrats—his accent alone was worth a paragraph. And is not the whole system worth a novel, worth a whole school of novels? Despite the recent indictment by Mr. H. G. Wells,[7] a railway corporation like the London and North Western represents the limit of modern powers of organisation. It is "made like a gun," disciplined like the British navy, and fifteen thousand pounds of

7. Wells' essay, "Locomotion in the Twentieth Century," appeared in the *Fortnightly Review*, Vol. LXIX (April, 1901). It was later published as Chapter One of *Anticipations* (London: Chapman and Hall, 1902).

net profit trickle into Euston every day! It glitters with the pride of life—it is as proud of itself as a girl in a new frock, or a certain regiment of Lancers. It is "crack." It throbs from end to end with "the human interest," you simply can't get away from humanity on a railway. Look into the cabin at the level crossing, where the venerable and maimed porter ends his days; look at the director's mansion, park, yacht, private car; look at the maiden lady at Cheltenham, whose happiness for the next twelve months depends on whether the company pays seven or seven-and-a-half! Crude contrasts, you say! Just so: a contrast cannot be too crude; the biggest effects are always crude. What we want is a little more crudeness and a little less fining and refining. Lord, give us plot: that is what the modern fashionable novelist should pray. We can fancy Providence directing him to a railway, and him protesting that there is no love in a railway system—as if Cupid was not seated on every signal-post! But of course he would not perceive these Cupids unless the General Manager fell in love with the signal-man's daughter!

So much for railways. Take a parish council. We know a village which is dominated by a single landowner, a plain man, who, by inheritance and purchase, has added acre to acre till he farms, personally farms, a superficies of mother-earth three times the size of the City of London. He owns all the houses in the village, and he employs nearly all the men in the village, directly or indirectly. And yet he is such a very plain man that once when he asked us our profession he exclaimed, on our reply: "An author, what's that?" Now there was an election of the parish council in that village, eight seats and nine nominations. The great landlord was among the candidates. The milkman, the grocer, a little farmer, a horse-dealer, and three others were elected, and the great landlord was placed ninth. The thing was reported in three lines in the local newspaper. But what intense dramatic significance in that silent rebuke so effectively administered by the village to its lord! Can you not imagine him lying awake at night and trying to laugh off the un-answerable verdict of the ballot-box? If such things happen else-where, one may assume that they happen also in Wessex, and that Mr. Hardy knows of them. Yet none could guess from the noble series of Wessex novels that Wessex had any corporate life within its borders. Why should this be so? If any man asserts that corporate life is not a fit subject for fiction, we merely and flatly traverse the statement. We feel that it is, and we are convinced that, for example, the incident which we have briefly narrated contains the basis of an admirable short story; also that Balzac would have written that story had time and circumstances permitted. Go a step higher, and take the municipal life of an industrial town. If you wish to see a town alive, strenuously alive beneath a calm surface, see it immediately before the decennial assessment for local taxes. Then you will have glimpses of a thousand intrigues, knotted, interwoven, inexpressibly mixed, and all circling round the solitary and awful figure of the assessor. How difficult it is to believe, in these tense days, that the assessor is a human being like yourself; that he is not a sort of blind god! We remember the wind of rage and exasperation that roared through a town when it turned out that the assessment of the house of the assessor's brother had been lowered, while that of a precisely similar house next door was unaltered. And yet not a house-owner in the town—not a churchwarden, a local preacher, a magistrate, or Sunday-school superintendent—but had been ready to jeopardise his immortal soul if, by so doing, he could have got five pounds off *his* house or factory! If the principal aim of the novel should be, as it is, to show forth character under circumstances of drama, there are few phenomena that could surpass in suitability for it the assessment of property in a town that sends a Radical to Parliament.

We might roam further, and discover many more fallow fields which await their tillage. But space forbids, and if we have not already said enough to prove our point, we could never prove it, and we have spoken in vain. Naturally, the literary superstition that a man ceases to be interesting when he ceases to be idle (in the ordinary sense of the word "idle"), and that the novelist must not follow him into the serious affairs of his life, the affairs which force him into this community or that, the affairs which will absorb him long after he has forgotten that he ever kissed a girl behind a haystack or said Bo! to another gander—this superstition will expire slowly. Still, we think it will expire.

In conclusion, let us repeat what we stated in our first article, namely, that we have no wish to deride Love, either as an activity of man or as a subject of the novelist's art. We think it is the best. But we emphatically demur to the proposition that Love is Life. It is a part of Life, and of most lives only a very small part.

Academy, No. 1519 (June 15, 1901), pp. 517–518; No. 1521 (June 19, 1901), pp. 557–558; No. 1524 (July 20, 1901), pp. 57–58.

The Novel-Reading Public (1909)

As a novelist, a creative artist working in the only literary "form" which widely appeals to the public, I sometimes wonder curiously what the public is. Not often, because it is bad for the artist to think often about the public. I have never by enquiry from those experts my publishers learnt anything useful or precise about the public. I hear the word "the public," "the public," uttered in awe or in disdain, and this is all. The only conclusion which can be drawn from what I am told is that the public is the public. Still, it appears that my chief purchasers are the circulating libraries. It appears that without the patronage of the circulating libraries I should either have to live on sixpence a day or starve. Hence, when my morbid curiosity is upon me, I stroll into Mudie's or the Times Book Club, or I hover round Smith's bookstall at Charing Cross.

The crowd at these places is the prosperous crowd, the crowd which grumbles at income-tax and pays it. Three hundred and seventy-five thousand persons paid income-tax last year, under protest: they stand for the existence of perhaps a million souls, and this million is a handful floating more or less easily on the surface of the forty millions of the population. The great majority of my readers must be somewhere in this million. There can be few hirers of books who neither pay income-tax nor live on terms of dependent equality with those who pay it. I see at the counters people on whose foreheads it is written that they know themselves to be the salt of the earth. Their assured, curt voices, their proud carriage, their clothes, the similarity of their manners, all show that they belong to a caste and that the caste has been successful in the struggle for life. It is called the middle-class, but it ought to be called the upper-class, for nearly everything is below it. I go to the Stores, to Harrod's Stores, to Barker's, to Rumpelmeyer's, to the Royal Academy, and to a dozen clubs in Albemarle Street and Dover

Street, and I see again just the same crowd, well-fed, well-dressed, completely free from the cares which beset at least five-sixths of the English race. They have worries; they take taxis because they must not indulge in motor-cars, hansoms because taxis are an extravagance, and omnibuses because they really must economise. But they never look twice at twopence. They curse the injustice of fate, but secretly they are aware of their luck. When they have nothing to do, they say in effect: "Let's go out and spend something." And they go out. They spend their lives in spending. They deliberately gaze into shop windows in order to discover an outlet for their money. You can catch them at it any day.

I do not belong to this class by birth. Artists very seldom do. I was born slightly beneath it. But by the help of God and strict attention to business I have gained the right of entrance into it. I admit that I have imitated its deportment, with certain modifications of my own; I think its deportment is in many respects worthy of imitation. I am acquainted with members of it; some are artists like myself; a few others win my sympathy by honestly admiring my work; and the rest I like because I like them. But the philosopher in me cannot, though he has tried, melt away my profound and instinctive hostility to this class. Instead of decreasing, my hostility grows. I say to myself: "I can never be content until this class walks along the street in a different manner, until that now absurd legend has been worn clean off its forehead." Henry Harland was not a great writer, but he said : *Il faut souffrir pour être sel.* [1] I ask myself impatiently: "When is this salt going to begin to suffer?" That is my attitude towards the class. I frequent it but little. Nevertheless I know it intimately, nearly all the intimacy being on my side. For I have watched it during long, agreeable sardonic months and years in foreign hotels. In foreign hotels you get the essence of it, if not the cream.

Chief among its characteristics—after its sincere religious worship of money and financial success—I should put its intense self-consciousness as a class. The world is a steamer in which it is travelling

---

1. "One must suffer to be salt." Henry Harland (1861–1905), an American author, was editor of the *Yellow Book*. His best-known novel is *The Cardinal's Snuff-Box* (1900).

saloon. Occasionally it goes to look over from the promenade deck at the steerage. Its feelings towards the steerage are kindly. But the tone in which it says "the steerage" cuts the steerage off from it more effectually than many bulkheads. You perceive also from that tone that it could never be surprised by anything that the steerage might do. Curious social phenomenon, the steerage! In the saloon there runs a code, the only possible code, the final code; and it is observed. If it is not observed, the infraction causes pain, distress. Another marked characteristic is its gigantic temperamental dullness, unresponsiveness to external suggestion, a lack of humour—in short, a heavy and half-honest stupidity: ultimate product of gross prosperity, too much exercise, too much sleep. Then I notice a grim passion for the status quo. This is natural. Let these people exclaim as they will against the structure of society, the last thing they desire is to alter it. This passion shows itself in a naive admiration for everything that has survived its original usefulness, such as sail-drill, uniforms, physical courage. Its mirror of true manhood remains that excellent and appalling figure, the Brushwood Boy.[2] The passion for the status quo also shows itself in a general defensive sullen hatred of all ideas whatever.

You cannot argue with these people. "Do you really think so?" they will politely murmur, when you have asserted your belief that the earth is round, or something like that. And their tone says: "Would you mind very much if we leave this painful subject? My feelings on it are too deep for utterance." Lastly, I am impressed by their attitude towards the artist, which is mediaeval, or perhaps Roman. Blind to nearly every form of beauty, they scorn art, and scorning art they scorn artists. It was this class which, at inaugurations of public edifices, invented the terrible toast-formula, "The architect *and contractor*." And if epics were inaugurated by banquet, this class would certainly propose the health of the poet and printer, after the King and the publishers. Only sheer ennui sometimes drives it to seek distraction in the artist's work. It prefers the novelist among artists because the novel gives the longest surcease from ennui at the least expenditure of money and effort.

2. A story by Kipling, first published in 1895, and later included in *The Day's Work* (1898). The "Boy" is a stock Kipling hero, half soldier and half schoolboy.

It is inevitable that I shall be accused of exaggeration, cynicism, or prejudice: probably all three. Whenever one tells the truth in this island of compromise, one is sure to be charged on these counts, and to be found guilty. But I too am of the sporting race, and forty years have taught me that telling the truth is the most dangerous and most glorious of all forms of sport. Alpine climbing in winter is nothing to it. I like it. I will only add that I have been speaking of the solid *bloc* of the caste; I admit the existence of a broad fringe of exceptions. And I truly sympathize with the *bloc*. I do not blame the *bloc*. I know that the members of the *bloc* are, like me, the result of evolutionary forces now spent. My hostility to the *bloc* is beyond my control, an evolutionary force gathering way. Upon my soul, I love the *bloc*. But when I sit among it, clothed in correctness, and reflect that the *bloc* maintains me and mine in a sort of comfort, because I divert its leisure, the humour of the situation seems to me enormous.

II

I continue from last week my notes on the great stolid comfortable class which forms the backbone of the novel-reading public. The best novelists do not find their material in this class. Thomas Hardy never. Eden Phillpotts, never. H. G. Wells, almost never; now and then he glances at it ironically, in an episodic manner. Hale White (Mark Rutherford), never. Rudyard Kipling, rarely; when he touches it, the reason is usually because it happens to embrace the military caste, and the result is usually such mawkish stories as "William the Conqueror" and "The Brushwood Boy." J. M. Barrie, never. W. W. Jacobs, never. Murray Gilchrist, never. Joseph Conrad, never. Israel Zangwill, never. Leonard Merrick, very slightly. Frank Harris, never. George Moore, in a "Drama in Muslin," wrote a masterpiece about it twenty years ago; "Vain Fortune" is also good; but for a long time it has ceased to interest the artist in him, and his very finest work ignores it. George Meredith was writing greatly about it thirty years ago. Henry James, with the chill detachment of an outlander, fingers the artistic and cosmopolitan fringe of it. In a rank lower than these, we have

William De Morgan and John Galsworthy.[3] The former does not seem to be inspired by it. As for John Galsworthy, the quality in him which more than any other vitiates his right to be considered a major artist, is precisely his fierce animosity to this class. Major artists are never so cruelly hostile to anything whatever as John Galsworthy is to this class. He does in fiction what John Sargent does in paint; and their inimical observation of their subjects will gravely prejudice both of them in the eyes of posterity. I think I have mentioned all the novelists who have impressed themselves at once on the public, and genuinely on the handful of persons whose taste is severe and sure. There may be, there are, other novelists alive whose work will end by satisfying the tests of the handful. Whether any of these others deal mainly with the superior stolid comfortable, I cannot certainly say; but I think not. I am ready to assert that in quite modern English fiction there exists no large and impartial picture of the superior stolid comfortable which could give pleasure to a reader of taste. The best novelists who now sympathetically occupy themselves with the superior stolid comfortable are writers of the calibre of Anthony Hope, E. F. Benson, Mrs. Humphry Ward, Miss May Sinclair: peers of Henry Arthur Jones, and slightly better than Arthur Wing Pinero.[4] Rather hard

3. All of the writers mentioned found subjects outside the urban middle classes, though in very different ways. Bennett's views on a number of them are included in this book: on Eden Phillpotts, see pp. 166–181; on Wells, pp. 186–202; on Kipling, pp. 182–185; on Frank Harris, pp. 155–158; on George Moore, pp. 135–154; on Galsworthy, pp. 203–210. W. W. Jacobs (1863–1943) was best known for his humorous tales of sailors, though he also wrote the classic horror story *The Monkey's Paw*. Murray Gilchrist (1868–1917) was a regional novelist of the English Peak District. Israel Zangwill (1864–1926), the Jewish writer and Zionist leader, wrote about Jewish life in the London East End. Leonard Merrick (1864–1939) wrote novels set in Paris. William De Morgan (1839–1917) was a potter of the Burne-Jones, William Morris circle, who took to writing in his sixties, and wrote seven novels of working-class and artists' lives.

4. Bennett's examples, with the odd exception of May Sinclair, are late-Victorian and Edwardian popular second-rate writers. Anthony Hope Hawkins (1863–1933) was the author of the "Ruritanian" romances *The Prisoner of Zenda* (1894) and *Rupert of Hentzau* (1898). Mrs. Humphry Ward is best known for her novel *Robert Elsmere*. May Sinclair (1879–1946), an altogether better novelist than any of these, was at the beginning of her career and had not yet written the

on the class that alone has made novel-writing a profession in which a man can earn a reasonable livelihood!

The explanation of this state of affairs is obscure. True, that distinguished artists are very seldom born into the class. But such an explanation would be extremely inadequate. Artists often move creatively with ease far beyond the boundaries of their native class. Thomas Hardy is not a peasant, nor was Stendhal a marquis. I could not, with any sort of confidence, offer an explanation. I am, however, convinced that only a supreme artist could now handle successfully the material presented by the class in question. The material itself lacks interest, lacks essential vitality, lacks both moral and spectacular beauty. It powerfully repels the searcher after beauty and energy. It may be in a decay. One cannot easily recall a great work of art of which the subject is decadence.

The backbone of the novel-reading public is excessively difficult to please, and rarely capable of enthusiasm. Listen to Mudie subscribers on the topic of fiction, and you will scarcely ever hear the accent of unmixed pleasure. It is surprising how even favourites are maltreated in conversation. Some of the most successful favourites seem to be hated, and to be read under protest. The general form of approval is a doubtful "Ye-es!" with a whole tail of unspoken "buts" lying behind it. Occasionally you catch the ecstatic note, "Oh! *Yes*; a *sweet* book!" Or, with masculine curtness: "Fine book, that!" (For example, "The Hill," by Horace Annesley Vachell.[5]) It is in the light of such infrequent exclamations that you may judge the tepid reluctance of other praise. The reason of all this is two-fold; partly in the book, and partly in the reader. The backbone dislikes the raising of any question which it deems to have been decided: a peculiarity which at once puts it in opposition to all fine work, and to nearly all passable second-rate work. It also dislikes being confronted with anything that it considers "unpleasant";

psychological novels that made her reputation. Henry Arthur Jones (1851–1929) and Arthur Wing Pinero (1855–1934) were the founders of the English school of "problem drama," modeled—though at some distance—on Ibsen. (See Jones's *The Case of Rebellious Susan* [1894] and Pinero's *The Second Mrs. Tanqueray* [1893]).

5. Horace Annesley Vachell (1861–1955). His novel *The Hill* (1905) was a school story set at Harrow.

that is to say, interesting. It has a genuine horror of truth neat. It quite honestly asks "to be taken out of itself," unaware that to be taken out of itself is the very last thing it really desires. What it wants is to be confirmed in itself. Its religion is the status quo. The difficulties of the enterprise of not offending it either in subject or treatment are, perhaps, already sufficiently apparent. But incomparably the greatest obstacle to pleasing it lies in the positive fact that it prefers not to be pleased. It undoubtedly objects to the very sensations which an artist aims to give. If I have heard once, I have heard fifty times resentful remarks similar to: "I'm not going to read any more bosh by *him*! Why, I simply couldn't put the thing down!" It is profoundly hostile to art, and the empire of art. It will not willingly yield. Its attitude to the magic spell is its attitude to the dentist's gas-bag. This is the most singular trait that I have discovered in the backbone throughout all my agreeably sardonic observation of it. My curious joy in it will never diminish.

Why, then, does the backbone put itself to the trouble of reading current fiction? The answer is that it does so, not with any artistic, spiritual, moral, or informative purpose, but simply in order to pass time. Lately, one hears, it has been neglecting fiction in favour of books of memoirs, often scandalous, and historical compilations, for the most part scandalous sexually. That it should tire of the fiction offered to it is not surprising, seeing that it so seldom gets the fiction of its dreams. The supply of good, workmanlike fiction is much larger to-day than ever it was in the past. The same is to be said of the supply of genuinely distinguished fiction. But the supply of fiction which really appeals to the backbone of the fiction-reading public is far below the demand. The backbone grumbles, but it continues to hire the offensive stuff, because it cannot obtain sufficient of the inoffensive,—and time hangs so heavy! The caprice for grape-nut history and memoirs cannot endure, for it is partially a pose. Besides, the material will run short. After all, Napoleon only had a hundred and three mistresses, and we are already at Mademoiselle Georges.[6] The backbone, always loyal to its old beliefs,

6. Marguerite Josephine Wemmer Georges (1787–1867), a French actress, was a favorite of Napoleon.

will return to fiction with a new gusto, and the cycle of events will recommence.

But it is well for novelists to remember that, in the present phase of society and mechanical conditions of the literary market, their professional existence depends on the fact that the dullest class in England takes to novels merely as a refuge from its own dullness. And while it is certain that no novelist of real value really pleases that class, it is equally certain that without its support (willing or unwilling—usually the latter), no novelist could live by his pen. Remove the superior stolid comfortable, and the circulating libraries would expire. And exactly when the circulating libraries breathed their last sigh the publishers of fiction would sympathetically give up the ghost. If you happen to be a literary artist, it makes you think—the reflection that when you dine you eat the bread un-willingly furnished by the enemies of art and of progress! Still, there is a holy joy even in that.

III

I want to dig a little deeper through the strata of the public. Below the actual fiction-reading public which I have described, there is a much vaster potential public. It exists in London, and it exists also in the provinces. I will describe it as I have found it in the industrial midlands and north. Should the picture seem black, let me say that my picture of a similar public in London would be even blacker. In all essential qualities I consider the lower middle-class which regards, say, Manchester as its centre, to be superior to the lower middle-class which regards Charing Cross as its centre.

All around Manchester there are groups of municipalities which lie so close to one another that each group makes one town. Take a medium group comprising a quarter of a million inhabitants, with units ranging from sixty down to sixteen thousand. I am not going to darken my picture with a background of the manual workers, the immense majority of whom never read anything that costs more than a penny—unless it be Gale's Special Finals.[7] I will deal only with the comparatively enlightened crust—employers, clerks,

7. A newspaper devoted to horse racing, published in Birmingham.

officials, and professional men and their families—which has formed on the top of that crust, with an average income of possibly two hundred per annum per family. This crust is the élite of the group. It represents its highest culture, and in bulk it is the "lower middle-class" of Tory journalism. In London some of the glitter of the class above it is rubbed on to it by contact. One is apt to think that because there are bookshops in the Strand and large circulating libraries in Oxford Street, and these thoroughfares are thronged with the lower middle-class, therefore the lower middle-class buys or hires books. In my industrial group the institutions and machinery perfected by the upper class for itself do not exist at all, and one may watch the lower without danger of being led to false conclusions by the accidental propinquity of phenomena that have really nothing whatever to do with it.

Now in my group of a quarter of a million souls there is not a single shop devoted wholly or principally to the sale of books. Not one. You might discover a shop specialising in elephants or radium; but a real bookshop does not exist. In a town of forty thousand inhabitants there will be a couple of stationers, whose chief pride is that they are "steam printers" or lithographers. Enter their shops, and you will see a few books. Tennyson in gilt. Volumes of the Temple Classics or Everyman. Hymn books. Bibles. The latest cheap Shakespeare. Of new books no example except the brothers Hocking.[8] The stationer will tell you that there is no demand for books; but that he can procure anything you specially want by return of post. He will also tell you that on the whole he makes no profit out of books; what trifle he captures on his meagre sales he loses on books unsold. He may inform you that his rival has entirely ceased to stock books of any sort, and that he alone stands for letters in the midst of forty thousand people. In a town of sixty thousand there will be a largeish stationer's with a small separate book department. Contents similar to the other shop, with a fair selection of cheap reprints, and half a dozen of the most notorious new novels, such as novels by Marie Corelli, Max Pemberton, Mrs.

8. Silas Hocking and his brother Joseph (1860–1937) were both ordained ministers in the United Methodist Free Church. Each wrote more than ninety novels, mostly religious, generally set in Cornwall.

Humphry Ward.[9] That is all. Both the shops described will have two or three regular book-buying clients, not more than ten in a total of a hundred thousand. These ten are book-lovers. They follow the book lists. They buy to the limit of their purses. And in the cult of literature they keep themselves quite apart from the society of the town, despising it. The town is simply aware that they are "great readers."

Another agency for the radiation of light in the average town first mentioned is the Municipal Free Library. The yearly sum spent on it is entirely inadequate to keep it up-to-date. A fraction of its activity is beneficial, as much to the artisan as to members of the crust. But the chief result of the penny-in-the-pound rate is to supply women old and young with outmoded, viciously respectable, viciously sentimental fiction. A few new novels get into the Library every year. They must, however, be "innocuous," that is to say, devoid of original ideas. This is, of course, inevitable in an institution presided over by a committee which has infinitely less personal interest in books than in politics or the price of coal. No Municipal Library can hope to be nearer than twenty-five years to date. Go into the average good home of the crust, in the quietude of "after-tea," and you will see a youthful miss sitting over something by Charlotte M. Yonge or Charles Kingsley. And that something is repulsively foul, greasy, sticky, black. Remember that it reaches from thirty to a hundred such good homes every year. Can you wonder that it should carry deposits of jam, egg, butter, coffee, and personal dirt? You cannot. But you are entitled to wonder why the Municipal Sanitary Inspector does not inspect it and order it to be destroyed. . . . That youthful miss in torpidity over that palimpsest of filth is what the Free Library has to show as the justification of its existence. I know what I am talking about.

A third agency is the book-pedlar. There are firms of publishers who never advertise in any literary weekly or any daily, who never publish anything new, and who may possibly be unknown to Simpkins themselves. They issue badly-printed, badly-bound, showy editions of the eternal Scott and the eternal Dickens, in many

9. Max Pemberton (1863–1950), journalist, novelist, and playwright, was the author of several historical adventure stories.

glittering volumes with scores of bleared illustrations, and they will sell them up and down the provinces by means of respectably dressed "commission agents" at prices much in excess of their value, to an ingenuous, ignorant public that has never heard of Dent and Routledge. The books are found in houses where the sole function of literature is to flatter the eye. The ability of these sub-terranean firms to dispose of deplorable editions to persons who do not want them is in itself a sharp criticism of the commercial organisation of the trade.

Let it not be supposed that my group is utterly cut off from the newest developments in imaginative prose literature. No! What the bookseller, the book-pedlar, and the Free Library have failed to do, has been accomplished by Mr. Jesse Boot, incidentally benefactor of the British provinces, who is the brain of a large firm of chemists and druggists, with branches in scores, hundreds, of towns.[10] He has several branches in my group. Each group is a circulating library, patronised by the class which has only heard of Mudie, and has not heard of the Grosvenor.[11] Mr. Jesse Boot has had the singular and beautiful idea of advertising his wares by lending books to customers and non-customers at a loss of ten thousand a year. His system is simplicity and it is cheapness. He is generous. If you desire a book which he has not got in stock he will buy it and lend it to you for twopence. Thus in the towns of my group the effulgent centre of culture is the chemist's shop. The sole point of contact with living literature is the chemist's shop. A wonderful world, this England! Two things have principally struck me about Mr. Jesse Boot's clients. One is that they are usually women, and the other is that they hire their books at haphazard, nearly in the dark, with no previous knowledge of what is good and what is bad.

It is to be added that the tremendous supply of sevenpenny bound volumes of modern fiction, and of shilling bound volumes

10. The shops of Boots the Chemists included circulating libraries from 1899 to 1966. The service supplied popular books to many areas which had no other library facilities; at its peak, during World War II, it had a million subscribers.

11. Mudie's Select Library was an older and more expensive circulating library, which charged a quarterly minimum subscription, and would therefore have been beyond the means of some of Boots' customers. The Grosvenor Gallery Library, in New Bond Street, London, was still more fashionable and expensive.

of modern belles-lettres (issued by Nelsons and others) is producing a demand in my group, is, in fact, making book-buyers where previously there were no book-buyers. These tomes now rival the works of the brothers Hocking in the stationer's shop. Their standard is decidedly above the average, owing largely to the fact that the guide-in-chief of Messrs. Nelsons happens to be a genuine man of letters. I am told that Messrs. Nelsons alone sell twenty thousand volumes a week. Yet even they have but scratched the crust. The crust is still only the raw material of a new book public. If it is cultivated and manufactured with skill it will surpass immeasurably in quantity, and quite appreciably in quality, the actual book-public. One may say that the inception of the process has been passably good. One is inclined to prophesy that within a moderately short period—say a dozen years—the centre of gravity of the book market will be rudely shifted. But the event is not yet.

New Age, IV (February 4, 11, and 18, 1909), 304, 325, 347.

Is the Novel Decaying? (1923)

If I have heard it once I have heard it fifty times during the past year, the complaint that no young novelists with promise of first-rate importance are rising up to take the place of the important middle-aged. Upon this matter I have two lines of thought:

What makes a novel important enough to impress itself upon both the discriminating few and the less discriminating many? (For first-class prestige is not obtained unless both sorts of readers are in the end impressed.) The first thing is, that the novel should seem to be true. It cannot seem true if the characters do not seem to be real. Style counts; plot counts; invention counts; originality of outlook counts; wide information counts; wide sympathy counts; but none of these counts anything like so much as the convincingness of the characters. If the characters are real, the novel will have a chance; if they are not, oblivion will be its portion.

The Sherlock Holmes stories have still a certain slight prestige. Because of the ingenuity of the plots? No. Because of the convincing-ness of the principal character? No. The man is a conventional figure. The reason is in the convincingness of the ass Watson. Watson has real life. His authenticity convinces every one, and the books in which he appears survive by reason of him. Why are *The Three Musketeers* and *Twenty Years After* the most celebrated of Dumas' thousand volumes? Many other novels of Dumas have very marvellous and brilliant plots. For instance, *Monte Cristo*. But the Musketeer volumes outshine them easily, because of the superior convincingness of the characters. Why is Sinclair Lewis's *Babbitt* a better book than his *Main Street*? Because in the latter the chief character (heroine) is a sentimental stick, while in the former the chief character, Babbitt himself, is a genuine individual that all can recognise for reality.

To render secure the importance of a novel it is necessary that the characters should clash one with another, so as to produce strong emotion, first in the author himself and second in the reader. This strong emotion cannot be produced unless the characters are *kept* true throughout. You cannot get strength out of falsity. The moment the still small voice whispers to the reader about a character, "He wouldn't have acted like that," the book is imperilled. The reader may say: "This is charming. This is amusing. This is original. This is clever. This is exciting." But if he also has to say, "It's not true," the success of the book cannot be permanent.

The foundation of good fiction is character-creating, and nothing else. The characters must be so fully true that they possess their own creator. Every deviation from truth, every omission of truth, necessarily impairs the emotional power and therefore weakens the interest.

I think that we have to-day a number of young novelists who display all manner of good qualities—originality of view, ingenuity of presentment, sound common sense, and even style. But they appear to me to be interested more in details than in the full creation of their individual characters. They are so busy with states of society as to half-forget that any society consists of individuals; and they attach too much weight to cleverness, which is perhaps the lowest of all artistic qualities. I have seldom read a cleverer book than Virginia Woolf's *Jacob's Room*, a novel which has made a great stir in a small world. It is packed and bursting with originality, and it is exquisitely written. But the characters do not vitally survive in the mind, because the author has been obsessed by details of originality and cleverness. I regard this book as characteristic of the new novelists who have recently gained the attention of the alert and the curious; and I admit that for myself I cannot yet descry any coming big novelists.

But nevertheless—and here is my second line of thought— I am fairly sure that big novelists are sprouting up. Only we do not know where to look for them. Or we cannot recognise them when we see them. It is almost certain that the majority of the great names of 1950 are writing to-day without any general appreciation. They have not been spotted as winners by the sporting prophets, and publicity paragraphs are not published about them. Few or none recognised the spring of greatness in the early Hardy, or in the early Butler, or in the early George Moore, or in the early Meredith. And there is scarcely a permanently great name in the whole history of fiction who was not when he first wrote overshadowed in the popular and even in the semi-expert esteem by much inferior novelists. The great did not at first abound in glitter and cleverness. As a rule they began by being rather clumsy, poor dears! Hence I am not pessimistic about the future of the novel.

Cassell's Weekly, March 28, 1923, p. 47. Reprinted, *Things That Have Interested Me*, *Third Series* (New York: George H. Doran Co., 1926), pp. 160–163.

The Progress of the Novel (1929)

I

A serious novelist may write either gravely or humorously, or both. Some of the least serious novelists have had no humour; and some of the most serious novelists have laughed all the time. The chief mark of the serious novelist, after fundamental creative power, is that he has a definite critical attitude towards life. Life being imperfect, the novelist's attitude must be not merely critical, but critical, often, in an adverse sense. Scratch a serious novelist, and you will find a preacher with a moral message. I doubt whether there is any exception to this rule. If you lay bare the preacher without scratching fairly deep, then the novelist has concocted a story out of a message, instead of distilling a message from a story.

A novelist should be interested first in people. When his interest in an idea gets the better of his interest in people, the idea lays a curse upon his art. ("Ideas are the curse of art," said Edmund de Goncourt, too loosely.) The serious novelist's message should never be stated, only implied; it should emerge, as one might say, of its own accord from the body of the story, like a sanitary odour, which gradually condenses into something concrete. Now and then a serious novelist is discomfited by the moral demon within him: a misfortune which happened to Tolstoi in *Resurrection*. Certain parts of *Resurrection* might have been taken from, or might have gone into, Tolstoi's moral essays. These are the worst parts of the book, and blots on a masterpiece. Gogol, Dostoievsky, Turgenev, and Schedrin, all moralists, had more control over their demons. So had Hardy.

All serious novels are based on the assumption that something is wrong. Hence the novelist's need to mingle adverse with favourable criticism. Perfection, happily unattainable, is the end of progress, is death. Imperfection is life, which springs from the clash

90

of opposing principles. Without a clash, there can be no drama; there would be nothing to write about. In the Hebraic heaven novels would be impossible; but hell is full of material for exciting and edifying fiction.

II

Serious novelists may be classified in various ways. And one way is to place them in categories according to the breadth of their outlook. Some novelists, and some of the finest, confine their critical attitude to a small section of the world. They ignore the rest. They build an imaginary wall round a tiny expanse of life and say: "Let's pretend that nothing exists on the other side of the wall." Such a novelist was Jane Austen. The pretence upon which she worked involved a more or less complete blindness to all sorts of phenomena within the tiny expanse itself. She had a definite critical attitude both favourable and adverse towards what, as a novelist, she saw; but she saw only what it suited her to see; and her job was thereby drastically simplified. (No blame to her!) What is true of Jane Austen is true of the great majority of novelists to this day.

Nevertheless the outlook of the novelist has been widening since the Jane epoch. And some of her forerunners had enclosed much larger expanses of life. For instance, Swift. From *Gulliver's Travels* you can get a more integral idea of the social organism in which the author lived than from any other novelist up to the time of Balzac. Swift's criticism was tremendously effective.

But the mighty, all-embracing, comprehensive critic of life was Balzac. Though he did not and could not put it completely into practice, Balzac's ideal of fiction might be described in two words: No walls. He took all France for his kingdom, every class of French citizen, and every activity of each class. He related one province to another, one class to another, one activity to another. Scarcely any of his books but are connected with, and illuminate, other books. His whole work coheres and is indivisible. Among novelists he was the first big sociologist. His most important subject was love; but he bound up love with other subjects which till he began to handle them no other novelist had supposed to be amenable to dramatic employment. The law of bankruptcy, for example.

He beheld the human spectacle romantically, and also, in so far as his conception of realism allowed, realistically. His researches were as prodigious as his imaginative insight was miraculous. In industry he surpassed Anthony Trollope. His creative verve has never been approached. As he himself explained, his mind had two compartments of manufacture; in the front compartment dwelt the book which he was writing, and in the back compartment the book which he would write next. He was not a man but an all-assimilating monster. He organised the novel more elaborately than any of his predecessors. He lifted it to a new and higher plane. Indeed, he may be said to have invented the modern novel.

Admittedly he fell short of his aim. His aim was to make the novel as infinite as life. But in fact he has his limitations; and walls were not unknown in the wide Balzacian landscape. In particular, like lesser novelists, he would be content to give a new name to an old type of character, persuading himself that the type was new. The Balzacian types are hardly numerous. His passionately amorous aristocratic ladies have a somewhat monotonous resemblance to one another. Nor did he deal adequately with children. Though no novelist has described a baby's bath more exquisitely than Balzac, the novelist lacked interest in those important and egotistical creatures, boys and girls. The Balzacian world is almost childless. Yet if as a man it had occurred to him to be a father, he might as a novelist have brought into his world children destined to be as famous or notorious as Madame de Sérizy, Diane de Maufrigneuse, Horace Bianchon, or Lucien de Rubempré.

The unique achievement of Balzac seems to have frightened novelists for fifty years after his death. It was as if he had said to future generations with his last breath: "Go one better—if you can." Nobody did. Nobody attempted to do so. And only one man attempted even to rival Balzac. That man was Zola. Zola's scheme was comparable in scope and magnitude to Balzac's. He planned it, he began it, and he finished it. It comprises at least three first-rate novels, and the architecture of it is more logical and more shapely than Balzac's. But Zola created not a single character that has stamped itself as deeply on the memory of western mankind as any one of a dozen or a score of Balzac's characters. Moreover, Zola carried the novel no farther than Balzac. He did nothing new. He was not a pioneer, an explorer, a discoverer. He was merely a super-craftsman of unsurpassed industry and tenacity of purpose who knew how to organise his terrific energy, and who had hours of genius.

III

Then, at the end of the century, came the next pioneer, H. G. Wells. If Wells thought of Balzac at all, which I doubt, he smiled at the low, short flights of the Frenchman's imagination. Wells dashed with extraordinary daring into the fiction business and created whole societies, civilisations, worlds, moons, stars. He knew no fear, and did not hesitate, by means of huge mundane disasters, to set one civilisation against another and show the results of the fray. In the creation of individual characters he has had many superiors. But Wells's imagination is not retail: it is wholesale. He has created societies first, and individuals second. "He lisped in *numbers*, and the numbers came." With him the fate of individuals is a trifle to the fate of societies.

Balzac, by nature, had a scientific habit of mind: he had a vague vision of societies; he was a considerable sociologist according to his lights. But Wells had a scientific habit of mind which was disciplined and developed by a scientific self-education. He based himself on biology, and turned all science into romance. Through-out his writing career he has yearned after the perfecting of the structure of societies and the abolition of all inefficiency. He has, incidentally, made Utopias. Other authors have made Utopias, from More to William Morris. But no novelist before Wells brought to the making of Utopias the tenth part of Wells's knowledge, sociological insight, and realism. You may be glad that you have not been compelled by destiny to live in one of his Utopias; but his Utopias exist in the mind. They have opened your eyes, broad-ened your outlook, awakened your conscience, and influenced your opinions. No imaginative author of modern times has exerted an influence equal to that of Wells. It is a world-influence; for he has been translated into every civilised language, and has adherents and opponents in every land, from Argentina to Japan. His fiction has a more tremendous sweep than any other; his imagination is more audacious and surer; his reiterated didacticism far more formidable. Like Balzac, whatever his demerits, he has not left the novel where he found it. As a phenomenon he stands by himself. His predecessors in his own line were his inferiors, and as yet he has had no followers worth talking about.

IV

Another way of classifying serious novelists is to divide them into categories according to the amount of constructiveness, explicit or implicit, in their criticism of the life they portray. Simply to ask whether they are image-breakers or image-makers would be too simple and too crude. Since every serious novelist founds his work on the assumption that something is wrong, every serious novelist must be an image-breaker. And of late years the practice of image-breaking has increased with the rapid growth of the general uneasy sense of political and social injustice. Fiction follows the trend of political and social thought, and the curve of that trend has been and is very marked. The racial conscience, even the world-conscience, has been awakened into a new disquiet. Hence adverse criticism multiplies, and image-breakers are having a grand time, with the approval of a perturbed public. They go forth slashing with stick and sword; the ground is strewn with the fragments of their wrath. Which wrath is often too facile. If certain novelists had their way, not an ideal would be left intact in a bereaved world.

It is not difficult to destroy; to reconstruct is a harder task. And to be constructive is especially difficult for a novelist, because he is forbidden to be openly didactic. Withal, adverse criticism constructive by implication may always be discovered in serious fiction. Disraeli was a forerunner on this path. In *Sybil* and *Coningsby* he laid about him with brilliant violence, but with equal brilliance he indicated forms of ideal which might be built out of the scattered fragments. The best novels of John Galsworthy contain much evidence of the activity of a mind which could not be content only to destroy.

There is, I think, no other outstanding example of the constructive spirit in modern fiction—either political or social. With, of course, the great exception of H. G. Wells! Perhaps no novelist was ever so constructive as H. G. Wells, though few have been so destructive. Of all English novelists he has the most sensitive conscience and is the most fertile in constructiveness, particularly schematic constructiveness. America, in Sinclair Lewis and Theodore Dreiser, possesses a pair of mighty destroyers; but their rage for explicit destruction has not left them a lot of energy for implicit reconstruction.

V

Still another way—and it is the last I shall mention—of classifying serious novelists is to divide them into categories according to the amount of sympathy which they show towards their characters. The majority of novelists separate their characters into sheep and goats, and portray the former as better, and the latter as worse, than any human being could possibly be. They forget that no man is consistent, that no individuality holds logically together, that every character in action displays an endless series of contradictions. Their naïve zeal for righteousness leads them to magnify such virtue as they perceive and to pursue with vindictive whips such vice as they perceive. If there is truth—and there is—in the maxim that to understand everything is to forgive everything, then it follows that these novelists have not understood what it was their first artistic duty to understand. Had they understood they would have shown compassion. (Which does not mean that they would have tolerated.) At least they would not have hated.

A great deal too much hatred is abroad in fiction, and always has been. Hatred of individuals which he has created springs less from the novelist's natural naughtiness than from his inability to grasp the scientific fact that every real individual is a result, and that every result has a cause, partly or wholly beyond the control of the individual.

As a rule, but not always, the greatest novelists have been the greatest sympathisers. The greatest sympathiser of all was Dostoievsky, whose nature had for human imperfections that universal, Christ-like, uncondescending pity which should be the ideal of all novelists. Balzac had few hatreds and very wide sympathies. Hardy was rarely malevolent. Galsworthy is full of compassion. But Wells can hate with a fire which is not always sacred; upon occasion he will bring every device of implacable hostility to annihilate the reputation of some unhappy sinner. Some novelists, however, adopt a worse attitude than this, namely, the aloof attitude of an observer watching insects of some interest but no importance under a microscope. Wells never takes it.

VI

Let us now come to the young, the post-Wells novelists, by which I mean those who started their careers after Wells had begun to put his mark on the mind of Europe and America.

Of course the first name that comes to the mind is Marcel Proust. Proust invented no new form, but he is said by distinguished French critics, whose views deserve deep respect, to have opened a new field of psychology. For myself I cannot honestly admit this claim. At his best he is, in my opinion, a great novelist (and at his worst a tedious); he discloses a passion for the minutiae of psychology; but that he is original in psychology I have failed to see. As for his scope, it is unquestionably narrow; no novelist has built walls higher than his.

I think that James Joyce has both invented a new method and enlarged the field of psychology. Joyce is a genuine innovator; the influence of *Ulysses* has already been, and doubtless will in the future be, considerable. But he too is a wall-builder. Also he lacks discipline and decency. I would call him the noble savage of the novel. Two other names are D. H. Lawrence and R. H. Mottram (author of *The Spanish Farm Trilogy*). Lawrence has treated sexual emotion with a mastery exceeding that of even any Frenchman; but his scope is limited by his obsession with the everlasting clash between man and woman. His walls enclose a narrow space. Like Lawrence, Mottram has genius and style. Every genius is original; every genius introduces something new into his art; but Mottram has not widened the scope of the novel, nor done anything that has not been done, differently, before. He is no pioneer, in either form or content. Virginia Woolf has passionate praisers, who maintain that she is a discoverer in psychology and in form. Disagreeing, I regard her alleged form as the absence of form, and her psychology as an uncoordinated mass of interesting details, none of which is truly original.

All that I can urge in her favour is that she is authentically feminine, and that her style is admirable. Both these qualities are beside my point. Of the above-mentioned five, only Joyce is of the dynasty of precursors and sure of a place in the history of the development of the novel.

Of the still younger novelists, a few, such as Henry Williamson, author of *The Pathway*, may emerge from the ruck of competence. *The Pathway*, while a very fine novel indeed, and covering a large expanse, shows absolutely no symptom of an innovating mind. In attitude and technique it looks backward instead of forward. One younger novelist, however, has quite definitely emerged from the ruck: Aldous Huxley. Among novelists under forty (he is thirty-five) Aldous Huxley rises high above everybody else as a figure in the world of imaginative prose literature. His novels are anticipated with eagerness; and it is impossible for anybody critically interested in fiction to ignore them. He has matured gradually and surely, which is a good sign. What he will ultimately achieve no one can foretell. What he has so far achieved is one sound and complete novel, *Point Counter Point*, issued last autumn. He is immensely well-informed about the social structure; his intelligence is acute; he has generally, but not always, a scientific mode of thought; he has taste and erudition; he has power and style; he is courageous, perhaps more courageous than he feels himself to be. He influences his contemporaries, and it may be said that, in the matter of the progress of the novel as an artistic vehicle, he stands for his generation; his generation may fairly be judged by him.

We will therefore test *Point Counter Point* by settling its place in the three groups of categories. The task is easy.

First: breadth of outlook—particularly sociological outlook. No fresh progress is to be observed, but rather a retrogression from the standard of Balzac, and certainly from the standard of Wells. (I do not mean here merely the Wells of the Utopias.) I do not see how the contrary can be argued with any hope of success. The novel deals with authors and their mates; three of the principal characters are authors; and yet I remember in *Point Counter Point* not a single passage in which are broadly treated the repercussions of literature upon life, or vice versa. Here, if ever in a novel, was an opportunity for imaginatively and dramatically portraying those relations. It was refused.

Second: destructiveness and constructiveness. The book is almost, if not quite, wholly destructive. It is a very formidable and uncompromising attack on the society which it depicts, and there are few or no implications which might pass for constructive criticism. The ground is littered with the shapeless rubble of demolished images. Never was ruin so ruthlessly accomplished.

Third: sympathy or antipathy towards individual characters. The attitude is almost uniformly hostile. In one case, that of Burlap, the treatment accorded amounts to virulent persecution. Of all the chief personages, one alone is sympathetically drawn. Indeed, the author gives the impression that he hates and despises his characters. He is without pity in the exposure of their weaknesses and their turpitudes, and his censure can only be justified on the assumption that their iniquity and absurdity are the fruits of individual naughtiness and original sin, and not in any degree to be attributed to ancestry, to environment, or to the mysterious but unescapable influences of a defective social structure.

Hence I do not see in the representative serious novel by a young man any appreciable sign of evolutionary development of the vehicle. I am judging it comparatively, not positively. As a positive achievement it ranks high; it has rightly aroused enthusiasm. The author is entitled to be proud of it. And one willingly admits that it contains a large dose of antiseptic straight talking—corrective of the pervading, timid sentimentalism of the British novel. Personally I exulted in its tonic brutality. But it is not a progressive book, save in the respect just noted. I should call it reactionary, in both a spiritual and a technical sense. And the milk of human kindness is not in it. Having read it—yes, and having sardonically enjoyed it— one comes to the conclusion that Jesus may have preached the Sermon on the Mount in vain.

Realist, I (April, 1929), 3–11. The magazine, which was subtitled "A Journal of Scientific Humanism," was published from April, 1929, to January, 1930. Bennett was a member of the editorial board, along with H. G. Wells, Harold Laski, Rebecca West, and Aldous and Julian Huxley.

II. NOVELS AND NOVELISTS

Ivan Turgenev (1899)

I

The approaching completion of an English version, in fifteen volumes, of the "Works" of Ivan Turgenev, translated by Mrs. Constance Garnett, introduced by Mr. Edward Garnett, and published by Mr. William Heinemann, deserves more than that passing and perfunctory notice which is usually accorded to such achievements. The decade now drawing to a close has been rather remarkable for newly translated and worthily produced editions of great foreign novelists. We have had Dumas, Balzac, Victor Hugo, Björnson, and d'Annunzio. And we have had Turgenev. But the case of the author of *Virgin Soil* differs from the rest. Dumas, Balzac, Hugo—these are names which have a very definite meaning to the public. Björnson, too, is renowned among us, and already the youthful d'Annunzio has raised a general curiosity. Translations of any of these men could be sure in advance of at least a moderate acceptance; in some instances the acceptance has amounted to enthusiasm. The late Sergius Stepniak, in his introduction to the English translation of *Smoke* (1894), said that Turgenev, "during the last fifteen years of his life, won for himself the reading public, first in France, then in Germany and America, and finally in England." The statement is certainly not correct as regards England and America, and it is only true in a very limited sense of France and Germany. Except in Russia, Turgenev has not even to-day captured the "reading public." He has everywhere captured the men of letters; but these constitute only a fraction of "the reading public." Men of letters who happen to have genius do not write for men of letters. They write, as Wagner was proud to say he composed, for the ordinary person. From the Russian magazines Turgenev used to receive £24 a "leaf" for serial rights. Stevenson never got as much, and Mr. Kipling has not greatly surpassed the figure. When genius commands such a price, it is fame; it is to "capture the reading public." Compare this vogue with the condition of affairs in England, and in France, the ultimate home of Turgenev's adoption. It is extremely improbable that any of his novels has reached a sale of ten thousand copies even in France. As for England, I do not hesitate to say that half-a-dozen years ago Turgenev was barely a name to our "reading public." It was Tolstoi who had made the capture. The more honour, and a very special esteem, therefore, to Mrs. Garnett and her colleagues in this undertaking of an approximately complete Turgenev in English. They have worthily laboured, they have courageously accepted risks, with a single eye to the cause of art. And, whatever the immediate result, they are to be vehemently congratulated upon their work. The *format* is admirable; considering the price, it is wonderful. Mr. Garnett's introductory essays contain much subtle and just appreciation. A complete ignorance of the Russian language prevents me from measuring the excellence of the translation. But decidedly it has the air of being faithful; it is good English, and quite apart and aloof from the ruck of translations. Stepniak, who should be an authority, said it was "as near an approach to the elegance and poetry of the original" as any he had encountered. Certainly, the same scholarship and the same enormous pains have not before been brought to an English rendering of Turgenev. It would be unfair to match it with the French translation, in fourteen volumes, published by Hetzel, Charpentier, and Hachette. The most eminent of his contemporaries were glad to help Turgenev in that translation; parts of it he did with his own hand, and every volume had the incomparable advantage of his minute revision. No other novelist was ever translated with such literary pomp. But, circumstance for circumstance, our English edition will hold its own. We have the right to boast of it. Possibly, as volume of it succeeded volume, with but scant expression of gratitude from either Press or public, those who had it in hand may have been a little discouraged and set back. They may have imagined that their efforts were thankless; in part wasted. Not so. What they have done they have done; and it was always good in the sight of the few whose unspoken applause is above the sound of trumpets.

II

Any attempt to examine the relations between Turgenev and his Western publics must suffer at its very inception by the fact that in neither French nor English is there a proper biography of the man; a full account of his life, his opinions, and his methods. The Vicomte E. M. de Vogüé's essay prefixed to the *Œuvres Dernières* is masterly, but it is only an essay. Renan's funeral oration, included in the same volume, is a majestic and lovely tribute, but it is only a discourse. For the rest, there are Deline's *Tourgueneff Inconnu*, fragmentary and mediocre; Pavlovsky's *Souvenirs sur Tourgueneff*, said to be very unreliable; the volume of letters, useful as far as it goes, edited by Halperine-Kaminsky under the title *Tourguéneff and his French Circle*; and critical studies by Paul Bourget and Ernest Dupuy. Strangely enough, Turgenev's own *Souvenirs Littéraires* are not obtainable in French. At some future date Mrs. Garnett might well crown her work by adding to it a translation of these *Souvenirs*. Such extracts therefrom as may be found here and there are of the highest interest and value.

The most important event in Turgenev's career was, of course, his self-exile from Russia. He was born in 1818. Russia is a place of sorrow for artists and thinkers to-day; it was more sorrowful then. You will get many glimpses of it in *A Sportsman's Sketches, First Love*, and other tales. If his mother had been sympathetic, it is conceivable that he might have stayed at home. But Turgenev's mother is already notorious. The Vicomte de Vogüé points out that in Turgenev's novels all the mothers are either wicked or grotesque. We learn from the Journal of Mme. Turgenev's adopted daughter that when Ivan took home his first book—*Paracha* (1841)—"the tiny blue-covered volume lay about mamma's room; it was never mentioned." A little incident touching this adopted daughter shows at once what manner of woman Mme. Turgenev was, and what the times were. The girl had fallen ill, and a serf-physician was ordered to attend her. "Remember," said the terrible mistress, "if you don't cure her—Siberia." Then there was the mighty censor, whose antics, performed apparently out of pure love of the ridiculous, are almost incredible. Turgenev wrote: "The young girl was a flower."

In the interests of law and order, the censor altered this to: "The young lady resembled a splendid rose." One can sympathise with an author's desire to put a thousand miles between himself and the mere physical presence of that official. But indeed authors have never been recognised of the powers in Russia. Turgenev told Edmond de Goncourt that at a dinner given by Count Orloff to celebrate the emancipation of the serfs, he was placed forty-seventh, after the despised priest. To catch the full beauty of this anecdote it is necessary to remember that Turgenev was then of European renown; that he was an intimate friend of the host, and that his books had helped to bring about the emancipation. It was from such a land that Turgenev fled. He explains the flight thus:

> For myself, I can say that I felt very keenly the disadvantages of this wrenching-away from my native soil, of this violent rupture of all the bonds which held me to the land of my youth; but there was nothing else to be done. That existence, that environment, and in particular that sphere to which I belonged—the sphere of country landowners and of serfdom—offered me no inducement to stay. On the contrary, nearly everything I saw around me awoke in me a feeling of disquiet, of revolt—to be frank, of disgust. I could not hesitate long. Either I must wholly submit, and follow the common groove, the beaten path, or I must deracinate myself at a single stroke, and get away from everyone and everything, even at the risk of losing many things dear to my heart. I chose the latter course. I plunged head first into the "German Ocean"; it purified and regenerated me; and when at length I emerged from its waters, I found myself an Occidental, and an Occidental I have always remained.

("*Voilà le gros mot lâché*," comments de Vogüé—"*Occidental*.") [1]

It seems convincing—yet I am conscious of a desire to cry for more light upon the temperamental causes of Turgenev's exile. Other great Russian authors suffered infinitely more than he; but they stayed. And they stayed because, in spite of all, Russia was still Russia to them. Did Turgenev unconsciously anticipate Ibsen, and was it the artist in him demanding equanimity in order to create that drove him out of his own country? Or was his departure due simply to a revolt of outraged sentiments? In the latter case our

1. "There's the most slipshod word—Occidental."

estimate of the man would be somewhat lowered. Whatever the truth of the matter, it appears to me quite possible that the disadvantages of his exile outweighed the advantages. This voluntary banishment certainly intensified that pervading melancholy and that inflexible reserve which have operated against the popularity of his novels among Western readers. To some extent it even interfered with his productiveness. Of Paris he once said: "It is impossible for me to work here." During the whole of his maturity he was a wanderer, without a hearth. He led a life of restaurants. He had acquaintances with whom he was on very familiar terms, and who liked and admired him immensely—the Viardots, Flaubert, de Goncourt, Daudet, and doubtless others in Germany and England—but had this pseudo-Occidental a single veritable *friend* outside Russia? Did he ever, in spite of his marvellous conversational powers, so freely exercised, ever fully reveal himself to his "French circle"? For myself, I suspect not. He was lonely, this man to whom all the most exalted doors in western Europe were open. He continually regretted his original sacrifice. For ever haunted by obscure racial longings, he retired within himself and became a mystery. As with many talkative men, his secret thoughts were his own.

What, other than Russia, were the things that lay next his heart? There was sport, we know. At the age of fifty-five he speaks, in a letter to Flaubert, of "my boundless passion for sport, the only pleasure which is left to me." He had made a definite appointment to meet Flaubert at Croisset; but "a very pleasant fellow, called Bullock" (who "possessed the finest partridge shooting in the whole of England"), had invited him to go and "kill mountains of partridges"; and though he would probably not be able to accept the invitation, there was a possibility of his doing so; therefore Flaubert must kindly postpone the appointment, on the chance. "There is something shocking," he observes, " in an old greybeard like myself crossing the sea twice in order to pour a lot of lead into a lot of partridges." As a sportsman Turgenev certainly had the large grandiose manner of Dumas *père*. He must have been the sort of sportsman to whom keepers, so prone to scoff, pay the homage of their sincere respect. He resembled Dumas, too, though one might easily not have suspected it, on another point: an intense predilection for the feminine. This man who was never married remarked at Flaubert's dinner-table, when Flaubert and de Goncourt were contesting the importance of love to an author, that his existence was "saturated with femininity":

> With me, neither books nor anything whatever in the world could take the place of woman. How can I make that plain to you? I find it is only love which produces a certain expansion of the being, that nothing else gives . . . eh? Listen! When quite a young man I once had a mistress, a miller's girl in the neighbourhood of St. Petersburg, whom I used to see when out hunting. She was charming, very fair, with a flash of the eye rather common among us. She would accept nothing from me. But one day she said to me: "You must give me a present."
>
> "What is it you want?"
>
> "Bring me some scented soap from St. Petersburg."
>
> I brought her the soap. She took it, disappeared, came back blushing, and murmured, offering me her hands, delicately scented:
>
> "Kiss my hands, like you kiss the hands of ladies in drawing rooms at St. Petersburg."
>
> I threw myself on my knees—and, you know, *that was the finest moment of my life.*

We owe this *histoire* to the de Goncourt *Journal*, which from 1872 to 1883 is full of references to Turgenev. Some of the best things in that famous but untranslatable collection of curios were gathered from Turgenev. But even the all-embracing *Journal*, to which nothing came amiss, is silent or nearly so on the supreme question: Turgenev's methods of work and the origin and growth of that consummate skill which places him in one respect above all other novelists. Guns and women: he would discuss these. What of writing, and those intimate details about actual *pen-work* which, as in the case of Stevenson, must always fascinate the admirers of a great literary artist? In eleven years Turgenev seems to have mentioned this matter to de Goncourt only once. Here is the passage:

> "In order to work I must have winter, a frost such as we have in Russia, an *astringent* cold, the trees all covered with crystals, then. . . . But I work still better in autumn, you know; on days when there is no

wind, no wind at all, and the ground is elastic and the air has a taste
of wine. My place—it is a little wooden house with a garden full of
yellow acacias—we have no white acacia. In the autumn the earth is
covered with pods, which crackle when you tread on them, and the
air is filled with mocking-birds . . . yes, shrikes. In there, all alone. . . ."

Turgeneff did not finish, but a contraction of the hands closed over
his chest told us of the joy and intoxication of the brain which he experienced in that little corner of old Russia.

There is not much substance in this. A solitary passage in Pavlovsky's *Souvenirs* is rather better:

I have various plans in my head [said Turgenev], but I can do
nothing; and the saddest part of it is that work is no longer a joy to me.
Once I liked to work as one likes to caress a woman. I experienced a
veritable pleasure in dreaming over a work or correcting it. When I
was writing I wanted no society. I isolated myself on my estates. There
I had a little room in the outbuildings, something like a peasant's cabin,
furnished only with a deal table and a chair; and there I used to work
fairly well for months at a time. Often I would carry on literary make-
believes with great zest. When I was writing *Fathers and Children* I kept
Bazarov's diary. If I read a new book, if I met an interesting man, if
there occurred any important political or social event, I always
described the thing in the diary from Bazarov's point of view. The
result was a large and very curious volume. Unfortunately, I have
lost it. Someone borrowed it to read and never returned it.

This is interesting, but it is like a crumb to the ravenous. The
man must inevitably have had a passion for technique and all the
thousand and one niceties of form. He must have spent years in the
sedulous cultivation of the craftsman in himself. The author of a
miracle like *On the Eve* may be born, but he is also made. In the
matter of condensation alone Turgenev was unique among the
great literary artificers. He could say more in a chapter of two
thousand words than any other novelist that ever lived. What he
accomplishes again and again in a book of sixty thousand words,
Tolstoi could not have accomplished under a quarter of a million.
His genius for choosing the essential and discarding everything else,
was simply unparalleled. What Ibsen did for European drama,
Turgenev did for European fiction: he uttered the last word of pure

artistry. And it is precisely of his life as a practical working novelist that we know nothing, or next to nothing.

Our information about his literary opinions is scarcely less meagre, and may be set out in a few lines. It is strange that Turgenev, whose work marks him as a hater of exaggeration in any form, was an enthusiastic admirer of Dickens. He put Dickens above Balzac, and was never tired in his praise. He did not care for the author of *Eugénie Grandet*. "Balzac," he is stated to have remarked, "is an ethnographer, not an artist." It is absurd, but there is criticism in it. Turgenev's reported adverse *dicta* about his contemporaries—Flaubert, Daudet, de Goncourt—are probably in the main aprocryphal. That his critical ideals remained fluid to the end is proved by his appreciation of de Maupassant. *La Maison Tellier* enchanted him. Among his own books he preferred *First Love*, of which he said his father was the hero. He considered that *A Sportsman's Sketches*, with certain exceptions, showed him at his weakest. There is a diversity of view as to the order of excellence in his novels. Mr. Edward Garnett would possibly put *On the Eve* first, and I could not disagree with him. The Vicomte de Vogüé unhesitatingly gives the palm to *A House of Gentlefolk*. Certainly the epilogue to that book and the love scene in Chapter XXXIV, are unforgettable art. Yet, when I reflect upon the mass of Turgenev's work, not these, but the sketch entitled "Byezhin Prairie," in *A Sportsman's Sketches*, stands out most prominent. The picture of the pony-boys by their watch-fire discussing ghosts—their artless talk, the effect and mystery of night, the ultimate dawn and sunrise . . . . . when a thing is supreme there is nothing to be said.

III

It seems to me that there are three reasons why Turgenev, despite the unaffected and zealous support everywhere extended to him by men of letters, should have failed to grip the public as Tolstoi and even Dostoievsky have gripped it. The first is, that as an artist he has hardly a fault; in particular, he never showed the least inclination to either flamboyance or vulgarity. He was always restrained and refined. Now the public may, and generally does, admire a great artist. But it begins (and sometimes ends) by admiring him for the wrong things. Shakespeare is more highly regarded for his philosophy than for his poetry, as the applause at any performance of "Hamlet" will prove. Balzac conquers by that untamed exuberance and those crude effects of melodrama which are the least valuable parts of him. And it is natural that people who concern themselves with art only in their leisure moments, demanding from it nothing but a temporary distraction, should prefer the obvious to the recondite, and should walk regardless of beauty unless it forces itself upon their attention by means of exaggerations and advertisement. The public wants to be struck, hit squarely in the face; then it will take notice. Most of the great artists, by chance or design, have performed that feat. But Turgenev happens not to have done so. Look through all his work, and I doubt if you will find a scene which in the theatrical sense could be called "powerful." There is no appeal by force to the soul; no straining, no grandiloquence, no distortion; nothing but the flawless chastity of perfect art. His best books are like an antique statue, and their beauty, instead of delivering a blow, steals towards you and mildly penetrates the frame. As well expect the public to admire the Venus de Milo as to admire *On the Eve*. Refinement is mistaken for coldness, and restraint for mediocrity. And so it will ever be.

Yet Turgenev, it may be said, is popular in Russia—why not also in the West? This brings me to the second point. A work of art will sometimes triumph for reasons neither artistic nor inartistic, but by means of the moral ideas upon which it happens to be founded. Every work of art must have a moral basis, and Turgenev's novels have a moral basis beyond the ordinary. They are the muffled but supreme utterance of a nation's secret desire. But what is that to the West? The West cannot feel what Russia feels—cannot even intellectually comprehend the profound surge of emotion which barely agitates the surface of that giant's life. It is nothing to the West, for instance, that "the chief figure of *On the Eve*, Elena, foreshadows and stands for the rise of young Russia in the sixties"; but it is everything to Russia, with her ears sensitive to catch the least echo of her own scarce-whispered aspirations. The proportion of readers who appreciate the artistic significance of Turgenev is as small in Russia as in France and England; but every literate east of the Baltic can, and does, grasp his moral significance. Here lies the difference between Turgenev and Tolstoi. Apart from his fiery vehemence, which compels attention, Tolstoi has the advantage over Turgenev in the race for popularity, because the moral basis of his work is less exclusively Russian, and nearer the universal. The inner meaning of *Anna Karenina* is plain to every country. The lessons of *War and Peace* need no searching. *The Kreutzer Sonata* would apply itself as well to Salt Lake City as to Moscow. Tolstoi speaks to humanity, Turgenev to Russia. But for all that Tolstoi is the lesser artist.

The third reason against Turgenev's general acceptance in the West is that Russia has something about her of the Orient, and that Turgenev had the Oriental melancholy and other attributes intensified to a special degree. Far from being completely occidentalised, as he imagined, the tinge and texture of his mind never abated their original quality. Oriental he was born, and (unlike Tolstoi, again) Oriental he remained. Though he preached an evangel, it was not an evangel of revolt and attack; rather an evangel of vague and quiescent hope, with dreamy eyes upon the furthest future. "Russian writers," says the Vicomte de Vogüé, "by reason as much of the circumstances in which they are placed as by the particular turn of their genius, do not openly attack; they neither argue nor declaim; they depict without arriving at a conclusion, and appeal more to pity than to anger." It is just the qualities of melancholy, inconclusiveness, and patient inactive faith which do not commend themselves to the Western mind, comparatively so strenuous, eager, and restive under abuses. We can neither understand nor sympathise with this policy of waiting and meditation. With us, to think is to act, and to act is to fight. When Uvar Ivanovitch answers the question: "Will there be men among us?" by "flourishing his fingers and fixing his enigmatical stare into the far distance," we chafe, we get angry. We feel the need of a watchword and a battle-cry. The true Russian does not.

From such deep-seated causes Turgenev's novels fail—at any rate, partially—in their moral suasion over the Western mind. Absolute resignation we could comprehend, and open rebellion we could approve; but a sad, uneasy something between the two leaves us cold and puzzled. Turgenev, I fancy, was aware of the racial defect, and aware also that Tolstoi had it not. Perhaps it was this knowledge which caused him to send across Europe to Tolstoi that pathetic and moving document.

"Very dear Léon Nikolaievitch," the missive ran,—"It is a long time since I wrote to you. I was then, and I am now, on my deathbed. I cannot recover; there is no longer the least chance of it. I am writing to you expressly to tell you how happy I have been to be your contemporary, and to make you a last urgent prayer. My friend, return to literary work. This gift has come to you from there whence everything comes to us. Ah! how happy I should be if I could know that you would listen to my prayer!... My friend, great writer of our Russian land, hear my prayer. Let me know if this letter reaches you. I clasp you for the last time to my heart— you and all yours. . . . I can write no more. . . . I am tired."

Academy, No. 1435 (November 4, 1899), pp. 514–517. Reprinted, *Fame and Fiction* (London: Grant Richards, 1901), pp. 211–230.

Turgenev and Dostoievsky (1910)

I have read with very great interest Mr. Maurice Baring's new volume about Russia, "Landmarks in Russian Literature" (Methuens. 6s. net). It deals with Gogol, Turgenev, Dostoievsky, Tolstoi, and Chekhov. It is unpretentious. It is not "literary." I wish it had been more literary. Mr. Baring seems to have a greater love for literature than an understanding knowledge of it. He writes like a whole-hearted amateur, guided by commonsense and enthusiasm, but not by the delicate perceptions of an artist. He often says things, or says things in a manner, which will assuredly annoy the artist. Thus his curt, conventional remarks about Zola might have been composed for a leading article in the "Morning Post," instead of for a volume of literary criticism. Nevertheless, I cannot be cross with him. In some ways his book is illuminating. I mean that it has illuminated my darkness. His chapters on Russian characteristics and on realism in Russian literature are genuinely valuable. In particular he makes me see that even French realism is an artificial and feeble growth compared with the spontaneous, unconscious realism of the Russians. If you talked to Russians about realism they probably would not know quite what you meant. And when you had at length made them understand they would certainly exclaim: "Well, of course! But why all this fuss about a simple matter?" Only a man who knows Russia very well, and who has a genuine affection for the Russian character, could have written these chapters. And I am ready to admit that they are more useful than many miles of appreciation in the delicate balancing manner of say an Arthur Symons.[1]

1. Arthur Symons (1865–1945), critic and poet, was principally associated with the Decadent movement of the 1890's, and was one of the principal interpreters of French Symbolism in England. His "appreciations" include *The Symbolist Movement in Literature* (1899) and *Studies in Seven Arts* (1906).

Mr. Baring raises again the vexed question of Turgenev's position. It is notorious that Turgenev is much more highly appreciated outside Russia than in it. One is, of course, tempted to say that Russians cannot judge their own authors, for there is a powerful and morally overwhelming cult for Turgenev in France, Germany, and England. I have myself said, sworn, and believed that "On the Eve" is the most perfect example of the novel yet produced in any country. And I am not sure that I am yet prepared to go back on myself. However, it is absurd to argue that Russians cannot judge their own authors. The best judges of Russian authors must be Russians. Think of the ridiculous misconceptions about English literature by first-class foreign critics! . . . But I am convinced that Mr. Baring goes too far in his statement of the Russian estimate of Turgenev. He says that educated Russian opinion would no more think of comparing Turgenev with Dostoievsky than educated English opinion would think of comparing Charlotte Yonge with Charlotte Brontë. This is absurd. Whatever may be Turgenev's general inferiority (and I do not admit it), he was a great artist and a complete artist. And he was a realist. There is all earth and heaven between the two Charlottes. One was an artist, the other was an excellent Christian body who produced stories that have far less relation to life than Frith's "Derby Day" has to the actual fact and poetry of Epsom.[2] If Mr. Baring had bracketed Turgenev with Charlotte Brontë and Dostoievsky with the lonely Emily, I should have credited him with a subtle originality.

About half of the book is given to a straightforward, detailed, homely account of Dostoievsky, his character, genius, and works. It was very much wanted in English. I thought I had read all the chief works of the five great Russian novelists, but last year I came across one of Dostoievsky's, "The Brothers Karamazov," of which I had not heard. It was a French translation, in two thick volumes. I thought it contained some of the greatest scenes that I had ever encountered in fiction, and I at once classed it with Stendhal's "Chartreuse de Parme" and Dostoievsky's "Crime and Punishment"

2. W. P. Frith (1819–1909), a painter of Victorian genre scenes. His *Derby Day* (1858) is a huge painting of the crowds at the Epsom race course; it hangs in the National Gallery, London.

as one of the supreme marvels of the world. Nevertheless, certain aspects of it puzzled me. When I mentioned it to friends I was told that I had gone daft about it, and that it was not a major work. Happening to meet Mrs. Garnett, the never-to-be-sufficiently-thanked translator of Turgenev and of Tolstoi, I made inquiries from her about it, and she said: "It is his masterpiece." We were then separated by a ruthless host, with my difficulties unsolved. I now learn from Mr. Baring that the French translation is bad and incomplete, and that the original work, vast as it is, is only a pre-liminary fragment of a truly enormous novel which death prevented Dostoievsky from finishing. Death, this is yet another proof of your astonishing clumsiness! The scene with the old monk at the beginning of "The Brothers Karamazov" is in the very grandest heroical manner. There is nothing in either English or French prose literature to hold a candle to it. And really I do not exaggerate! There is probably nothing in Russian literature to match it, outside Dostoievsky. It ranks, in my mind, with the scene towards the beginning of "Crime and Punishment," when in the inn the drunken father relates his daughter's "shame." These pages are unique. They reach the highest and most terrible pathos that art has ever reached. And if an author's reputation among people of taste depended solely on his success with single scenes Dostoievsky would outrank all other novelists, if not all poets. But it does not. Dostoievsky's works—all of them—have grave faults. They have especially the grave fault of imperfection, that fault which Turge-nev and Flaubert avoided. They are tremendously unlevel, badly constructed, both in large outline and in detail. The fact is that the difficulties under which he worked were too much for the artist in him. Mr. Baring admits these faults, but he does not sufficiently dwell on them. He glances at them and leaves them, with the result that the final impression given by his essay is apt to be a false one. Nobody, perhaps, ever understood and sympathised with human nature as Dostoievsky did. Indubitably nobody even with the help of God and good luck ever swooped so high into tragic grandeur. But the man had fearful falls. He could not trust his wings. He is an adorable, a magnificent, and a profoundly sad figure in letters. He was anything you like. But he could not compass the calm and

exquisite soft beauty of "On the Eve" or "A House of Gentlefolk."
... And now, Mr. Heinemann, when are we going to have a
complete Dostoievsky in English?

New Age, VI (March 31, 1910), 518. Reprinted, *Books and Persons* (New
York: George H. Doran Co., 1917), pp. 208–213.

Some Adventures Among Russian Fiction (1916)

The glory of Russian literature used to be dimmed for Englishmen by a veil of bad translation. Terrible English translations of Russian masterpieces exist to this day—rivalling in turpitude the French translations of Dickens—but of late years honest, courageous, and capable translators have begun to appear; at any rate one has appeared, and the glory is seen more brightly. I employ the words "honest" and "courageous" of the new school of translators, because so many of the old gang, whatever their equipment, had the cowardly habit of shirking difficulties and the dishonest habit of concealing that any difficulties had been shirked. However, my first recollections of Russian literature are not embittered by the sins of translators. The first Russian author I remember reading was Dostoievsky, about a quarter of a century ago. A series of Dostoievsky stories, mostly minor stories, was published in imperfectly bound greenish volumes at that period by, I think, Bickers of Leicester Square. There were, among others, *The Friend of the Family*, *Uncle's Dream*, and *The Gambler*. I cannot recall that the translations as such made any impression on me whatever; they certainly did not annoy me. As for the stories themselves, they did not make much impression on me either, but I can remember that Dostoievsky seemed to me to be chiefly remarkable for mild humour. That he was a novelist of the first rank assuredly did not occur to me. At one time, later, I wondered how in the first stage it could have seemed to me that Dostoievsky was chiefly remarkable for mild humour. But now that my acquaintance with his works is more complete, I have to admit that the first impression was not utterly wrong. Dostoievsky *is* often mildly (if very subtly) humorous. His *Journal of an Author*, for example, not yet translated into English,

116

is often most determinedly humorous in style, and in such tales as the man who was accidentally swallowed by a crocodile (also not yet translated) he becomes positively farcical. . . . I dropped Dostoievsky, and thought no more of him for many years.

Of course I read Tolstoi, in the translations of the epoch. I raved fashionably about *Anna Karenina* and *The Death of Ivan Ilyitch*, but I could not embark upon *War and Peace*,—it was too formidably long. When, after a considerable interval, I re-read *Anna Karenina* and *Ivan Ilyitch*, in the excellent translations of Mrs. Constance Garnett, I was forced to modify my ancient enthusiasm for *Anna Karenina*. I had always deemed it vitiated by an excessively faulty construction; and now I found it hard, often otiose, dull in its exactitudes, and too concerned about externals. For me, on the whole, it lacked poetry. To this judgment I still adhere, while not denying its huge masterfulness nor its good title to a European reputation. I then came to grips with *War and Peace*, which is a finer book than *Anna Karenina*. *War and Peace* is nearly as fine as anything there is. It is a staggering production for a young man,— Tolstoi was in the thirties when he wrote it. It makes you comprehend that there simply are no novels in English, and very few in French. The effect of the unsentimentalised annals of the home life of Pierre and Natasha after all the battles are over is one of the finest tonic effects in the entire range of fiction. No "great" English novelist would have even begun to get it, because he would have sentimentalised the situation and made his helpless puppets live happily ever afterwards. I suppose that there is no historical novel to compare with *War and Peace*. Gogol's *Taras Bulba*, a jolly boyish tale with a contemptible plot and some splendid, roaring mediaeval pictures, cannot compare with it. But Gogol may not yet be judged in English. Though I am willing to believe that *Dead Souls* is a colossal masterpiece of sardonic humour, absolute conviction must abide the issue of an English version that can be read without tears of exasperation. We need a complete Gogol in this country. *Ukraine Nights* is a strange and wonderful book.

Some time after the publication in the Pseudonym Library of small books by less than great writers, such as Goncharov and Korolenko, the great Turgenev vogue began in Britain. It was due in the main to Edward and Constance Garnett. Mrs. Garnett's translations gave confidence; Mr. Garnett's introductions constituted something new in English literary criticism; they cast a fresh light on the art of fiction, completing the fitful illuminations offered by the essays of Mr. George Moore. In a short time *On the Eve* was, for eager young Englishmen of letters, the greatest novel ever written, and Bazarov, in *Fathers and Children*, the most typical character ever created by a novelist. Tolstoi receded, and Dostoievsky went clean out of sight. We knew that the Russians put Dostoievsky first and Turgenev third of the three, but we had no hesitation in deciding that the Russians did not thoroughly understand their own literature and that we did. We found social and political reasons why the Russians could not truly appreciate Turgenev. We were utterly convinced that Turgenev had carried imaginative narrative art further than any man, and that Balzac was clumsy by the side of him.

I still hold to this opinion. I do not think that any artist ever achieved more immaculate results with a more exquisite economy of means than Turgenev. Even in mere adroitness neither de Maupassant nor Chekhov is his match. And yet I have gradually come round to the Russian estimate of Turgenev. It was in Paris that the first doubts as to Turgenev's pre-eminence were sown in my mind. I met there a growing body of opinion whose oriflammes were Dostoievsky and Stendhal. Naturally I pitied these youthful Frenchmen for falling into the same error as the Russians. Then I lay awake at nights with the horrid thought: Is it conceivable that *On the Eve* is not the greatest novel ever written, and that Turgenev lacked some quality? Then I read *The Brothers Karamazov* in French—there was no English translation. The French translation was bad—markedly inferior to the admirable French translations of Turgenev—and the translator (as I afterwards learnt) had had the infelicitious idea of omitting, among other things, the whole of the first part of the book. The perusal of *The Brothers Karamazov*, even in the shorn and unfaithful French version, left me a changed man, for the novel is both more true and more romantic than any other whatsoever. The change has been slowly consolidated by the appearance of volume after volume of Mrs. Constance Garnett's translation (the only complete translation in any language). Turgenev's value has not lessened for me, but Dostoievsky's has enormously increased.

Just as Stendhal cured me and many others of Flaubertism, so Dostoievsky cured us of Turgenevism. These two authors have survived throughout the period of the idolatry of technique inaugurated by Flaubert and closed by the flawless failures of Élémir Bourges.[1] Both of them were free of that perverse self-consciousness of the artist which at bottom is the cover for a lack of inspiration and of interest in life itself. Both were far too interested in life to be unduly interested in art. Both were the truculent enemies of dilettantism in any form. Stendhal jeered at preciosity by deliberately imitating the style of the Code Napoléon; and Dostoievsky's portrait of Turgenev is vicious,—it is indeed a blot on the magnanimity of the most benevolent of novelists.[2] Dostoievsky in particular wrote hurriedly; he tumbled the stuff out of himself pell-mell. He excelled in sheer impressiveness because he had a more universal and authentic sympathy and a deeper comprehension of human nature than anybody else. Dostoievsky abhorred artifice, if he ever thought about artifice. He never tried for effects. He did not know what it was to be "literary." He wrote novels as if he was eagerly talking to you, neither artlessly nor artfully, but in full bursting possession of his subject. Some novelists perform as though they were conjurors in evening-dress. Dostoievsky worked like a skilled workman with his sleeves rolled up and his hairy forearms showing. Or he may be likened to the master of a great sailing-ship. He will bring a novel safely to a climax and a close amid terrific stresses as a Scotch captain rounds Cape Horn in a gale,—and you are on board!

It is characteristic of the baffling variousness of art that the next great Russian influence was Chekhov, who happened to be a supreme example of the dandiacal conjuring school. As Dostoievsky may be linked with Stendhal, so may Chekhov with de Maupassant. Chekhov was every bit as accomplished a virtuoso as de Maupassant. He beat de Maupassant in range because, unlike de Maupassant,

1. Elémir Bourges (1852–1925), author of long symbolic novels.
2. Dostoievsky attacked Turgenev in the character of Karmazinov, a vain, second-rate novelist in *The Possessed* (Chapter 3).

he was free from the erotic obsession. Chekhov wrote a vast quantity of sketches which have no permanent value, but at his best he is unequalled in the technique of the short story, and his only rival in impressiveness on the same scale is Joseph Conrad. Finer stories than *The Moujiks, Ward No. 6, The Ravine*, and a few others have never been written. They have all the qualities of de Maupassant plus the unique poignancy of Chekhov. We must, however, await a critical and adequate edition of Chekhov before we can arrive at a full judgment of him. (It is coming.) Some of his tales have been tolerably translated, other execrably. The best have been "done into English" several times, and reappear in different volumes under different titles by different translators. Grave trouble awaits the bibliographers of the future, and the readers of the present are sometimes involved in needless expense, and so regard themselves as swindled.

I might have mentioned many other Russian novelists of value, but it has been my fortune to encounter only one who can be ranked with the five great ones. I mean Schedrin, whose masterpiece, *The Golovlev Family*,[3] seems to me to be a work of the very first order. It has just been translated into English, but I have read it only in the French version, *Les Messieurs Golovleff*, by Polonsky and Debesse, published by Savine, Paris.

From Winifred Stephens (ed.), *The Soul of Russia* (London: Macmillan, 1916), pp. 84–88. The volume was a collection of essays published in aid of a fund for Russian refugees.

3. Mikhail Evgrafovich Saltykov (1826–1889), a Russian novelist and satirist, wrote under the pseudonym of M. Schedrin. *The Golovlev Family* was written in 1876, and translated into English in 1916.

George Meredith: On His Death (1909)

The death of George Meredith removes, not the last of the Victorian novelists, but the first of the modern school. He was almost the first English novelist whose work reflected an intelligent interest in the art which he practised; and he was certainly the first since Scott who was really a literary man. Even Scott was more of an antiquary than a man of letters—apart from his work. Can one think of Dickens as a man of letters, as one who cared for books, as one whose notions on literature were worth twopence? And Thackeray's opinions on contemporary and preceding writers condemn him past hope of forgiveness. Thackeray was in Paris during the most productive years of French fiction, the sublime decade of Balzac, Stendhal, and Victor Hugo. And his Paris sketchbook proves that his attitude towards the marvels by which he was surrounded was the attitude of a grocer. These men wrote; they got through their writing as quickly as they could; and during the rest of the day they were clubmen, or hosts, or guests. Trollope, who dashed off his literary work with a watch in front of him before 8:30 of a morning, who hunted three days a week, dined out enormously, and gave his best hours to fighting Rowland Hill in the Post Office[1]— Trollope merely carried to its logical conclusion the principle of his mightier rivals. What was the matter with all of them, after a cowardly fear of their publics, was simple brutish ignorance. George Eliot was not ignorant. Her mind was more distinguished than the minds of the great three. But she was too preoccupied by moral questions to be a first-class creative artist. And she was a woman. A woman, at that epoch, dared not write an entirely honest novel; nor a man either! Between Fielding and Meredith no entirely

1. Sir Rowland Hill (1795–1879), creator of the modern British postal system, and secretary to the Post Office, 1854–1864. Trollope worked for the Post Office from 1834 to 1867.

honest novel was written by anybody in England. The fear of the public, the lust of popularity, feminine prudery, sentimentalism, Victorian niceness—one or other of these things prevented honesty. Mind, I do not wish to belittle the Victorians quite out of existence. I can read Jane Austen for ever. The others please me less, in the following order: Dickens, Trollope, Emily Brontë, Charlotte Brontë, George Eliot. Thackeray I regard as chiefly despicable, save in one or two short works; an arrant craven and snob, with a style absurdly overpraised. Many years have passed since I could read from end to end of any book by either Dickens or Thackeray. Yet I have sincerely tried.

To read "Richard Feverel" after, say, "Pendennis" or "Esmond," is like eating grapes after turnips or bread-and-Crosse-and-Blackwell. What a loosening of the bonds! What a renaissance! Nobody since Fielding would have ventured to write the Star and Garter chapter in "Richard Feverel." It was the announcer of a sort of dawn. But there are fearful faults in "Richard Feverel." The book is sicklied o'er with the pale cast of the excellent Charlotte M. Yonge. The large constructional lines of it are bad. The separation of Lucy and Richard is never explained, and cannot be explained. The whole business of Sir Julius is grotesque. And the conclusion is quite arbitrary. It is a weak book, full of episodic power and overloaded with wit. "Diana of the Crossways" is even worse. I am still awaiting from some ardent Meredithian an explanation of Diana's marriage that does not insult my intelligence. Nor is "One of our Conquerors" very good. I read it again recently, and was sad. In my view, "The Egoist" and "Rhoda Fleming" are the best of the novels, and I don't know that I prefer one to the other. The latter ought to have been called "Dahlia Fleming," and not "Rhoda." When one thinks of the rich colour, the variety, the breadth, the constant intellectual distinction, the sheer brilliant power of novels such as these, one perceives that a Thackeray could only have succeeded in an age when all the arts were at their lowest ebb in England, and the most middling of the middle-classes ruled with the Bible in one hand and the Riot Act in the other.

Meredith was an uncompromising Radical, and—what is singular —he remained so in his old age. He called Mr. Joseph Chamberlain's nose adventurous at a time when Mr. Joseph Chamberlain's nose had the ineffable majesty of the Queen of Spain's leg. And the "Pall Mall" haughtily rebuked him. A spectacle of history! He said aloud in a a ball-room that Guy de Maupassant was the greatest novelist that ever lived. To think so was not strange; but to say it aloud! No wonder this temperament had to wait for recognition. Well, Meredith has never had proper recognition; and won't have yet. To be appreciated by a handful of writers, gushed over by a little crowd of "thoughtful young women," and kept on a shelf uncut by ten thousand persons determined to be in the movement— that is not appreciation. He has not even been appreciated as much as Thomas Hardy, though he is a less fine novelist. I do not assert that he is a less fine writer. For his poems are as superior to the verses of Thomas Hardy as "The Mayor of Casterbridge" is superior to "The Egoist." (Never in English prose literature was such a seer of beauty as Thomas Hardy.) The volume of Meredith's verse is small, but there are things in it that one would like to have written. And it is all so fine, so acute, so alert, courageous, and immoderate.

A member of the firm which has the honour of publishing Meredith's novels was interviewed by the "Daily Mail" on the day after his death. The gentleman interviewed gave vent to the usual insolence about our own times. "He belonged," said the gentleman, "to a very different age from the *modern* writer—an age before the literary agent; and with Mr. Meredith the feeling of intimacy as between author and publisher—the feeling that gave to publishing as it was its charm—was always existent." Charm—yes, for the publisher. The secret history of the publishing of Meredith's earlier books (long before Constable's had ever dreamed of publishing him) is more than curious. I have heard some details of it. My only wonder is that human ingenuity did not invent literary agents forty years ago. Then the person interviewed went grandly on: "In his manner of writing the great novelist was very different from the *modern* fashion. He wrote with such care that judged by *modern* standards he would be considered a trifle slow." Tut-tut! It may interest the gentleman interviewed to learn that no modern writer would dare to produce work at the rate at which Scott, Dickens, Trollope, and Thackeray produced it when their prices were at their highest. The rate of production has most decidedly declined, and upon the whole novels are written with more care now than ever they were. I should doubt if any novel was written at a greater speed than the greatest realistic novel in the world, Richardson's "Clarissa," which is eight or ten times the length of an average novel by Mrs. Humphry Ward. "Mademoiselle de Maupin" was done in six weeks. Scott's careless dash is notorious. And both Dickens and Thackeray were in such a hurry that they would often begin to print before they had finished writing. Publishers who pride themselves on the old charming personal relations with great authors ought not to be so ignorant of literary history as the gentleman who unpacked his heart to a sympathetic "Daily Mail."

New Age, V (May 27, 1909), 98. Reprinted under the title "Meredith," *Books and Persons* (New York: George H. Doran Co., 1917), pp. 134–139.

The Meredith Centenary (1928)

George Meredith was born a hundred years ago, and has been dead nearly nineteen years. We have had opportunity, therefore, to make up our minds about him. But a writer's posterity, occupied with its own affairs, is apt, like a millionaire, to keep the suppliant waiting in ante-rooms, and apparently we have not yet decided to receive Meredith. All that can be said with certainty is that at present we do not even read him. That is to say, he is read only by those few whose passionate interest in what they believe to be good keeps the flame of renown alive through ages of general neglect.

There are misconceptions concerning Meredith. People say that he was the son of an ordinary tailor. So he was. But he was the grandson of a most extraordinary tailor, a character, a figure in a large town, a diner-out and a sportsman; a fellow of the grand manner. George Meredith took after the grandfather. Also his aunts were the mistresses of opulent homes. Also he made many distinguished and educated friends who understood how to combine high thinking with material comfort. Thus, though he had the bad habit of being poor, his pictures of leisured and luxurious life are probably not the fanciful inventions which some of us once supposed them to be. He knew what he was writing of when he collected his characters, intellectual or smart or both, in a country house where wine and philosophy were appreciated with equal expertise.

He was a fine sight for any beholder. A born comedian, he loved in later years to play the part of a great man, and he played it perhaps to exaggeration but with the sense of style. He had the evil temper of a tyrant; I am willing to attribute this to ill-health, despite which he lived very long.

He was not, in my opinion, a novelist by either birth or inclination. The first business of a novelist is to tell a story, and Meredith never learnt it. (Hardy did.) He halts his stories in order to give a performance—of otiose psychological analysis or unnecessary description. He wanders vaguely around. He gets lost. Even when going straight he often goes too slowly. So that the reader says impatiently to himself: "Yes. This is brilliant and sound stuff, but it irritates me, and I almost wish I hadn't begun the thing. Still, having begun it, I'll struggle with it till I finish it or it finishes me." More than one of Meredith's novels has finished me.

Worse, Meredith wrote obscurely—not always, but frequently. Now obscurity of writing can be due to nothing but obscurity of thought. Oscar Wilde said that Meredith had mastered everything except language. This was an understatement. He had not mastered thought. And, worser and worser, he had not mastered construction —the prime constituent of a work of art. None of his novels is really well constructed, except "Beauchamp's Career" and "Evan Harrington." These two works, and no others, hold you. No! It is not that they hold you. There are indeed others which hold you, but by your exasperated neck. "Beauchamp's Career" and "Evan Harrington" persuade you, draw you easily forward in their wake. The heavenly powers watched over the author as he wrote them, saying: "Just twice we will make you better than you are."

Meredith began with verse and ended with verse. I suspect that he preferred verse to prose, and felt himself more at home in verse. To mere narrative he was assuredly at heart indifferent. His fundamental desire was not to narrate, but to be lyrically static, or static in the comic vein. (By comic I of course do not mean farcical.) He is at his best in ecstasy, and in the comic exposure of weak characters. And when he slips into one of these moods he sends the story to the devil. He knows he can do what he chooses with you then, and naughtily makes you pay for two pages of perfection by inflicting on you twenty pages of face-scratching, trackless jungle. I exaggerate, but the truth is in me.

The popular judgment on Meredith is that his two best books are "The Ordeal of Richard Feverel" and "The Egoist." With one reservation I concur in this judgment. His literary career, which stretched over sixty years, can be divided into two parts. "Feverel" opens the first part and "The Egoist" the second. Twenty years separate them (1859–1879). He had written two prose things before

"Feverel"—"Farina," which is a short and tedious pastiche, and "The Shaving of Shagpat," which is a longer and less tedious pastiche aiming to outdo the Oriental extravagance of "The Thousand and One Nights."

Then came "Feverel." It has the fine Meredithian characteristics: rapture and high comedy. The chapter, "A Diversion played on a Penny Whistle," one of the most celebrated passages in English fiction, is as wondrous and faultless to me to-day as it was when I first read it forty years ago. Odd how this scene recalls the shepherd's piping in "Tristan," Act III. (But it preceded "Tristan" by several years.) There is, amid the ecstacy, the same touch of realism in both. Meredith: "The self-satisfied sheep-boy delivers a last complacent squint down the length of his penny-whistle." Wagner, having caused his sheep-boy to hit on a pleasing phrase, makes him repeat the phrase again and again with a naive self-complacency.

But "Feverel" has also the less satisfactory Meredithian characteristics. The author gets lost in the maze of his tale; and the motivation goes to bits. Why did Richard leave Lucy? Every admirer finds a different reason, but nobody finds a good one and Meredith never gives a clear one. You have another example of these inexplicable separations in "Diana of the Crossways." But Diana was a clever fool, while Lucy had the wisdom of simplicity.

"Feverel" waited nineteen years for a second edition. By that time Meredith was well sick of the British public, and he determined to write solely at his own sweet wilfulness. "The Egoist" was the first result. Despite its faults of technique, no finer and richer comedy than this novel exists in English. The next book, "The Tragic Comedians," is dense and heavy. The last three novels, of his autumn and old age, are disfigured by too much of Meredith's own sweet wilfulness. Utterly occidental, they yet show the oriental extravagance of the writer of "The Shaving of Shagpat."

Of all Meredith's novels I like best "Evan Harrington." It has few faults and a hundred virtues. It is solid, restrained, shapely, and of an ample and continuous inspiration. Nothing unduly stands out in it. Perhaps that is why it has made less noise in the world than great but inferior books. It was written next after "Feverel," when Meredith was thirty-three. A marvellous achievement for so young a writer. When I first read "Evan Harrington" I began it after supper and finished it just in time for breakfast—without one moment of exasperation. This is praise.

No space left for my idiosyncratic and doubtless inexpert ideas about Meredith's poetry. Some of the best of it is sanely bitter.

Evening Standard, February 9, 1928, p. 7.

Henry James's *Embarrassments* (1896)

The first story in Mr. Henry James's new volume of *Embarrass-ments* (Heinemann, 6*s*.) is one of the best he has given to us for many years. It is exceedingly subtle and exceedingly clear, and the effective simplicity of the narrative arrangement could not possibly be bettered. The remaining stories, it seems to me, will delight only that select circle of admirers (of whom, be it understood, I am one) which regards him as a great, though peculiar, master. For myself, my adoration is placid, and, therefore, discriminating; and, al-though I still worship, I can plainly see that the great man's mere ingenuity, not only of construction, but of expression, must strike the absolutely unprejudiced as tedious. Also his colossal *cautiousness* in statement cannot fail to be very trying. If only he would now and then contrive to write a sentence without a qualifying clause! But at the worst there aren't two Henry Jameses; though many have imitated the cut of his mantle, he has never been approached. He can accomplish certain things more finely than anybody else, can render to the reader certain sensations which the reader cannot obtain from any other source. To review him is futile.

"Book Chat," signed "Barbara," *Woman*, VII (June 24, 1896), 9.

Henry James's *The Finer Grain* (1910)

At the beginning of this particularly active book season, reviewing the publishers' announcements, I wrote: "There are one or two promising items, including a novel by Henry James. And yet, honestly, am I likely at this time of day to be excited by a novel by Henry James? Shall I even read it? I know that I shall not. Still, I shall put it on my shelves, and tell my juniors what a miracle it is." Well, I have been surprised by the amount of resentment and anger which this honesty of mine has called forth. One of the politest of my correspondents, dating his letter from a city on the Rhine, says: "For myself, it's really a rotten shame; every week since 'Books and Persons' started have I hoped you would make some elucidating remarks on this wonderful writer's work, and now you don't even state why you propose not reading him!" And so on, with the result that when "The Finer Grain" (Methuen, 6s.) came along, I put my pride in my pocket, and read it. (By the way, it is not a novel but a collection of short stories, and I am pleased to see that it is candidly advertised as such.) I have never been an enthusiast for Henry James, and probably I have not read more than 25 per cent. of his entire output. The latest novel of his which I read was "The Ambassadors," and upon that I took oath I would never try another. I remember that I enjoyed "The Other House"; and that "In the Cage," a short novel about a post-office girl, delighted me. A few short stories have much pleased me. Beyond this, my memories of his work are vague. My estimate of Henry James might have been summed up thus: On the credit side:— He is a truly marvellous craftsman. By which I mean that he constructs with exquisite never-failing skill, and that he writes like an angel. Even at his most mannered and his most exasperating, he conveys his meaning with more precision and clarity than perhaps any other living writer. He is never, never clumsy, nor dubious, even in the minutest details. You would never catch him, for example, beginning a sentence as the "Westminster Gazette" began one the other day, thus: "Further, the Duke of Albany's only and posthumous son by a family arrangement"! Also he is a fine critic, of impeccable taste. Also he savours life with eagerness, sniffing the breeze of it like a hound . . . But on the debit side:—He is tremendously lacking in emotional power. Also his sense of beauty is over-sophisticated and wants originality. Also his attitude towards the spectacle of life is at bottom conventional, timid, and undecided. Also he seldom chooses themes of first-class importance, and when he does choose such a theme he never fairly bites it and makes it bleed. Also his curiosity is limited. It seems to me to have been specially created to be admired by super-dilettanti. (I do not say that to admire him is a proof of dilettantism.) What it all comes to is merely that his subject-matter does not as a rule interest me. I simply state my personal view, and I expressly assert my admiration for the craftsman in him and for the magnificent and consistent rectitude of his long artistic career. Further I will not go, though I know that bombs will now be laid at my front-door by the furious faithful. As for "The Finer Grain," it leaves me as I was—cold. It is an uneven collection, and the stories probably belong to different periods. The first, "The Velvet Glove," strikes me as conventional and without conviction. I should not call it subtle, but rather obvious. I should call it finicking. In the sentence-structure mannerism is pushed to excess. All the other stories are better. "Crafty Cornelia," for instance, is an exceedingly brilliant exercise in the art of making stone-soup. But then? I know I am in a minority among persons of taste. Some of the very best literary criticism of recent years has been aroused by admiration for Henry James. There is a man on the "Times Literary Supplement" who, whenever he writes about Henry James, makes me feel that I have mistaken my vocation and ought to have entered the Indian Civil Service, or been a cattle-drover. However, I can't help it. And I give notice that I will not reply to scurrilous letters.

New Age, VII (October 27, 1910), 614–615. Reprinted under the title "Henry James," *Books and Persons* (New York: George H. Doran Co., 1917), pp. 163–166.

A Candid Opinion on Henry James
(1927)

On two occasions in my maturer life have I blushed. The first
occasion was when, sitting in the stalls of a theatre, someone lightly
touched my shoulder from the row behind, and, turning, I heard a
remembered voice say: "You don't know me, Mr. Bennett, but I
know you." This was Ellen Terry. The second was when, in the
coffee-room of a club to which we both belonged, a stoutish man
accosted me and said: "You won't recall me. I'm Henry James.
May I join you upstairs later?"

Yes, I did fairly blush—I suppose because I was flattered. Such
is the mysterious influence of immense artistic prestige on my
blood vessels. Not that I quite believed that Ellen Terry really
thought I shouldn't know her, or that Henry James really thought
I shouldn't recall him. As regards Henry James, he did join me
upstairs later. The first thing he said was: "For me this room is full
of ghosts." And he went on to talk in highly-finished phrases of
James Payn and other lions, and of asses in lions' skins. He was at
once sardonic and gloomy; and marvellously courteous to the boy
—for, although about fifty, I felt just like a boy in his presence.
It seemed to me that the mournful light of the setting sun was in
his eyes; he was certainly in bad health.

And now another book has been written upon Henry James, this
time by Professor Pelham Edgar ("Henry James, Man and Author").
It resembles most American books about books; it is painstaking,
thorough, ingenious, infrequently illuminating—and not succulent.
Reading it, you have the terrible suspicion that the author does not
entirely understand what he is talking about. I don't assert that he
doesn't, but I am not securely convinced that he does.

Artistic prestige has an influence not only on my blood-vessels
but on my critical faculty. It took me years to ascertain that Henry

132

James's work was giving me little pleasure. I first had a glimpse of the distressing fact when "What Maisie Knew" began to appear serially in "The New Review" ages ago, somewhere in the Ninth Dynasty.[1]

By the one thousand persons (including myself) in England who are genuinely interested in the art of literature this serial was anticipated with a religious eagerness. I could not get on with it. My fault, of course. Impossible to credit that anything of Henry James's was not great!

But when I was immovably bogged in the middle of "The Golden Bowl" and again in the middle of "The Ambassadors" (supposed, both of them, to mark the very summit of Henry James's achievement) I grew bolder with myself. In each case I asked myself: "What the dickens is this novel *about*, and where does it think it's going to?" Question unanswerable! I gave up.

To-day I have no recollection whatever of any characters or any events in either novel. And I will venture to say that I have honestly enjoyed, and been held by, only two of James's novels— "In the Cage" and "The Other House." The former is very short and the latter is not interminable.

I am willing to admit for the sake of argument, that Henry James knew more about the technique of the novel than any other novelist (save Turgenev). He was fond of saying that a novel, to be artistically satisfactory, must be "organised," and he "organised" his own with unique and inhuman elaboration. I will also admit, without any reserve, that his style, though unduly mannered, is very distinguished, and that he said what he so subtly meant with unsurpassed accuracy. I will admit that he knew everything about writing novels—except how to keep my attention.

My doubt is whether he had actually much to say, in a creative sense, that needed saying. I think that he knew a lot about the life of one sort of people, the sort who are what is called cultured, and who do themselves very well both physically and intellectually, and very little indeed about life in general. I think that in the fastidiousness of his taste he rather repudiated life.

1. *What Maisie Knew* ran serially in the *New Review* from February to September, 1897.

He was a man without a country. He never married. He never, so far as is commonly known, had a love-affair worthy of the name. And I would bet a fiver that he never went into a public-house and had a pint of beer—or even half-a-pint. He was naive, innocent, and ignorant of fundamental things to the last. He possessed taste, but his taste lacked robustness. He had the most delicate perceptions; but he perceived things with insufficient emotion. He was mortally afraid of being vulgar, and even of being carried away. My notion is that most first-rate creative artists simply do not know what vulgarity is. They go right on, and if it happens to them to be vulgar in the stress of emotion, well, it happens to them—and they are forgiven.

Henry James's short stories have received high praise. I think they are the thinnest of all his work, and essentially commonplace in essence. As for his recollections, such as "The American Scene," and "A Small Boy and Others," I think they push uncompromising unreadableness further than it was ever pushed before. His letters are a disturbing revelation of the man.

I offer these views with respect and with reserve; because I am harried by doubts. My eye may have a blind spot for the alleged supreme excellencies of Henry James. But, if so, the eyes of a vast number of other people no plainer than myself are similarly afflicted. I extol him as a literary critic. He was perhaps the first important English-writing critic to deflate the balloon of Gustave Flaubert. His essays on the younger English novelists are masterly, and packed close with vitamines. I have read them twice, and may read them again. But never shall I set out afresh into the arid desert of "The Golden Bowl." No!

Evening Standard, January 27, 1927, p. 5.

Mr. George Moore (1901)

I

It was not until the publication of *Esther Waters* in 1894 that Mr. George Moore received from the general public and its literary advisers the candid recognition of his eminence as a serious novelist. At that date he had been writing for sixteen years and had produced some dozen books, including—besides fiction—verse, drama, and criticism; several of these volumes had had a large and steady sale, and one of them—indubitably a masterpiece—had been translated into French; as far back as 1885 he was in a position to inform Mr. Mudie (in that militant pamphlet *Literature at Nurse, or Circulating Morals*) that the support of the libraries was not vital to his existence as an author. But in some mysterious way the just laurels of his achievement were denied to him. The press, while witnessing faithfully enough to the extraordinary power and merit of his work, assumed an attitude of pained reproach, confronted him with arguments in which recur those notorious phrases, "photographic realism," "nose in the gutter," and "true mission of art," and would on no account explicitly acknowledge his entire probity. Though this powerful and meritorious work sold freely, the respectable bookshops, instead of displaying it on the shelf of popularity, preferred to bring it forth, on demand only, from some shy corner. In compensation, to be sure, it was thrust before your gaze, along with translations of Paul de Kock,[1] confessions of ladies'-maids, and physiological treatises, on the façades of dubious marts in Holywell Street and elsewhere; and so came to be bought at nightfall by youths who imagined that they were indulging a taste for naughtiness. In the early nineties, when Mr. Moore published two volumes of essays, it began to be rumoured that he was our

1. Paul de Kock (1794–1871), French author of a large number of amusing, sometimes improper novels. He was very popular in France and England during the nineteenth century.

foremost art-critic; but none referred to his novels. Then, after a silence as regards fiction of five years, came *Esther Waters*. Its author must have felt a certain scornful embarrassment at the largesse of praise with which this book was saluted. He had abated not one of his principles; he had made no compromises, offered no apologies. On the contrary, here were precisely the themes and precisely the methods which before had disadvantaged him to such an extent that once, in order to get printed serially, he had been compelled to use a pseudonym. Yet *Esther Waters* was called, without any sort of reservation, a *chef d'oeuvre*. The most discreet critics lauded it with the whole fervour of their souls. It was discussed everywhere with open doors. Not to have read it amounted to a social solecism, and those timid discerning ones who in secretness had previously given Mr. Moore his true rank, were now able to confess their belief. I am not concerned here to inquire into the causes of this strange revulsion of a prejudice. It is enough to note that owing to developments on the part of one or two writers who were fortunate enough or wise enough to establish themselves before developing, the cult of the Young Person had been for some time on the wane.

That Mr. Moore is a vigorous individuality, from the first stubbornly bent upon the realisation of a revolutionary theory, need not be affirmed. Were it otherwise the opposition which he encountered had been far less acrid and less persistent. But he has never, so far as I am aware, formally enunciated his artistic creed. *Literature at Nurse* was merely the expression of an annoyance which resolved itself into the complaint: "If I am punished, why are others who have transgressed more deeply allowed to go free?" He is not, like the brothers de Goncourt, given to *préfaces et manifestes*. And when one seeks in the history of his career for a clue to his idiosyncrasy, one discovers that his career is unpublished. Even the latest compendium of facts, which boasts of so many thousand biographies, gives nothing but the briefest bibliography of his works; other annuals of reference ignore him. Happily there appeared, first in a magazine called *Time*, now extinct, and afterwards in book form, that singularly vivacious, vivid fantasy of reminiscence, criticism, and philosophy, *The Confessions of a Young Man* (1888). In form, *The Confessions of a Young Man* is a novel, with a hero named Dayne, but one may be permitted to assume that in essence it is an autobiography. Mr. Moore cares so little for the mere name of his hero that he styles him Edward or Edwin indifferently; and it is impossible to regard either the minute details of Parisian studio life or the literary criticisms in which the book abounds as other than personal to the author himself.

Dayne went to Paris as a youth, and almost became a Parisian. "The English I love, and with a love that is foolish—mad, limitless; I love them better than the French, but I am not so near to them." And again: "With Frenchmen I am conscious of a sense of nearness; I am one with them in their ideas and aspirations, and when I am with them I am alive to a keen and penetrating sense of intimacy." He sketches for us, with a frankness now gay, now cynical, the luscious *vie de Bohème* that Paris alone can offer to the young man of health and wealth whose love of art exceeds his love of virtue. Here, amid scenes splendid, squalid, or bizarre, move students, *cabotins*, painters, poets, pale enthusiasts starving for the sake of an idea, actresses, women of fashion, courtesans, clubmen, and mere spectators. Artistic endeavour and perfumed vice mingle in a complete fraternity unknown elsewhere; everything is unusual, irregular, fantastic. Dayne emerges from the ordeal of this environment but little changed. For him the enticements of the flesh are not more powerful than those of art. One week he is beguiling the hours in some salon or alcove, the next he is incandescent with aspiration. So the years pass; and at last, having saturated himself with the French theories of literary and graphic art which are bound up with the names of Flaubert, the de Goncourts, Zola, Degas, and Manet, he one day learns with tragic certainty that he is not destined to be a painter, and he courageously admits that all this periodic, frenzied effort has been misdirected. Then we have interludes of philosophy and literary criticism; the philosophy perhaps not of much account; the criticism often crude, hasty, and shallow, but original, epigrammatic, sometimes of an astounding penetration, and always *literary*—remarkable enough at a period when Englishmen had apparently lost the purely literary point of view.

Later, Dayne is driven by adverse circumstances to London and to a lodging in the Strand. He gives himself seriously to literature, and now we have incidents which beyond doubt are taken from life. That "The Magazine" must be Tinsley's is patent to everyone familiar with the Grub Street of the eighties; and in the tall man whom Mr. Tinsley accepted for a second Dickens it is not difficult to recognize a novelist who, though he seems to write no longer, has accomplished at least one excellent story. The book ends on a curiously wistful note, and we leave the hero, who has dipped into and withdrawn from the luxurious Bohemianism of London, at work on a novel.

The general tendency of Dayne's ideas about art and the cast of his temperament may be gathered from such characteristic passages as the following:

> For art was not for us then as it is now—a mere emotion, *right or wrong only in proportion to its intensity*; we believed then in the grammar of art, perspective, anatomy, and *la jambe qui porte*.[2]
>
> In contemporary English fiction I marvel, and I am repeatedly struck by (*sic*) the inability of writers, even of the first class, to make an organic whole of their stories. Here, I say, the course is clear, the way is obvious, but no sooner do we enter on the last chapters than the story [Mr. Hardy's *Far from the Madding Crowd*] begins to show incipient shiftiness, and soon it doubles back and turns, growing with every turn weaker like a hare before the hounds. From a certain directness of construction, from the simple means by which Oak's ruin is accomplished in the opening chapters, I did not expect that the story would run hare-hearted in its close, but the moment Troy told his wife that he never cared for her I suspected something was wrong; when he went down to bathe and was carried out by the current I knew the game was up, and was prepared for anything, even to the final shooting of the rich farmer and the marriage with Oak, a conclusion which, of course, does not come within the range of literary criticism.
>
> *The Story of an African Farm* was pressed upon me. I found it sincere and youthful, disjointed but well written; descriptions of sandhills and ostriches sandwiched with doubts concerning a future state and convictions regarding the moral and physical superiority of women: but of art nothing; that is to say, art as I understand it, rhythmical sequence of events described with rhythmical sequence of phrase.

2. "The leg that carries."

For it (*Les Palais Nomades*) is in the first place free from those pests and parasites of artistic work—ideas. Of all literary qualities the creation of ideas is the most fugitive. . . .

But in me the impulse is so original to frequent the haunts of men that it is irresistible, conversation is the breath of my nostrils. I watch the movement of life, and my ideas spring from it uncalled for, as buds from branches. Contact with the world is in me the generating force; without it what invention I have is thin and sterile, and it grows thinner rapidly, until it dies away utterly.

Although Mr. Moore had issued four novels, three of these being works of the first importance, before the appearance of the *Confessions*, the latter is probably a youthful work. At any rate it represents an early stage of the author's development. For our guidance in following the subsequent progress of his ideas, Mr. Moore has thoughtfully introduced into nearly all his novels a novelist named Harding, a character whom his creator eyes with unmistakable complacency. Harding holds advanced views on most things, and he is intimate with one Thompson, the leader of a school of painters styled "the Moderns," whose theories Harding endeavours to realise in literature. Whenever Harding appears the dialogue turns upon literature and art, and his remarks thereupon are full of interesting suggestion. In *A Modern Lover*, for example, he is made to state his position clearly, thus:

> We do not always choose what you call unpleasant subjects, but we try to go to the roots of things; and the basis of life, being material and not spiritual, the analyst invariably finds himself, sooner or later, handling what this sentimental age calls coarse. But, like Thompson, I am sick of the discussion. If your stomach will not stand the crudities of the moral dissecting-room, read verse; but don't try to distort an art into something it is not, and cannot be. *The Novel, if it be anything, is contemporary history, an exact and complete reproduction of social surroundings of the age we live in.*

But the most notable and dignified utterance upon the function of the novel is made by the author himself in *A Drama in Muslin*:

> Seen from afar all things in nature are of equal worth; and the meanest things, when viewed with the eyes of God, are raised to

heights of tragic awe which conventionality would limit to the deaths of kings or patriots. The history of a nation as often lies hidden in social wrongs and domestic griefs as in the story of revolution, and if it be for the historian to narrate the one, it is for the novelist to dissect and explain the other.

Here indeed is the voice of one who sees in the novel something more than diversion for weary brains.

II

After two small volumes of verse, *Flowers of Passion* and *Pagan Poems*, of which nothing need be said except that they contain some experiments in irregular rhythms more curious than successful, Mr. Moore published his first novel, *A Modern Lover*, in 1883.

This is the story of a painter who prospered and flourished, not from innate ability of force of character, but solely by reason of the magnetic, persuasive, physical influence which he unconsciously exerted upon his fellow-creatures—and in particular upon those of them who happened to be women. Men despised him for his femininity, but they served towards his advancement: women adored him. Had he been an actor in New York he would have been styled "the matinée girls' idol." "He was one of those creatures," said Harding to a group of "the Moderns," "who exercise a strange power over all with whom they come in contact, a control that is purely physical, yet acting equally on the most spiritual as on the most gross natures, and leading us independently of our judgment. How can we blame the women for going mad after him, when even we used to sacrifice ourselves, over and over again, to help him." He had "exquisite beauty, his feminine grace seemed like a relic of ancient Greece saved by some miracle through the wreck and ruin of ages. He leaned against an oak bureau, placed under a high narrow window, and the pose defined his too developed hips, always, in a man, the sign of a weak and lascivious nature."

The career of Lewis Seymour is disposed with a certain large simplicity round the figures of three women, each of whom abased herself that he might rise, and each of whom was cast behind him when her usefulness had ceased. At the beginning we find him, a starving art-student, lacking even the means to engage the model necessary for the execution of a very remunerative commission which chance has brought to him. In the same mean lodging-house lives a work-girl, Gwynnie Lloyd, modest, pure, and warm-hearted, with whom he has relations of sentiment. A model is essential; but he has no money; he makes a suggestion to Gwynnie, and after a fierce conflict with her instincts she accepts the igno-minious misery of sitting to him for the nude. The commission is carried out, to the great worldly advantage of Lewis, and Gwynnie is forgotten; for him she no longer exists.

The second woman is Mrs. Bentham, rich, and living apart from an impossible husband. Lewis is invited to her country house in order that he may decorate the ball-room, and from the inception of their acquaintance, she scarcely hides from him the influence of his spell; nevertheless it is a long while before she becomes his mistress. They meet in Paris, where Lewis is studying, and the emotional climax of the book is reached upon an evening which the lovers spend together driving about the city. No other English writer has expressed the peculiar enchantment of Paris as Mr. Moore does in this sensuous and glowing scene. It is a beautiful summer night:

> Drawing up close to her in the captivating ease of the victoria, he endeavoured to attune his conversation to the spirit of the hour. And what a delightful hour it was! The tepid air was as soft and luxurious as silk on their faces, and the swing of the swiftly-rolling carriage treacherously rocked to quietude all uneasy thoughts. . . . The victoria was now passing through the wide and mournful Place Vendôme into the brilliantly lighted Rue de la Paix. Upon a vast plain of moonlight blue sky was stretched the façade of the opera house; with its rich per-spectives extending down the shadow-filled Rue Auber and Meyerbeer. On each side and atop of the highest roofs two gold figures spread their gold wings, whilst below in the blanching glow of clustering electric lights, the passers went like an endless procession of marionettes march-ing to the imagined strain of an invisible orchestra. . . .
>
> The beauty of the city acted on Mrs. Bentham and Lewis as a nar-cotic; and, in spirit, they had already stepped into the pleasures which Paris, in her capacity of fashionable courtesan, holds upon to all comers. The measure of expectant waltzes beat in their feet, the fumes of un-corked champagne arose to their heads, and the light wings of unkissed

kisses had already touched their lips, and their thoughts and bodies swayed by the motion of the carriage, watched deliciously the flashing and gleaming of the thousand lights that moved around them, seeing nothing distinctly but the round back of the coachman as he sat, his shoulders set, steering faultlessly through an almost inextricable mass of whirling wheels.

At a late hour the drive out to the Arc de Triomphe, and when the *détour* had been accomplished:

> They descended the avenue towards Paris. The chaplets of light that glowed through the leaves of the chestnut trees were now all extinguished; but Paris blazed at the bottom of the great white road. Far away by the Place de la Concorde, the terraces of the Orangerie— the dark running Seine with its bridges and beautiful buildings, lay extended like a lover-awaiting courtesan, and Mrs. Bentham watched the city beaming distinct as they descended the long incline. Chameleon-like it changed every hour, now it appeared in her eyes like an infamous alcove full of shames and ignominies into which she was being dragged; she would fain have shut out the sight with her hands, she longed to fly from it; but she was whirled in a current she could not combat, and wearily she wished to sink to sleep, and then to awake to find that all was over, that all had been decided for her.

At last, after midnight, they reach the door of Mrs. Bentham's hotel. Lewis wishes to enter. She begs him to go away, and complains that the *concierge* will be coming out to reconnoitre:

> The moment was a critical one. There was no time for further words. Mrs. Bentham pushed past him; but determined not to be beaten he followed her. *It was the bravest act of his life.*

In that last sentence we have a specimen of the ferocious humour Mr. Moore has permitted himself about a dozen times in as many years.

This amour has rather a long existence, for all the resources of Mrs. Bentham's wealth and position are lavished upon Lewis. She even spends a thousand a year in secretly buying his pictures through a dealer. And so Lewis grows independent. He patronises the author of his successes, and laments in privacy that the hand of time is laid upon her. The end comes when Lewis meets Lady

Helen, a daughter of a distinguished peer, and falls passionately, genuinely in love for the first time in his life. He instantly abandons Mrs. Bentham; while she, for her part, recognising that his future prosperity must depend upon an advantageous marriage, sorrowfully yields him to the third woman, and is content thereafter to watch over his interests with a solicitude which is only maternal.

The third woman was decorative, and it was the painter in Lewis that she entranced:

> The light filled Lady Helen's saffron-coloured hair with strange flames, and the red poppies in her straw hat echoed, in a higher key, the flowers embroidered on her dress. She was quite five feet seven, and very slender. She was the type of all that is elegant, but in her elegance there was a certain hardness; her face seemed to have been squeezed between two doors. Lady Helen was very pale, and in the immaculate whiteness of her skin there was scarcely a trace of colour; it was pure as the white of an egg, only around the clear eyes it darkened to the liquid velvety tint which announces a passionate nature. The head, beautifully placed on a long, thin neck, fell into ever-varying attitudes; the waist, which you could span with your hands, swayed deliciously, and the slight hips recalled more those of Bacchus than the Venus de Milo.

Lady Helen more than returns the fervency of Lewis, and in spite of terrible difficulties with her relatives (all of whom are drawn with remarkable skill—the mother is a superb sketch) she becomes his wife. Lewis is married in "a church filled with women he has deceived." His star continues to ascend. By degrees he grows weary of his once adored wife; and she, discovering in him a being more selfish than herself, bows to his egotism and becomes a slave. She closes her eyes to his peccadilloes; she uses the fascination of her individuality in order to obtain orders for portraits; she relaxes the exclusiveness of her drawing-room to the end that Lewis may become an A.R.A.[3] And Lewis amuses himself, always extending the long record of his facile conquests.

> He remained ever the same. He was now three-and-thirty, but he did not look more than six-and-twenty, and he grew daily more delightful

3. Associate of the Royal Academy; thus an established academic painter.

and seductive. Experience and necessity had perfected the social talents with which nature had endowed him. Better than ever he knew how to interest, how to move. He knew the words that touched, the words that caressed, the words that tickled; and, smiling and graceful, he continued to persuade ladies to sit for their portraits.

No discerning student could read *A Modern Lover* in 1883 without being impressed by the profound difference between it and all previous English novels. It was candidly erotic; it depressed; it presented a group of principal characters so unsavoury that one cannot possibly respect any of them; it scorned to be either bright or breezy or wholesome or anything that might secure the approbation of a great and enlightened public. But the quality which isolates it is deeper than these. It is written throughout with that religious, punctilious regard for major and minor truth which entitles it to be called "realistic." It was the first realistic novel in England. By the term "realistic novel" I simply mean, of course, one whose aim is to be *real*, regardless of any conventions which would involve a divergence from life itself. And I do not forget that the realism of one age is the conventionality of the next. In the main the tendency of art is always to reduce and simplify its conventions, thus necessitating an increase of virtuosity in order to obtain the same effects of shapeliness and rhythm. But so far as we are concerned, Mr. Moore achieved realism. Steeped in the artistic theories of modern France, he contrasted the grave and scientific fiction of Flaubert and his followers with the novels of Englishmen, and he saw in the latter, by comparison, only so many fairy tales devised for the pleasure of people who would not take art seriously. (For not even the finest English novelists had attempted to reproduce life in its entirety; the notion of doing so possibly never occurred to them.) He sought to do in English the thing which he had seen done in French. Casting away every consideration of usage, precedent, "propriety," popular taste, and impelled only by the desire to render with absolute fidelity life as he observed it, he wrote *A Modern Lover*. And though the ideas which urged him forward were already trite in France, they were startlingly new in this country. Thanks to the insularity of our island, he was indeed a pioneer. Like most pioneers, he was earnest almost to truculence.

Knowing that sexuality was anathema, he chose a theme accordingly, and developed it in detail with an air sublimely unconscious of the frightful outrage he was inflicting. During the greater part of it *A Modern Lover* is purely sexual—as sexual as Guy de Maupassant's *Bel Ami*, to which it bears a remarkable resemblance; indeed one could be certain that *A Modern Lover* was directly inspired by *Bel Ami* were it not for the fact that it preceded *Bel Ami* by two years.

We may imagine the horror and consternation which the book, suddenly cast like a bombshell into the midst of a sleepy hamlet, would create. We can perhaps sympathise with those who saw in it an infamy, a wanton and incredible provocation. Mr. Moore had prepared a shock which was almost too severe: since that time many events have occurred, and we are now less easily roused to the anger of grieved righteousness. Yet *A Modern Lover* has not a trace of pornography. Considering the opportunities for indelicacy, its delicacy is really marvellous, much beyond what any public could with reason expect from such a revolutionary. It would appear that the author, having satisfied spleen in the selection of a subject, was content not to carry his theories to their last limits. The book is not realistic in the common meaning of the term. For the average person, a realistic novel is one which gives an unadorned recital of facts mainly sordid and disgusting. *A Modern Lover* is full of poetic quality. Combined with and superimposed upon its cold exactitude, is that wide and absolute *vision* which, in verse as in prose, marks the loftiest form of art. It abounds with descriptions of urban and rural landscapes, of skies, and of passions, conceived and executed on the high plane of pure poetry. No richer, more glowing pictures of sunset can be found anywhere. The baser passions—those, for instance, of jealousy and of love which is not spiritual—are made grand by simple strength of imagination. One notes everywhere, also, the author's peculiar skill (the skill of a poet) in setting down a complex effect in one phrase. Thus, when Lewis, a starving and resourceless student, exasperated by the opulent luxury and dissipation around him, is walking one night through the West End, we read: *In his madness he fancied he heard the shower of gold and kisses that fell over the city.*

The psychology of the book is not less remarkable than its imagination. At each crisis in the development of the story the secret springs of human nature are exposed with the strict justice of a creator who regards his characters with divine indifference. Only sometimes does his icy impartiality give way to an attitude slightly sympathetic. The most effective example of such compassion is the scene of the ball where Mrs. Bentham, who has made the two tragic discoveries that she is old and that Lewis has withdrawn his affection, is presented to us in a light so touching that we almost love this frail, demoralised and self-ruined woman. All the characters except Gwynnie Lloyd and such minor persons as Thompson the artist and Harding the novelist, are either depraved or contemptible or ridiculous—and chiefly they are depraved. Their author, violently opposed to the practice of those novelists and painters who gain from subject an effectiveness which he preferred to get by treatment, had evidently determined to owe nothing to the mere intrinsic charm of his people. He was amazingly serious and conscientious. But he could not rid himself completely of the English tradition, for towards the end of the book, in making Gwynnie Lloyd the maid of Lady Helen, he is guilty of a scandalous sentimentality. The defection from his ideal is so gross and so unconscious as to be laughable. The last part of the tale is in several respects the least fine. After the honeymoon of Lewis and Lady Helen the theme is changed from love to art, the unity of the book is endangered, and the author scarcely escapes an anti-climax.

III

I have considered *A Modern Lover* at some length, not only because it is an extremely remarkable first novel, but also because it so plainly differentiates the aims and methods of Mr. Moore from those of his contemporaries. Compared with his next work, however, it is faulty and insignificant. For *A Modern Lover* has the flaws of youthfulness. Its outlook, though penetrating, is narrow: love, jealousy, and colour—the author has eyes for nothing else. Moreover it is languorous, often effeminate; persuasive rather than compelling; and once or twice somewhat rank in its luxuriance. *A Mummer's Wife* has none of these imperfections.

This second novel (1885) suffered the same fate as its predecessor at the hands of the libraries. It could not have been so distasteful to Mrs. Grundy, but it contained one scene of offence—a scene which Mr. Moore quotes in full in the pamphlet *Literature at Nurse*. Published to-day, the scene would arouse scarcely a comment, and one speculates in vain upon Mr. Moore's reason for omitting it from later editions of the book.

In *A Mummer's Wife* the author logically prosecuted his theory of fiction, using a finer austerity, a severer self-discipline. *A Modern Lover* was adolescent. *A Mummer's Wife* is absolutely mature. The tale is that of the wife of a small draper in the North Staffordshire Potteries—an inexorable record of decadence. Mr. Ede is asthmatical, and the story opens with one of his dreadful attacks. Kate Ede is passing her nights at her querulous husband's bedside, and her days in attending to the shop and her own dressmaking business. The household, which is completed by the figure of Ede's grim fanatic mother, is strictly religious, mean and sordid in its comforts, tedious and confined in the regularity of its movement. Kate's monotonous life, to quote Mr. Moore's own summary, "flows on unrelieved by hope, love, or despair." To make a few extra shillings a week the Edes let their front rooms, which are taken by Mr. Dick Lennox, the manager of an opera bouffe company on tour. He makes love to the draper's wife, seduces her (here occurred the eliminated scene), and she elopes with him. She travels about with the actors, and gradually becomes one of them; she "walks on" among the chorus, speaks a few words, says a few verses, and is eventually developed into a heroine of comic opera. This life, therefore, that up to twenty-seven knew no diversion, no change of thought or place, now knows neither rest nor peace. Even marriage, for Dick Lennox marries her when Ralph Ede obtains his divorce, is unable to calm the excitation of the brain that so radical a change of life has produced, and after the birth of her baby Kate takes to drink, sinks lower and lower, until death from dropsy and liver complaint saves her from becoming one of the street-walkers with whom she is in the habit of associating.

Here was a second, a stronger, and a still more dignified protest against the long-accepted methods of English novelists: a superb and successful effort to show that from life at its meanest and least decorative could be drawn material grand enough for great fiction. Mr. Moore in this book ascetically deprived himself of all those specious aids to effect—nobility of character, feminine grace, the sudden stroke of adverse fate, lovely scenic background, splendour of mere event—which the most gifted of his forerunners had found useful. His persons are in all respects everyday folk, lacking any sort of special individual charm, and at best full of paltry human faults. For scene he chooses one of the most unsightly towns in the kingdom, and the hero and heroine leave this only to wander through the frowsy theatres and theatrical lodging-houses of the north. He invents no tragic situations of conventional type. No one is much ill-used; even the wronged invalid husband recovers and marries again. There is no departure from daily existence at its most usual, no point at which we can say: "This was contrived for effect."

And, in practising such a unique austerity, George Moore produced a masterpiece. By the singleness of his purpose to be truthful, and by sheer power of poetical imagination, he has raised upon a sordid and repellent theme an epic tale, beautiful with the terrible beauty which hides itself in the ugliness of life. *A Mummer's Wife* is more than a masterpiece; it is one of the supreme novels of the century, a work which stands out, original, daring, severe, ruthless, and resplendent, even amongst the finest. It excels at all points. In the large masses of its form it is impeccable. It proceeds naturally and inevitably, without haste and without slur to a catastrophe from which there is no escape. The characters have the illusion of beings seen and known. In the matter of detail the book stands solitary in modern English fiction. Never before was the laborious scholarship of "local colour" used with such ease and skill. Mr. Moore is at home everwhere: in the little draper's shop of an obscure town; under the stages of provincial theatres; in the dressing-rooms of loose coryphées; in earthenware manufactories; in the purlieus of Islington. He knows the trivial routine of a dressmaking business, and how a comic opera is rehearsed. He can tell you the precise attitude of the working woman towards her fiction: He knows how a child is born and how it dies. He is acquainted with the minute phenomena of inebriety and of organic disease. He writes of nothing which he has not observed—but he has observed everything. In the hands of a lesser artist such prodigious lore might have resulted in an orgy of fact; in the hands of George Moore its effect is merely to give the reader a sense of security and confidence amid the tumult of imagination.

There is one charge to be laid against *A Mummer's Wife*, and it touches the question of style. George Moore's style presents a most curious literary problem. In the writing, not only of *A Mummer's Wife*, but of all his novels, the finest qualities and the meanest defects are mingled so curiously that one dares neither to bestow upon nor to withhold from him the title of stylist. From the outset his prose was interesting. The prose of *A Modern Lover* might be described by those two favourite adjectives of the author's own, "languorous" and "persuasive." It has an indolent voluptuous beauty which only seldom approaches the lyricism of great prose. It is, however, frequently emotional, and the best parts of the book are those dealing with passion and the excitations of nature. It is often vehement, scarcely once virile. *A Mummer's Wife* shows a development. Here the style is virile and generous. Take the admirable description of Dick Lennox:

> She yearned to bury her poor aching body, throbbing with the anguish of nerves, in that peaceful hulk of fat, so calm, so grand, so invulnerable to pain, marching amid, and contented in, its sensualities, as a stately bull grazing amid the pastures of a succulent meadow.

The word "succulent" in this passage is chosen with the nicest intention to illustrate the character.

For an example of lofty lyricism, observe the whole scene in which Kate's baby dies while its parents are asleep. It includes thus:

> Above the dark roof the moon had now become a crescent, and as an angel stealing and leaning forward, a white ray kissed with cold supernatural kisses the cheeks of the lonely child,—and instantly, as if in fear, the blue staring eyes were opened, the little legs were drawn up to the very chest, the weak wail ceased and the convulsions began. Would father or mother awake to soothe the pitiful struggle? No, the shivering little limbs stirred only to the hideous accompaniment of the drunken woman's snores; and even as heedless, majestic in naked golden

glory, the moon swam up through the azure peace of the skies, until brought face to face with the child.

Then, in a strange and luminous pause, a green presence took possession of the whole room, including every detail in its mysterious embrace. The meanest objects became weird and fearsome; form and sound were transfigured. Demon-like, the brandy bottle stood on the chest of drawers, and the huddled group in the dusky bed seemed as a vile world snoring, equally indifferent to life and to death. Yet for a moment there was hope, for, as if subdued by the magnetism of an unearthly power, the convulsions grew less, and a sweet calm came over the cradle. The respite, how brief it was! Soon the little blankets were cast aside, the legs were twisted on to the chest, and the eyes blinked convulsively. But no smile of joy, nor tear of grief, changed the mild cruelty of the amber-coloured witch at the window: softly as a drinking snake, she drank of this young life. Thou shalt be mine and mine only, she seemed to say; and in the devouring gleams the struggle was continued. Out of the flower-like skin black stains grew; all the soft roundnesses fell into distortions; chubby knees were wrenched to and fro, muscles seemed to be torn, and the bones beneath to be broken violently: as in the Laocoon, every movement spoke of pain.

So, for an inappreciable space of time, the white rays glorified the poetic agony; and then the little wan body lay still in a flood of passionless light. Not a star watched the bird-like remains: only the moon knew of the moon's tragedy; and after lingering an hour, the pale aureole moved up the sky, leaving the child to sleep in darkness for ever.

It would be difficult in the face of such prose to deny to the author most of the qualities which make for distinguished style: dignity, a rhythmical sense, a true feeling for words, and that delight in words *qua* words so characteristic of all modern stylists. Yet, an examination of his defects will give us pause. For all Mr. Moore's books are studded with passages that disclose stone-blindness to the niceties of diction and punctuation, an ignorance of common rules, of composition and even of grammar, indiscretions in the use of metaphor, and a general lack of literary good taste. Scores of examples might be selected, but I must be content with a few:

> They seemed like a *piece* of finished sculpture ready to be taken from the *peace* and meditation of the studio and placed in the noise and staring of the gallery.

She could not help but feeling ashamed.

A vision of Mrs. Bentham seated at supper by his side *rose to his lips.*

Mr. Carver only eyed him sharply and advised him to be very careful, to look before he leaped, *and,* better still, *not to leap at all,* but to *let things untie themselves* gradually.

Esther asked him after Mrs. Randal and her children (meaning, not that Esther asked Mrs. Randal and her children first and *him* afterwards, but that she inquired from him concerning Mrs. Randal and her children).

Re-see, re-finish, disassociate, ennuied.

One is accustomed to meet such solecisms only in prose which is absolutely worthless. But Mr. Moore plants them in the very midst of passages otherwise noble and dignified. The faults may be superficial, but they effectually tarnish. Only a man who, having developed in another art the higher qualities of the artist, had turned suddenly to literature without troubling to acquire the rudiments of its technique, could possibly have committed them.

IV

In the fifteen years which have elapsed since *A Mummer's Wife,* Mr. Moore has published six novels, including the book which gave him popularity. None of these, in my opinion, quite equals *A Mummer's Wife.* Even *Esther Waters* is colder, less richly inspired. Of the rest, one, *Vain Fortune,* is slight, obviously a minor work; and it seems to be Mr. Moore's desire that two others, *Spring Days* and *Mike Fletcher,* should be forgotten. As to *Esther Waters,* and *Evelyn Innes* and its sequel, it is unnecessary to say anything; the first has been definitely accepted as a masterpiece, and the others are at present in the eye of the public. There remains, of the first importance, *A Drama in Muslin.*

This novel, issued a year after *A Mummer's Wife,* is very different thematically from either of its predecessors. In it Mr. Moore deals with what is called "the marriage market." He has five heroines, all more or less of good birth, and he exposes the wild, breathless husband-hunt in its every aspect—sordid, strategic, crafty, base, sometimes almost epic. To accentuate the despicable meanness of this scramble for establishment and position, the scene is laid chiefly in provincial Ireland, with Dublin as the centre of all things, and a

Viceroy's kiss as the climax of social distinction. The terrible triviality of it is emphasised by basing it on a subsoil, as it were, of the revolt of the Irish peasants, the fatal machinations of the League. This under-theme is used sparingly; just a glimpse opens here and there to hint that all the artificialities which make husband-hunting possible, are tottering over a seismic disturbance of elemental things. Judge of the effect of a passage such as the following in the midst of the illusions of drawing-rooms:

> And now they saw that which they had taken to be eternal, vanishing from them even as a vapour. An entire race, a whole caste, saw themselves driven out of their soft, warm couches of idleness, and forced into the struggle for life. The prospect appalled them; birds with shorn wings could not gaze more helplessly on the high trees where they had built, as they thought, their nests out of the reach of evil winds. What could they do with their empty brains? What could they do with their feeble hands? Like an avenging spirit, America rose above the horizon of their vision, and the plunge into its shadowy arms threatened, terrified them now, as it had terrified the famine-striken peasants of Forty-nine.

And the tragic suggestiveness of such landscapes as this:

> Around them the barren country lay submerged in shadows; the ridge of the uplands melted into the drifting grey of the sky, and every moment the hearth-fire of a cabin started into or disappeared from sight. They burned, steadfast and solitary, in the dim wastes that stretched from hill to hill, or were seen in clusters between the dark-blowing foliage of the roadside poplars; and as the carriage passed, on a doorway full of yellow light the form of a man was often sketched in menacing black.

With its five heroines and involved complexity of intrigue, it is impossible here to discuss the enormous detail of *A Drama in Muslin*. I must be content to bring out, for the benefit of those who continually assert that only a single living novelist has mastered the feminine mind, one salient and indisputable fact concerning it: namely, that the book is a gallery of unsurpassed portraits of women. There are at least a dozen women in the book painted with absolute insight and fidelity. In particular, Mrs. Barton and her two daughters

Alice and Olive, triumphantly live. You cannot argue about them: they are as vital as yourself. In Alice Barton, the plain elder sister of the vapid beauty whom Mrs. Barton is determined to marry to a title, we have one of the very few "sympathetic" characters drawn by George Moore. Alice Barton is entirely lovable, full of sagacity and of "the grave and exquisite kindness of a beautiful soul." She will yield to none in sheer charm, and she is the good genius of the story. She alone can comfort the mystic Lady Cecilia whose loathing for men and the world amounts to a disease; she alone assists Mary Gould through her shameful motherhood; she alone can nurse the hysterical, beautiful Olive through an attack of fever; she alone comprehends the fineness of her father's twisted nature; she alone hates Lord Dungory. She is compact of sense and charity. And yet even she, while scorning the ignoble ideals which constitute husband-hunting the chief occupation of a girl's life, could not but tremble before the prospects of one who, brought up as girls were brought up, should fail in that grand campaign.

For her there is nothing, nothing, nothing! Her life is weak and sterile, even as the plain of moonlight-stricken snow. Like it she will fade, will pass into a moist and sunless grave, without leaving a trace of herself on the earth—this beautiful earth, built out of and made lovely with love. Yes, built out of love—for all is love. Spring, with amorous hands, will withdraw the chaste veil of winter's maidenhood, and the world, like a bride arrayed in flowers and expectation, will be but a universal shrine, wherein is worshipped the deity. All then shall be ministrants of love. Sweet winds shall join herb and flowers, and through the purple night soft-winged moths shall carry the desire of every plant and blossom; in the light air the wings of mating birds shall mingle, and upon the earth the lowliest animals be united; only woman is forbidden to obey the one universal instinct, coequal with the music of the spheres, and eternal even as it.

One is relieved from a painful apprehension when, towards the end of the story, Alice falls in love with the quiet, scholarly dispensary doctor, and, characteristically calm before her mother's angry denunciations, marries him.

A Drama in Muslin excels in character-drawing. Neither before nor since has Mr. Moore analysed types with such various and perfect skill. In the lyric and dramatic qualities it is perhaps somewhat inferior to *A Modern Lover* and *A Mummer's Wife*; here and there are signs of fatigue. But it is far from being without that generous lyricism which is the blossom of prose literature; and the middle of the tale is moving drama. The figure of the poor hunted Marquis, wandering by night about Dublin, torn between his passion for Violet Scully and Mrs. Barton's Napoleonic offer of £20,000 with Olive, cannot be forgotten. The book is completely serious, rigidly veracious—a brilliant instance of the modern tendency to bring history, sociology and morals within the dominion of the novelist's art. Quite as much as *Esther Waters* it is didactic. It teaches, as all true art must. It is more than a story; it seeks to do something more than please. And this seriousness, this religious devotion to truth, this proud scorn of every prejudice which might limit his scope: these qualities, occurring as they do everywhere in Mr. Moore's work, differentiate that work from that of almost all his contemporaries.

Fame and Fiction (London: Grant Richards, 1901), pp. 233–268. Bennett later wrote of this essay: "Twenty-five years ago I wrote a complete study of George Moore's work up to that date. No review would publish it. At that date the name of George Moore had a sinister odour in the nostrils of the mandarins. I had at last to include the essay in a volume of literary criticism" (*Evening Standard*, October 31, 1929, p. 9).

Frank Harris' *The Bomb* (1908)

It is eight years since the appearance of "Montes the Matador," a volume which contains one of the finest short stories ever written by Saxon, Russian, or Gaul. Mr. Frank Harris has at last thought fit to publish another book. I know not what he has done with himself in the meantime, but whatever his activity has been, I resent it, as it was not literary. "The Bomb" bears all the external marks of a publication by Messrs. Methuen. The name of Mr. John Long, however, is on the title-page. One may assert with confidence that "The Bomb" is the most serious work of imagination yet issued by the publisher-in-ordinary to Mr. Nat Gould and Mr. Hubert Wales.[1] I congratulate him. I wonder how many dilettanti of literature have preserved through eight years their enthusiasm for the author of "Montes the Matador" and "Elder Conklin." I wonder how many of them, when they saw the name of Frank Harris among "To-Day's Publications" in their newspaper, took instant and eager measures to procure his book. Not that for a moment I imagine "Montes the Matador" to have had a large sale. I am convinced that it was too true, sober, unsentimental, and distinguished to have had a large sale. But its contents were immensely and favourably talked about by people whose good opinion helps an author's works to sell among the sheep, and if "The Bomb" had appeared seven years ago it would have been sure of success. I shall watch with interest the remarks upon it of the mandarins. "A really great book," said Dr. Robertson Nicoll the other day, writing not, strange to say, of Mr. Clement Shorter's mausoleum for the Brontës, but of Sir Arthur Conan Doyle's recent

---

1. Nat Gould (1857–1919) wrote 130 novels, all of them about horse racing. "Hubert Wales" was the pen name of William Piggott, author of several sensational novels written before World War I. Both Gould and Piggott were published by John Long, Ltd.

collection of "Strand Magazine" stories.[2] Oh, face of Aberdeen granite! I could, if I would, predict his pronouncement upon "The Bomb."

"The Bomb" begins with these words: "My name is Rudolph Schnaubelt. I threw the bomb which killed eight policemen and wounded sixty in Chicago in 1886." The novel is the narrative of the events which culminated in the bomb, related in the first person by a Bavarian emigrant to the United States.[3] It is also Rudolph Schnaubelt's defence of anarchy, since it contains no apology for the bomb. Everyone who is in the habit of reading fiction is familiar with the sensation which occasionally makes one say of the author one is reading: "He must have been through that himself!"

"The Bomb" gave me this sensation at the start, and continued without intermission to give it me till the end. The illusion of reality is more than staggering; it is haunting. (I am not prepared to assert that to give the illusion of reality is the highest aim of fiction. I am quite sure that I never thought "On the Eve" or "The Mayor of Casterbridge" to be a relation of anything that actually happened.) Impossible not to believe that Frank Harris himself is the anarchist who threw the bomb in the Haymarket, Chicago, in 1886! Impossible not to believe that the whole business, in all its details, is not literally true to fact. My own ignorance of the flight of bombs is such that I did not know a bomb had been thrown at Chicago in 1886. On consulting Haydn's "Dictionary of Dates," I found that the rough outlines of the tale do indubitably coincide with fact, bombs and Socialism having been rife in Chicago in 1886. I am now more puzzled than ever to draw a line between what is fact and what is fiction in the book. The experiences, the intimate spiritual experiences, of the bomb-thrower between the moment of throwing and his arrival in England are crushing in their convincing-

2. Doyle's *Round the Fire Stories* was published in 1908. These stories of "the Grotesque and the Terrible" had appeared serially in the *Strand Magazine* between 1898 and 1906.

3. The Haymarket Riot occurred in Chicago on May 4, 1886. Police attempted to break up an anarchists' meeting, a bomb was thrown, and several persons were killed. Eight anarchists were convicted of conspiracy in the case, and four were hanged.

ness. The cry is drawn sharply out of the reader: "He simply *must* have been through this himself!" (I remember, in reading "Montes," the gradual growth in me of a belief that Frank H⌐ris had been a matador—and a matador in love! I am also sure, in spite of myself, that he once set fire to a dry-goods store in a western city.) Many passages are on the very highest level of realistic art. I state this as one who reckons to know, comprehensively and in detail, what realistic art is.

Mr. Harris has offered himself the luxury of grave difficulties in the accomplishment of the illusion of reality. There is, for instance, the difficulty of the language—for his narrator is a German journalist, who learnt "American" as a man. He disposes of this with adequate skill. The style is just what the style of such a man would be, save perhaps for a few phrases, such as "the blessed oblivion had knit up the ravelled sleeve of my thoughts!" I doubt whether the German's racial fondness for Shakespeare would carry him so far in a moment of intense narrative emotion. Another and a greater difficulty is that there is a superman in the book. Now, a superman, and especially an anarchist like Louis Lingg, is like seven devils in the path of a novelist. It may be said, I think, that Mr. Harris has made Louis Lingg convincing. Some of his sayings— such as that the worst fault of American civilisation is that it is not complex enough—are extremely suggestive, and in the supreme crises he does veritably conduct himself as a superman. His suicide and death are Titanic. But the greatest difficulty of all is in the sustentation of the character of the narrator. Here the author's triumph is prodigious and dazzling—such a triumph as can only be appreciated by those who have themselves tried to write a novel in the first person. Rudolph is German to his toes. A rather weak man, capable of immense and obstinate enthusiasms when tuned up by a stronger individuality; often sentimental; naïve; merry in his relations with women (there are pages which the late Ian Maclaren[4] would have blushed to sign); narrow in his view; violent and feeble by turns; the disciple, the honest and intelligent

4. Pseudonym of John Watson (1850–1907), Scottish novelist and clergyman. His sentimental novels and stories of Scottish life were a part of the "kailyard school," which also included James Barrie.

tool incarnate! A living man! In the closing passages the rank bitterness of his resentment against all America is wondrously done.

"The Bomb" is the work of an artist born. I feel nearly sure that the craftsmanship in it is chiefly instinctive and not acquired. Assuredly there is evidence in it that its author does not write enough, nor nearly enough. It is a book very courageous, impulsively generous, and of a shining distinction. In pure realism nothing better has been done—and I do not forget Tolstoi's "The Death of Ivan Ilyitch"! Some literary roué of the circulating libraries is bound to open his mouth and say that I have lost my head over "The Bomb." I am not a literary roué; but I am the author of some thirty books, and therefore likely to keep my nerve when confronted by other men's novels. I have said.

New Age, IV (November 5, 1908), 32.

George Gissing (1899)

The sound reputation of an artist is originally due never to the public, but to the critics. I do not use the word "critic" in a limited, journalistic sense; it is meant to include all those persons, whether scribes or not, who have genuine convictions about an art. The critic's first requisite is that he should be interested. A man may have an instinctive good taste; but if his attitude is one of apathy then he is not a true critic. The opinions of the public are often wrong; the opinions of the critics are usually right. But the fundamental difference between these two bodies does not lie here: it lies in the fact that the critics "care," while the public does not care. The public, by its casual approval, may give notoriety and a vogue which passes; but it is incapable of the sustained ardour of appreciation which alone results in authentic renown. It is incapable because it is nonchalant. To the public art is a very little thing—a distraction, the last resort against *ennui*. To the critics art looms enormous. They do not merely possess views; they are possessed by them. Their views amount to a creed, and that creed must be spread. Quiescence is torment to the devotee. He cannot cry peace when there is no peace. Passionate conviction, like murder, will out. "I believe; therefore you must believe": that is the motto which moves the world. Keats writes an ode: the critics read it; they are on fire; each is instantly transformed into a missionary. The wide earth must know of that ode; the sky must ring with it. And so the missionaries go about. "Can you not see it, O public? You must see it. You have got to see it. Here is a great ode!" And after thirty-and-three years the public mildly inquires: "What is all this noise about Keats?" And it buys the ode prettily bound, and regards it with a *moue*, and admits—partly for the sake of quietness, partly from a sense of propriety, and just a little bit from honest liking—that the thing is a masterpiece. And so, by vehement insistence, by unwearied harping, the reputation of Keats is made and kept alive. What applies to Keats applies some time to all artists, of whatever shade or degree. Even if the public happens to begin by acclaiming an artist, he must nevertheless come to the critics for that consolidating warmth of esteem, that *quasi*-religious devotion, without which there is no permanent security. It may be early, it may be late—the moment surely arrives when, but for the critics, the artist would fall into that neglect which is death. Byron needed no missionaries for half a century; but he needs them now. Keats could not have lived a week without those apostles of the faith.

And neither, to approach the subject at last, could Mr. George Gissing. The author of *Demos* enjoys a fame today which he certainly deserves, but which he owes to the critics exclusively. His novels contain less of potential popularity than those of almost any other living novelist of rank. They have neither the prettiness which pleases, nor the outward beauty which subdues, nor the wit which dazzles, nor the thematic bigness which overawes. And they are not soiled by any specious lower qualities which might have deceived an innocent public into admiration. There is nothing in them to attract, and much to repel, the general gaze. A West End bookseller and the proprietor of a circulating library said to me: "My ordinary public will have none of Gissing. But I stock his novels. They have a steady, very slow sale. I can tell my 'Gissing' customers at a glance. They may be divided into two classes, the literary and the earnest. By 'earnest' I mean interested in social problems. As for other sorts of people—no, not at all. You see, his subjects are so unattractive. My ordinary public simply doesn't care to read about that kind of thing." Thus the observant bookseller. Yet Mr. Gissing is renowned. He stands for something. His words have authority, and his name carries respect even among "my ordinary public" which will not buy him. He figures often in the magazines, and I have small doubt that he receives higher prices for serial rights than many authors whose editions far outnumber his own. The fact is, he has that peculiar moral significance and weight which exist apart from mere numerical popularity, and which yet have an assessable value in the commercial market. "My ordinary public" may be conceived as saying to him: "We often hear of you. We take you for a serious person of high motives. We are told you are rather fine, but we don't realise it ourselves; to us you are very grey and depressing. We prefer to be more cheerful. Still, we suppose there really is something in you, and since we have heard so much about you, we shall probably look at anything of yours that we may happen to see in the monthlies. In the meantime we leave your books to those who care for them."

It is, of course, just this "grey" quality of his subjects, so repellent to the public, which specially recommends Mr. Gissing's work to the critics. The artists who have courage fully to exploit their own temperaments are always sufficiently infrequent to be peculiarly noticeable and welcome. Still more rare are they who, leaving it to others to sing and emphasise the ideal and obvious beauties which all can in some measure see, will exclusively exercise the artist's prerogative as an explorer of hidden and recondite beauty in unsuspected places. Beauty is strangely various. There is the beauty of light and joy and strength exulting; but there is also the beauty of shade, of sorrow and sadness, and of humility oppressed. The spirit of the sublime dwells not only in the high and remote; it shines unperceived amid all the usual meannesses of our daily existence. To take the common grey things which people know and despise, and, without tampering, to disclose their epic signi-ficance, their essential grandeur—that is realism, as distinguished from idealism or romanticism. It may scarcely be, it probably is not, the greatest art of all; but it is art, precious and indisputable. Such art has Mr. Gissing accomplished. In *The Nether World*, his most characteristic book, the myriad squalid futilities of an in-dustrial quarter of London are gathered up into a large coherent movement of which the sinister and pathetic beauty is but tòo stringently apparent. After *The Nether World* Clerkenwell is no longer negligible. It has import. You feel the sullen and terrible pulse of this universe which lies beneath your own. You may even envy the blessedness of the meek, and perceive in the lassitude of the heavy laden a secret grace that can never be yours. Sometimes, by a single sentence, Mr. Gissing will evoke from the most obscure phenomena a large and ominous idea. The time is six o'clock, and the workshops are emptying. He says: "It was the hour of the unyoking of men." A simple enough phrase, but it lends colour to the aspect of a whole quarter, and fills the soul with a vague, beautiful sense of sympathetic trouble. This is a good example of Mr. Gissing's faculty of poetical constructive observation—a faculty which in his case is at once a strength and a weakness. He sees the world not bit by bit—a series of isolations—but broadly, in vast wholes. He will not confine himself to a unit, whether of the individual or the family. He must have a plurality, working in and out, mutually influencing, as it were seething. So he obtains an elaborate and complicated reflection of the variety and confusion of life impossible to be got in any other way. So also by grouping similar facts he multiplies their significance into something which cannot be ignored. That is his strength. His weakness is that he seems never to be able to centralise the interest. His pictures have no cynosure for the eye. The defect is apparent in all his books, from *The Unclassed*, a youthful but remarkable work, wherein several separate narratives are connected by a chain of crude coincidences, down to the recently-published *Crown of Life*, of which the story loses itself periodically in a maze of episodes each interrupting the others. Out of the fine welter of *The Nether World* nothing emerges paramount. There are a dozen wistful tragedies in this one novel, of which the canvas is as large as that of *Anna Karenina*—a dozen exquisite and moving renunciations with their accompanying brutalities and horror; but the dark grandeur which ought to have resulted from such an accumulation of effects is weakened by a too impartial diffusion of the author's imaginative power.

I have said that *The Nether World* is Mr. Gissing's most characteristic book. It is not, however, his best. In *Demos*, which preceded it by three years (appearing in 1886), the cardinal error of the latter work is avoided. *Demos* may be esteemed an unqualified success. The canvas is enormous, the characters a multitude, but as the narrative progresses it becomes, instead of a story of socialism as Mr. Gissing intended, the story of one woman. The figure of Adela Mutimer—a girl of race married by the wish of her family to an artisan—monopolises more and more the reader's anxiety, until at length the question of her happiness or misery dwarfs all else. Adela is Mr. Gissing's finest and loveliest creation, and the great scene in which she compels her husband to desist from a crime that could never have been discovered is unmatched in sheer force and conviction by any other in his work. It is, in truth, masterly. *Demos* has another point of particular interest in that the plot turns chiefly upon the differences which separate class from class. Many novelists have dealt with the consequences of a marriage between persons of unequal birth, but none has brought to the consideration of the matter that wide and exact documentary knowledge of caste and that broad outlook which mark Mr. Gissing's conception. His philosophy seems to be that social distinctions have a profounder influence upon the general human destiny than is commonly thought. The tendency of men of wide sympathies among all grades is to insist on a fundamental similarity underlying the superficial disimilarity of those grades; but Mr. Gissing by no means accepts the idealistic theory that the rank is but the guinea stamp and a man's a man for a' that. He may almost be said to be obsessed by social distinctions; he is sensitive to the most delicate *nuances* of them; and it would seem that this man, so free from the slightest trace of snobbishness, would reply, if asked what life had taught him: "The importance of social distinctions." Listen to this about Adela Mutimer and her husband:

> He was not of her class, not of her world; only by a violent wrenching *of the laws of nature* had they come together. She had spent years in trying to convince herself that . . . only an unworthy prejudice parted class from class. One moment of true insight was worth all her theorising on abstract principles. To be her equal this man must be born again . . .

Here is the spirit which informs the whole of Mr. Gissing's work. It crops out again and again in unexpected places. It is always with him. Yet he shows no aristocratic bias whatever: he holds an even balance. If he has a weakness it is for the class "created by the mania of education," consisting "of those unhappy men and women whom unspeakable cruelty endows with intellectual needs while refusing them the sustenance they are taught to crave." The words are the words of the Rev. Mr. Wyvern in *Demos*, but there are many indications that they express the thoughts of George Gissing. If his heart is hardened, it is against

> the commercial class, . . . the supremely maleficent. They hold us at their mercy, and their mercy is nought. Monstrously hypocritical, they cry for progress when they mean increased opportunities of swelling their own purses at the expense of those they employ and of those they serve; vulgar to the core, they exalt a gross ideal of well-being, and stink in their prosperity. The very poor and the uncommercial wealthy alike suffer from them; the intellect of the country is poisoned by their influence.

Mr. Gissing has often been called a pessimist: he is not one. He paints in dark tints, for he has looked on the sum of life, and those few who have done this are well aware that life is dark; Clerkenwell is larger than Piccadilly, and Islington than Brixton. The average artist stays at home in life; Mr. Gissing has travelled far, and brought back strange, troublous tales full of disturbing beauty; and he suffers for his originality. The audience is incredulous, and objects to anything which disturbs, even beauty. But Mr. Gissing is not thereby constituted a pessimist; he is merely a man who can gaze without blinking; he is not soured; he has, I fancy, the marvellous belief that happiness is evenly distributed among the human race; he may sup on horrors, but he can digest them without a headache the next morning; he is neither gay nor melancholy, but just sober, calm, and proud against the gods; he has seen, he knows, he is unmoved; he defeats fate by accepting it. When Sidney Kirkwood and Jane Snowdon, both beaten and both sad, meet by the grave of Grandfather Snowdon, he leaves them thus:

> To both was their work given. Unmarked, unencouraged save by their love of uprightness and mercy, they stood by the side of those more hapless, brought some comfort to hearts less courageous than their own. Where they abode it was not all dark. Sorrow certainly awaited them, perchance defeat in even the humble aims that they had set themselves; but at least their lives would remain a protest against those brute forces of society which fill with wreck the abysses of the nether world.[1]

1. *The Nether World* (London, 1889), III, 310.

This may be grievous, but it is not pessimism. The thoughtless may say that it is scarcely diverting to read after dinner; but those who can bear to reflect upon the large issues of life will be grateful that an artist of Mr. Gissing's calibre has used his art so finely for the inculcation of fortitude and serenity.

Academy, No. 1441 (December 16, 1899), pp. 724–726. Reprinted, *Fame and Fiction* (London: Grant Richards, 1901).

The Novels of Eden Phillpotts (1927)

I

Dartmoor uplifts itself in the middle of Devonshire in south-west England. It is a tract of country about twenty-four miles down the map and twenty miles across the map, with an area of over two hundred square miles. It is unlike, even spectacularly unlike, any other district in Great Britain. It is granitic and rises in a number of hills (called 'tors'), nearly all of which are capped by vast masses of outcropping granite. The elevation of these obdurate bumps varies from a few hundred to more than two thousand feet—which is a great height for a small and temperate island. The tors are the source of many streams. Because of its granitic composition Dartmoor resists agriculture, and in fights with persevering farmers the Moor often wins. It is an undulating moor with huge smooth slopes, morasses, bogs—and the stony peaks. The landscapes are beautiful, majestic, and intimidating. One may walk many miles in them without encountering anything more civilised than a troop of free ponies. Roads are few; villages are scarce; there is only one town near its centre, Princetown, a burg entirely insignificant—save for a state prison. There is only one railway—a picturesque single track to Princetown; there is no large hotel, and naught but somewhat early-English accommodation for tourists, on the whole of the Moor.

No other district in England can compare with Dartmoor in richness and variety of prehistoric remains; the 'old men' have left their marks on it everywhere. Few districts, if any, can compare with it in the variety of its minerals; gold has been found on Dartmoor; but far more important than its gold is its tin; and far more important than its tin is its china clay. On the other hand, the Moor can show very few trees—and those few not luxuriant and certainly not as old as the antique quasi-legal customs which still to some extent govern the tenures of moorland. Its inhabitants are sparse, its communities tiny, and necessarily cut off from one another and from the rest of England. The Moor is apart; its people are apart. By reason of their geographical situation, and the distinctiveness of their industries, the character of the people has a quite special savour and quality. What a district for a novelist—compact, complete, withdrawn, exceptional, traditional, impressive, and racy! Eden Phillpotts found it and annexed it.

II

The twenty volumes of the present definitive edition form what the novelist rightly calls a "Dartmoor Cycle." They all deal with the Moor, and their composition covers a period of exactly a quarter of a century. The first novel, *Children of the Mist*, was written in 1898; the last, *Children of Men*, was written in 1923. But, although they constitute the most important part of Eden Phillpotts' output, these novels by no means constitute the whole of it. I point this out in order to destroy the quite false legend that he is a writer of one idea and one field. On the contrary, the work of few living authors is as various and as wide-embracing as his. A Devon man, born in India, and educated at Plymouth, he lived first in London, indulging in business, journalism, and fiction; and then he returned to Devonshire, where, barring a few brief excursions afield, he has faithfully remained, either on his moor or on the further outskirts of it, and producing with immense and sustained industry a continuous succession of works in almost all branches of literature—novels, short stories, travel, philosophy, poetry, essays, studies of horticulture and of wild nature, plays, and pure fantasias based on classical themes.

His earliest novels, *The End of a Life* and *A Tiger's Cub*, gave no indication beyond their sincerity and their elaborateness that their author was to become a realistic novelist with a scientifically conceived philosophy and system of technique. They will divert and hold the reader who yields to them, for they contain scenes of marked emotional power; but they are not the efforts of a creative artist who knows exactly what he would be at. Later came *Some Everyday Folks*, and in the very title of the book we discern the first stirrings of the writer in the direction of realism. Evidently he had begun to suspect that in the unexaggerated dailiness of life the novelist may find material worthy of his most serious energies. *Some Everyday Folks* suffers from timidity; the author had not yet cultivated the courage of his convictions—convictions then indeed still rather undeveloped.

Three years later (1897) he published *Lying Prophets*, a Cornish story of the coast, and a most notable advance on its forerunner. *Lying Prophets*, if immature, is essentially a fine work, imagined and constructed with genuine distinction, and moving easily, throughout the greater portion of its course, on a high plane. The realist was fully disclosed in it, the man who would not deign to arrange life cunningly in a pattern of optimism, and the man also who had his own personal and disturbing vision of beauty. Its pictures of the sea, and the terrific description of the flood, are memorable, and nothing that Eden Phillpotts has since done or may hereafter do will render them second-rate. Good judges were as much struck by its promise as by its actual performance. But it has no connection whatever with Dartmoor; nor had the author, up to this date, handled the Moor at all, save in a few short stories. The truth probably is that he was awakening but slowly to the marvellous possibilities of the unique morsel of material which lay waiting for him in the shape of Dartmoor. No doubt he had been cautiously attending the moment of full inspiration.

The next year and the next book, *Children of the Mist*, brought the first large vision of the Moor. After that Eden Phillpotts prosecuted with regularity his great geographical scheme for covering all the Moor (omitting the high central wastes where men dwell not), until he had finished *Widecombe Fair*, the fourteenth novel. At this point he interrupted the series to write five extraneous novels displaying some of the minor industries of southern and south-western England: the Cornish slate quarries (*Old Delabole*), Essex horticulture and oyster fisheries (*The Nursery*), the Kentish hop industry (*Green Alleys*), spinning at Bridport (*The Spinners*), and Brixham trawl-fishing (*The Haven*). Then he went back to the Dartmoor Cycle and brought it to a magnificent close with *Children of Men*. Incidentally, I ought to mention, he had written no less than five volumes of fiction about "the human boy."

III

Like nearly all its successors, *Children of the Mist* deals exclusively with the peasantry and the farming class. The burden of the plot is upon what are generally called 'simple minds', though I have never been able to see that such minds are simpler (or shall I say less complex?) than our patronising own. Eden Phillpotts certainly has no illusion as to their simplicity. The hero is a water-bailiff, Will Blanchard. One of the heroines is his sister; the other is the miller's daughter. The most intellectual character is a sign-painter in a tiny Dartmoor town, and the most imposing are two brothers of low birth who have re-settled on the Moor after acquiring a fortune in the Colonies. The minor people are labourers and their women-folk. Not a soul in the story is either sophisticated or well-educated, or speaks correctly, or would be at ease in a drawing-room.

Here is to be noted a difference between Eden Phillpotts and his senior, Thomas Hardy. Thomas Hardy succeeds best when he centralises the interest on a sophisticated character. Tess is highly sophisticated. She is, within, a fine lady. And of the leading women in that masterpiece, *The Woodlanders*, Grace and Felice are far more alive than Marty South. Whereas Eden Phillpotts succeeds best when he centralises the interest on characters quite without any exotic or adventitious attractiveness.

Children of the Mist is first and chiefly a study of the character of Will Blanchard. "You're dealing with a curious temperament," says someone to Will's father-in-law, the miller. The miller replies: "I'm dealing with a damned fule. But there are fules and fules. . . ." And Will Blanchard is a fool. He is a headstrong, conceited, ignorant, irritable, rude, good-natured, warm-hearted, and generous fool. Meet such a peasant as Will in a Dartmoor village and you would not think twice about him. And he does not conquer either. He fails. He is a proved fool. Nevertheless, he is the hero of the tale, and a right hero, because the strength, the weakness, and the beauty of human nature are intensely made manifest in him. Simple—no! And the slowly unrolled psychological panorama of the development of his faulty and fine soul is more impressive than any of the exceedingly impressive situations which arise out of it.

You can perceive in this book, as in all the Dartmoor novels, that the author thinks first, and unshrinkingly, of character and the development of character, and only afterwards of situations. But he is fond of terrific situations—situations which bear their own weight without strain solely by virtue of the truth of the character-drawing that has preceded them.

Take the minor final situation of Clem Hicks the sign-painter and his seduced sweetheart, Chris Blanchard. Clem has put an end to his ceaseless arraignment of the eternal powers by suicide. His mother and Chris meet at night over his corpse. Chris means to kill herself, and she tells Mrs. Hicks that she is pregnant. "Wummon!" the little, insignificant, faded, sturdy creature bursts out in protest. "You'm a holy thing to me. . . . Go to un! Go to Clem and tell un, in his ear, that I know. It'll reach him if ye whisper it. His soul bain't so very far away yet. . . . An' ax God for a bwoy. . . . But for Christ's sake, ax like wan who has a right to, not fawning an' humble." The situation is lifted up to the heroic with tremendous emotional power.

And then Mrs. Hicks sinks back again. A hundred pages further on we have a last glimpse of the old woman. "She never talks of nothing but snuff. 'Tis the awnly bright spot in her life. She's forgot everythin' 'bout the past, an' if you went to see her she'd hold out her hand and say, 'Got a little bit o' snuff for a' auld body, dearie?' And that's all." An uncompromising touch, which retrospectively enhances in the memory the convincingness of the greatest moment in Mrs. Hick's life.

Children of the Mist is a long and intricate book. One leaves it with the sensation of having lived a long while with a whole community. Nobody and nothing is omitted. We have assisted at the operations of agriculture and the superstitious rites thereto pertaining. We have heard the peasants, and especially the ancient Billy Blee, discussing God. We have seen winter change to summer and summer to winter. We have seen deaths and births. We are closely acquainted with certain sheep-dogs, and with a Muscovy duck of solitary habits. We know all the reaches of the river from the lofty castle down to the mill-wheel. We have learnt to sympathise with the moor-men against the caprices of their mysterious overlord, the 'Duchy.' And, above all, we have seen the Moor in every kind of weather—the terrible, magnificent moor, which is at once the subsistence and the ruin of the men that toil like ants on its vast curving flanks. The recollection of the central wastes in winter, as rendered at length in the third part of the novel, freezes up the heart. It is appalling. And, let us admit, the quality of obduracy which human nature has caught from the Moor is equally appalling.

IV

After *Children of the Mist* came *Sons of the Morning* (in which the principal characters stand higher than peasants and small trades-men in the social scale) and another remarkable novel, *The River*—the titular stream being the Dart—as to which much might be said. But the book that followed *The River* showed an advance so con-siderable as to mark another definite stage in the author's develop-ment. *Children of the Mist* was a structure of genuine imaginative realism built on a foundation into whose composition had entered a certain amount of mere cleverness. In *The Secret Woman* the craftsman offers no display of youth openly exulting in the exercise of a virtuosity which it knows to be rare. The virtuosity is there all right, but it hides itself. *The Secret Woman* is mature—a tragedy scientifically conceived.

Children of the Mist opens with a description of a girl's face. *The Secret Woman* opens with a large description of that part of the Moor on which the story is to move. This very significant detail shows the direction of the author's progress. He was thinking scientifically—or, to use a more proper word, philosophically; that is to say, he was making an effort towards synthesis. The habit of novelists had been to place characters *against* a background. And in some novels we even have the singular sight of a set of figures realistically like life, but scarcely attached to the planet, existing, as it were, in the void.

Nothing of this method of approach in *The Secret Woman*! Here Eden Phillpotts has kept steadily before him, during the process of creation, the dominant truth that the most important factors in human life are the sun and the earth itself; he has remembered that human life is only a portion of a larger life. *The Secret Woman* is not a tragedy which happens to occur on Dartmoor. It is a part of Dartmoor on which a tragedy happens to occur. This distinction is of high importance to the understanding of the author's position. We used to divide the substance of a novel into 'character and event' and 'scenery.' But Eden Phillpotts has demonstrated in his work that such a division is unphilosophical and inept. His characters are henceforward part of his scenery and the scenery is part of the characters. He has put humanity into its right place in the universal scheme.

This book is primarily *mundane*. It deals with every form of vital energy on a particular portion of the earth's crust. Not with an air of apology does it describe the clouds over a man's head, or the shape of a larch by which stands a young girl. It is a novel chiefly about humanity, of course; but only because humanity is the leading theme in the great concerted movement of evolution, and not because humanity is the expression of a separate kind of force which by chance finds itself on the earth's surface. The unity, the correlation of all forms of vital energy—this is what Eden Phillpotts feels and what is the original and final source of his inspiration.

The plot of *The Secret Woman* is simple; it is austere. Ann Redvers, a woman of the highest respectability with two grown-up sons, catches her husband in adultery. In an impulsive moment of overmastering resentment she kills him, and then learns that her sons have witnessed the deed. Jesse is his father's son, Michael his mother's. Jesse urges her to confess. Michael savagely forbids her to confess. She is suspected by none. Then the tragedy begins slowly to work itself out, up there in the solitary farm on the Moor. Stage of it succeeds stage: the tension increases until it breaks suddenly, as it must break. While it lasts it achieves just that degree of 'intolerableness' which is the mark of first-class tragedy. The agony of the mother who is longing to confess and have peace, but does not confess because of her favourite son, finds vent in cries which stick in the memory like sharp swords.

Meanwhile, the identity of the adulteress (the 'secret woman') remains hidden, and she actually becomes affianced to Jesse. Here is a situation which, even though the girl had no intention of marriage, we of the Anglo-Saxon public would not have accepted at the beginning of the century.[1] The doings of the sleepy-eyed Salome, very close to earth as she is, would have shocked and angered us then. And the perfect naturalness with which episode follows episode, the impossibility of putting our finger on any spot and saying, "That is not true and not beautiful," would not have prevented the mass of readers from labelling its author as 'unhealthy.' Indeed, there is scarcely an aspect of this masterly and daring novel which is not a proof that the large public acclaiming it was a changed and enlightened public. Eden Phillpotts was continuing the great work of educating the public.

Everywhere, in its opening and its close, in its emotion and its humour, in its varying episodic moods and in its fundamental attitude towards the eternal mystery, *The Secret Woman* is plainly the creation of a philosophic mind that was fettered by nothing but a consideration for truth. The sentimentalist in search of facile comfort will not find it here, but he who is never afraid of beauty will be rewarded.

V

After *The Secret Woman* came *The Portreeve*, a novel in which, as in *Sons of the Morning*, the author departed from his custom of confining the main interest to the peasantry. And then *The Whirlwind*, which is one of the four or five major books of the Dartmoor Cycle. I would not assert that the psychological scheme of *The Whirlwind* is finer than that of *The Secret Woman*; but it is simpler; it is handled with an even nobler austerity; and, perhaps still more important, it has the advantage of stating and summing up with a sort of stark completeness the elements of the moral struggle which is the basis of all the author's principal works, namely, the conflict between traditional, dogmatic, religious faith and the profounder paganism of instinct. Wherever he may take us, in successive novels, in his 'perambulation' of the Moor, he always introduces us to characters who are preoccupied by problems of eternal import. An anthology

1. Bennett is here referring to historical fact. In 1912 *The Secret Woman* was adapted for the stage, but was refused a license by the Lord Chamberlain. The producer, Harley Granville-Barker, produced the play as a private performance, and it was a notable success.

might well be compiled from the sayings of his peasants, in the public-houses and elsewhere, about that which is the enigma of the universe, though they would call it by another name.

Now in the figures of Daniel Brendon, the gigantic farm-hand, who slowly develops religious mania, and his wife Sarah Jane, the unspoilt creature of earth, the two tendencies of human thought are personified in their most naïve and elemental form. Never, surely, was a more superb pagan than Sarah Jane, who first appears to us wearing a sack for an apron. Her beauty, her startling candour, her naturalness, her fierce pride, her innocence, her passionate belief in the righteousness of her own desires, render her easily the most enchanting among her author's creations; and of the originality and truth of the observation which must have gone to the conception of her, there can be no doubt. When Dan began to bring religion into his kisses she bluntly reproved him; "Leave God till after. Go on burning now. Love me. Hug me. There'll be black and blue bruises on my arms to-morrow." And again, when he suggests to her that she is fond of her kind because they are made in God's image, she corrects him with vehemence: "Not that! Not that! Because they are made in mine!" And yet she says once to a man whose love she had refused: "I'm a very modest woman, really, though you don't seem to think so." She was. She had the modesty of nature.

As for Daniel Brendon, he had every good quality except intelligence. He was industrious, upright, constant; but a fatal stupidity of prejudice marred his happiness from start to finish. And when his prejudice was engaged he could not see straight—even when he could see at all. And his prejudice was made homicidally dangerous by a jealousy which drives him to mad, to Greek excesses. The scene in which he strikes the corpse of the man who had dishonoured him is among the most terrible in fiction. And the other scene, in which the sinning woman dies by her own hand in order to spare the justly infuriated Daniel from killing her, is among the most sublime. Certainly it surpasses anything in the author's previous novels. The motive of jealousy complicates the central situation; but one may argue that Daniel's jealousy was one of the consequences of his religious prejudice.

The Whirlwind has been called a cruel book. It is neither cruel nor merciful. An author has no business with cruelty or with mercy. In his attitude he must try to follow, so far as a man may, the example of nature. But no author can hope to equal nature in the matter of this majestic indifference to the fate of the individual. And Eden Phillpotts has not done so. Just before the moment of Sarah's suicide he writes: "Her heart throbbed farewell to the only world she had known; and she was glad that the sky shone blue over her death. She turned her lovely eyes up to it. A million unclouded firmaments would not redeem the loss to earth when those eyes shut." The last sentiment shows that, in the emotional excitement of composing that tremendous page, his affection for the preferred creature of his imagination moved him actually to compassionate nature upon the woman's dissolution! Yet the artist in him was well aware, and must have told him so afterwards, that the shutting of those eyes was no loss whatever to earth.

VI

The Whirlwind was followed by eight novels: *The Mother*, *The Virgin in Judgment*, *The Three Brothers*, *The Thief of Virtue* (perhaps the most interesting of the eight), *Demeter's Daughter*, *The Beacon*, *The Forest*, and *Widecombe Fair*, which on account of considerations of space cannot here be discussed. It must suffice to point out that *Widecombe Fair* is significant in that it presents a comprehensive and complete picture of all the activities of a village. Here the community itself is, in a curious and original way, the protagonist of the story. Also the book is especially remarkable for the spoken wisdom and wit of the characters.

Then came *Brunel's Tower*, which might be classed equally in the Dartmoor Cycle and in the series of novels dealing with small industries. *Brunel's Tower* describes earthenware manufacture, as practised on the confines of the Moor, with extraordinary fullness and exactitude of detail; and the discerning reader will note the narrative virtuosity with which the processes of potting are throughout employed to subserve the purposes of the plot.

The hero, Harvey Porter, is very imperfect, like all the Dartmoor heroes—and like human nature, and the story is the story of his reclamation from a vicious origin. Harvey Porter (whose real name is something else) escapes as a boy from a reformatory and, by dint of effective lying, gets a situation in George Easterbrook's pottery, and soon makes a god of his master. But the god is as savage as a Hebrew deity. He judges and condemns the youth for a fault whose excuse was that it was committed for the glory of the god. Harvey Porter is cast out.

Mr. Easterbrook is startled and pained when his friends tell him that he was wrong to expect perfection from the partially reclaimed sinner; that he has impulsively abandoned his humane work before it was, or could have been, finished; and that therefore he ought to relent and to resume it. Mr. Easterbrook does relent, but before he brings himself to take back his worshipper the youth is killed in a successful attempt to save the life of the savage god.

Such are the bones of the tale, which is simple and comparatively quiet. Its interest, richly and variously maintained, is purely psychological, until the tragedy of the close. Pity is the note of this restrained and very moving book. The moral significance is well stated by the characters. Says one Mr. Pitts: "When a man goes through the door of death, Samuel, it may mean something far worse than death to those left behind him." And says Samuel Punchard: "A very good-natured boy—though queer—was Porter, and gone off in a blaze of glory, I'm sure, for it's the last thing he did that will be remembered about him, and that's the best. So, through his wrong-doing, he was put into the way of a bit of right-doing; and after being a rascal he swells up into a hero. And all inside six months. Now that's a bit out of the usual—eh?" "Why, no, Samuel," Mr. Pitts decides the matter. "An everyday thing, I reckon, and well inside the pattern of human nature."

VII

Miser's Money and *Orphan Dinah* succeeded *Brunel's Tower*, and then came *Children of Men*, the eighteenth and the last novel of the Dartmoor Cycle. For the most part these novels are tragedies, and terrible tragedies; and *Children of Men* is perhaps the most terrible of them all. Like *The Whirlwind*, *Children of Men* is a story of jealousy complicated by religious fervour; but with this difference, that the two passions are in two different persons, not mingled in a single individual; there is a further difference, that the woman is patently and utterly guiltless.

Jacob Bullstone, a professional breeder of terriers, married Margery Huxam, many years his junior. Jacob's tendency towards jealousy is early displayed. Margery's mother is an extreme example of the Dartmoor dogmatic die-hard, and her antipathy to her son-in-law is aroused by Jacob's carelessness and his freedom of speech in the matter of religion. Margery says to her mother that Jacob is "great on reason." Judith Huxam replies: "I'm sorry to hear it. Reason is well known for a faulty shift and the playground of the devil. Reason don't save no souls, but it damns a parlous number, and I wish I could feel a lot surer than I do where Jacob will spend his eternity." Mrs. Huxam is incapable of any compromise. She is one of those women who are born, who live, and who die without a doubt concerning the rightness of their convictions and the wrongness of all other convictions whatsoever.

Jacob also is incapable of compromise in the marital field. His wife is admired by, and is sympathetic to, Adam Winter, but there is absolutely nothing in the relations of these two to justify the least criticism. Jacob, however, is possessed by all the seven devils of jealousy. In this particular he is mentally sick. After seventeen years of placid married life, when four children in the house are approaching adolescence, he practically accuses his wife of infidelity. Her defence of herself makes a magnificent scene. Jacob is convinced of her innocence—or he would be convinced if reason directed his thoughts about marriage as it directs his critical thoughts about religious dogma.

On his own special preoccupation Jacob in fact is just as irrational as his mother-in-law on hers. His jealousy smoulders and then burns scorchingly up once more; and he leaves his house to begin an action for divorce. The sole defect in the whole formidable narration lies, to my mind, in the fact that the author fails to explain how Jacob found a solicitor, and how the solicitor found a barrister, to take the case into court on such a preposterous bit of evidence. The husband's behavior is rendered admirably convincing. The lawyer's behaviour is not. Inevitably Jacob loses his case. But habit forces him to return to the Moor and to his own community.

Margery, ill, has gone to live with her mother. Time does its work. Repentant Jacob wants tremendously to get his wife back, and Margery would go back. But Margery's ruthless mother will not hear of a reconciliation. For her a reconciliation would mean Margery's eternal damnation. Mrs. Huxam cannot trust her daughter's strength of mind; and to save Margery's soul Mrs. Huxam flies with Margery's sick body to the house of a relative at Plymouth. Jacob follows. Mrs. Huxam defends her daughter to the last. She locks herself in the bedroom of the dying Margery. Jacob, aided by Mrs. Huxam's brother, breaks into the bedroom. Margery is dead, and the sheet drawn up over her face. Behold indeed a situation to which the adjective Greek may properly be applied, as it may be applied to so many other situations in the Dartmoor novels.

But the story does not end at this point, where it would have ended in a Greek tragedy. The four children of the Bullstones begin to play major rôles in the development of the plot—and particularly Auna, her father's favourite child, whose changeless affection is Jacob's salvation. At the close of the book sadness still obtains, but a calm and restrained content is about to prevail over it. The older generation, wounded and permanently scarred, recedes very slowly into the background, and the younger generation, to whom the past is and must be after all only a tale, happily pushes forward nature's endless plan.

Here is mellowness. Here is the author grandly completing, with sternness, but a tempered and even tender sternness, the task of twenty-five years. It is a superb climax to an effort as large and as finely sustained as any in fiction. *Children of Men* may or may not be superior to all its forerunners. I cannot say. But it is most positively inferior to none.

VIII

In fiction, as in all literature, what most matters is the author's attitude towards the mystery of the universe. The attitude of Eden Phillpotts is scientific so far as science can go. Beyond that it is strictly agnostic. If he has any ruling dogma—and nearly all of us have—the dogma is not apparent in his books. He sees the workings of the primal cause as chiefly tragic in their results. The character of his mind is certainly grim. He thinks straight, and is always ready to face uncompromisingly the logical consequences of his thought. He puts humanity down to its proper place in the whole scheme of things. And that scheme is an orderly scheme. In other words, for him there *is* a scheme, and he takes it seriously; he takes it emotionally. He is an ironist; but his irony is subdued, often hidden. He seems to say to his readers: "Now I admit I feel this strongly, and I want you to feel it strongly." He stands or falls by his emotional quality. He has not the ironist's shame at being caught in an utterly serious mood.

In all this he differs from Thomas Hardy, with whom—for reasons which I do not comprehend—he is often compared. Thomas Hardy carries irony as far as the fantastic. He does not, artistically, regard the earth as an ordered, reasonable unit in the immense march of evolution. He regards it as a wondrous, lovely, disconcerting jocularity on the part of an Unknowable with sardonic leanings towards the absurd. In the invention of incident he shows again and again that this is the real posture of his mind. One never knows what is coming next in a novel by Thomas Hardy. The creator in him revels in sheer fantasy.

In that enchanting and unsurpassed novel, *The Woodlanders*, there is scarcely an episode which is not whimsical, capricious, bizarre. The obsession of old South about the tree; the result of Giles's effort to render the tree innocuous; Giles's singular interview from the height of the tree with Grace on the ground: these things reflected upon afterwards are amazingly curious. And they are followed by matters still more so. Who but Thomas Hardy would have drawn the first meeting of his hero and heroine out of a contract made by an old woman to sell her corpse to a doctor for dissection? Who but he would have made the heroine surprise her lover seemingly but not really asleep, and allowed her apparition to cause the hero to imagine that he in fact was asleep?

The connecting of Marty and Felice by means of false hair, and the wanton use of the circumstance at the close of the book, are further examples in the fantastic vein. And what shall be said of the re-awakening of Fitzpiers's passion for Felice by the device of his licking the court-plaster off her bruised arm? Or of Fitzpiers, after an escapade, arriving home on his horse fast asleep and remaining for hours undiscovered in the stable? Or of the accidental exchange of similar horses at night in the wood? Or of the meeting of Grace, Felice, and Suke outside the bedroom of the wounded Fitzpiers, and Grace's astounding exclamation: "Wives all, let us enter together"? Or of the man-trap and the loss of Grace's skirt therein? Or of the last tragic idyll of Grace and Giles outside and inside the solitary hut? The entire plot is woven out of Marty's hair, and the barber buying it is like a god who steps out of the machine at the beginning of the book, steps back into the machine immediately, and is never seen again.

This leads to another difference between the two artists of rural life. The very nature of Thomas Hardy's philosophy necessarily gives to his novels a certain picaresque quality, allying their technique to the technique of the eighteenth century. An astonishing hazard (which, however, compels acceptance of itself) is always at work in the Wessex novels. They are a mass of twists and turns. The sense of direction is rather vague, and so there occur in them few overshadowing, towering situations, which in narrative fiction cast their gloom before and after, situations which are foreseen and deliberately led up to. Impressive scenes occur in Thomas Hardy; but they spring forth suddenly, startlingly, and fade as suddenly away; they are never the *raison d'être* of the story. Eden Phillpotts' tactics, proceeding as they must from his philosophy, are quite the reverse. Nothing of the wayward spirit in his muse! The Dartmoor novels exist for, and by reason of, the major situations which dominate, and are intended to dominate, their surroundings.

Eden Phillpotts states or implies a definite problem at the commencement, and he solves it—so far as anything earthly may be solved—at the finish. Each of his books is raised on a clear, single, main foundation. The models for his primary inspirations and for the manner of their growth, are the classical tragedies. He is by principle as austere as Aeschylus. True, he adorns his work with the epigrammatic expression of worldly wisdom and with brilliant occasional humour. But these ornaments are not allowed to impair emotion or to influence in the least degree the straight and tragic course of the tale.

Introduction to *Widecombe Fair*, Vol. I of the Widecombe Edition of the Dartmoor Novels (London: Macmillan, 1927), pp. vii–xxxi.

Kipling's *Actions and Reactions* (1909)

After a long period of abstention from Rudyard Kipling, I have just read "Actions and Reactions." It has induced gloom in me; yet a modified gloom. Nearly a quarter of a century has passed since "Plain Tales from the Hills" delighted Anglo-Indian, and then English society. There was nothing of permanent value in that book, and in my extremest youth I never imagined otherwise. But "The Story of the Gadsbys" impressed me. So did "Barrack-room Ballads." So did pieces of "Soldiers Three." So did "Life's Handicap" and "Many Inventions." So did "The Jungle Book," despite its wild natural history. And I remember my eagerness for the publication of "The Seven Seas." I remember going early in the morning to Denny's bookshop to buy it. I remember the crimson piles of it in every bookshop in London. And I remember that I perused it, gulped it down, with deep joy. And I remember the personal anxiety which I felt when Kipling lay ill of typhoid in New York. For a fortnight, then, Kipling's temperature was the most important news of the day. I remember giving a party with a programme of music, in that fortnight, and I began the proceedings by reading aloud the programme, and at the end of the programme instead of "God Save the Queen" I read, "God Save Kipling," and everybody cheered. "Stalky and Co." cooled me, and "Kim" chilled me. At intervals, since, Kipling's astounding political manifestations, chiefly in verse, have shocked and angered me. As time has elapsed it has become more and more clear that his output was sharply divided into two parts by his visit to New York, and that the second half is inferior in quantity, in quality, in everything, to the first. It has been too plain now for years that he is against progress, that he is the shrill champion of things that are righteously doomed, that his vogue among the hordes of the respectable was due to political reasons, and that he retains his authority over the said hordes because he is the bard of their prejudices and of their clayey ideals. A democrat of ten times Kipling's gift and power could never have charmed and held the governing classes as Kipling has done. Nevertheless, I for one cannot, except in anger, go back on a genuine admiration. I cannot forget a benefit. If in quick resentment I have ever written of Kipling with less than the respect which is eternally due to an artist who has once excited in the heart a generous and beautiful emotion, and has remained honest, I regret it. And this is to be said: at his worst Kipling is an honest and painstaking artist. No work of his but has obviously been lingered over with a craftsman's devotion! He has never spoken when he had nothing to say—though probably no artist was ever more seductively tempted by publishers and editors to do so. And he has done more than shun notoriety—Miss Marie Corelli does that—he has succeeded in avoiding it.

The first story, and the best, in "Actions and Reactions," is entitled "An Habitation Enforced," and it displays the amused but genuine awe of a couple of decent rich Americans confronted by the sæcular wonders of the English land system. It depends for its sharp point on a terrific coincidence—as do many of Kipling's tales; for instance, "The Man who Was"—the mere chance that these Americans should tumble upon the very ground and estate that had belonged to the English ancestors of one of them. It is written in a curiously tortured idiom, largely borrowed from the Bible, and all the characters are continually given to verbal smartness or peculiarity of one kind or another. The characters are not individualised. Each is a type, smoothed out by sentimental handling into something meant to be sympathetic. Moreover, the real difficulties of the narrative are consistently, though I believe unconsciously, shirked. The result, if speciously pretty, is not a bit convincing. But the gravest, and the entirely fatal fault, is the painting of the English land system. To read this story, one could never guess that the English land system was not absolutely ideal, that tenants and hereditary owners did not live always in a delightful patriarchal relation, content. There are no shadows whatever. The English land system is perfect, and no accusation could possibly be breathed against it. And the worst is that for Kipling the English land system probably *is* perfect. He is incapable of perceiving that it can be otherwise. He would not desire it to be otherwise. His sentimentalisation of it is gross—there is no other word—and at bottom the story is as wildly untrue to life as the most arrant Sunday School prize ever published by the Religious Tract Society. Let it be admitted that the romantic, fine side of the English land system is rendered with distinction and effectiveness; and that the puzzled, unwilling admiration of the Americans is well done, though less well than in a somewhat similar earlier story, "An Error in the Fourth Dimension."

An example of another familiar aspect of Kipling is "With the Night Mail." This is a story of 2,000 A.D., and describes the crossing of the Atlantic by the aerial mail. It is a glittering essay in the sham-technical; and real imagination, together with a tremendous play of fancy, is shown in the invention of illustrative detail. But the whole effort is centred on the mechanics of the affair. Human evolution has stood stock-still save in the department of engineering. The men are exactly the same semi-divine civil service men that sit equal with British military and naval officers on the highest throne in the kingdom of Kipling's esteem. Nothing interests him but the mechanics and the bureaucratic organisation and the *esprit de corps*. Nor does he conceive that the current psychology of ruling and managing the earth will ever be modified. His simplicity, his naïveté, his enthusiasms, his prejudices, his blindness, and his vanities are those of Stalky. And, after all, even the effect he aims at is not got. It is nearly got, but never quite. There is a tireless effort, but the effort is too plain and fatigues the reader, forcing him to share it. A thin powder of dullness lies everywhere.

When I had read these stories, I took out "Life's Handicap," and tasted again the flavour of "On Greenhow Hill," which I have always considered to be among the very best of Kipling's stories. It would be too much to say that I liked it as well as ever. I did not. Time has staled it. The author's constitutional sentimentality has corroded it in parts. But it is still a very impressive and a funda-mentally true thing. It was done in the rich flush of power, long before its creator had even suspected his hidden weaknesses, long before his implacable limitations had begun to compel him to imitate himself. It was done in the days when he could throw off exquisite jewels like this, to deck the tale:—

> To Love's low voice she lent a careless ear;
> Her hand within his rosy fingers lay,
> A chilling weight. She would not turn or hear;
> But with averted face went on her way.
> But when pale Death, all featureless and grim,
> Lifted his bony hand, and beckoning
> Held out his cypress-wreath, she followed him.
> And Love was left forlorn and wondering,
> That she who for his bidding would not stay,
> At Death's first whisper rose and went away.[1]

New Age, VI (November 4, 1909), 14–15. Reprinted under the title "Kipling," *Books and Persons* (New York: George H. Doran Co., 1917), pp. 160–166.

1. "Rivals," set as an epigraph to "On Greenhow Hill," in *Life's Handicap* (London, 1891).

Herbert George Wells and His Work
(1902)

"The aim and the test and the justification of the scientific process is prophecy."

The prophet whose *Anticipations* have so profoundly impressed thoughtful people that no less serious a person than Mr. William Archer has proposed in a London newspaper that he should be endowed with an annual income on condition of continuing to prophesy, has hitherto somewhat suffered, in the public estimate, under the disadvantage of being wrongly labelled. It is a fact that his work is at least as diverse as that of any living prose-writer. In the seven years since he ascended into the literary firmament he has given forth "scientific romances" such as *The Time Machine, The Invisible Man, The Island of Doctor Moreau, The War of the Worlds, When the Sleeper Wakes,* and *The First Men in the Moon;* satiric fantasias, such as *The Wonderful Visit* and *The Sea Lady;* a naturalistic romance, in *The Wheels of Chance;* a realistic novel of modern life, in *Love and Mr. Lewisham;* a couple of volumes of sketches and essays; about half a hundred "strange stories," in all veins, from that of Poe to that of Guy de Maupassant; and finally the aforesaid *Anticipations,* which are as a lamp to the feet of the twentieth century. Nevertheless, and despite all this, if you mention the name of H. G. Wells to the man in the street, he is fairly sure to exclaim, "Oh, yes, the disciple of Jules Verne." Even critics who think to render the acme of praise call him "the English Jules Verne." And critics who wish to patronize refer to his *"pseudo-*scientific romances."

Now, I may usefully begin to define Mr. Wells by showing what he is not. He is not the English Jules Verne; he does not belong to the vast Jules Verne school; and his scientific romances are not pseudo-scientific. It conveniently happens that both Jules Verne and Mr. Wells have travelled to the moon, and therefore I will come down to particulars by contrasting the famous *From the Earth to the Moon* and its sequel *Around the Moon*, with Mr. Wells's *First Men in the Moon*. Jules Verne, by the way, did not invent the moon as a place of celestial resort; Jean Baudoin, Cyrano de Bergerac, Fontenelle and Edgar Allan Poe had been there before him.[1] In Jules Verne's lunar romance, the note of farcical humour is struck at the commencement and it sounds with increasing mirth to the very end. His city of Baltimore is a farcical city; his Yankees, Impey Barbicane and J. T. Maston, are uproarious puppets of the vaudeville stage; even his Frenchman, Michel Ardan, is a "type" of the broadest. His Gun Club is magnificently farcical. You will remember how, at the notorious mass-meeting of thousands of savants at 21 Union Square, the president's chair, "supported by a carved gun-carriage, was modelled upon the ponderous proportions of a thirty-two-inch mortar. It was pointed at an angle of ninety degrees, and suspended upon trunions, so that the president could balance himself upon it as upon a rocking-chair, a very agreeable fact in the hot weather"; and how the inkstand was made out of a gun, and order was kept by means of a bell that gave a "report equal to that of a revolver"; and how at the conclusion of his speech the orator, overcome with "emotion, sat down and applied himself to a huge plate of sandwiches." Jules Verne troubles but little about science. He talks with naïve and large satisfaction about "the immutable laws of mechanics," but the immutable laws of mechanics are only dragged into the story here and there to give it a fictitious sanction. We find, for instance, the secretary "rapidly tracing a few algebraical formulae upon paper, among which n^2 and x^2 frequently appeared."

1. Jean Baudoin (1590–1650) translated Francis Godwin's *Man in the Moone* (1638) into French as *L'Homme dans la Lune, ou le Voyage chimérique fait au monde de la lune nouvellement decouvert par D. Gonzales* (Paris, 1648). Baudoin's translation was used by both Poe and Verne. Cyrano de Bergerac (1619–1655) wrote *Histoire comique des Etats et Empires de la Lune* (pub. 1656). *Entretiens sur la Pluralité des Mondes* (1686), by Bernard de Bovyer de Fontenelle (1657–1757), was one of the most popular of the cosmic-voyage tales. Edgar Allan Poe (1809–1849) wrote his tale of a moon journey, *The Unparalleled Adventures of One Hans Pfaal* (1835), as a hoax. The literature of the genre is treated in Marjorie Hope Nicolson's *Voyages to the Moon* (New York, 1948).

The immutable laws of mechanics are no longer immutable when the projectile, full of air, is opened to emit the dead dog into spatial vacuum and practically no air escapes; nor are they absolutely changeless when the rockets are fired to give impetus by their recoil; nor when a thermometer is hung out on a string to measure an interstellar frostiness of 140° Centigrade below zero. Moreover, Jules Verne's airy argonauts do not achieve the moon; had they done so, they could never have returned to tell the tale. They circle round what the author in a Hugoesque mood calls the Queen of Night; and that detail alone serves to illustrate Jules Verne's propensity to shirk serious scientific problems. In saying this, my aim is, not to depreciate Jules Verne, but simply to differentiate him from Mr. Wells. *From the Earth to the Moon* and *Around the Moon* are delightful and indeed unique books. They exhibit an extraordinary gift of narrative; a free and fantastic grace of style, and a rich, broad humour which no imitator has ever approached. They are entirely delicious. But they live by their humour and verve and not at all by their illusion of reality or their dexterous handling of the immutable laws of mechanics. They never convince—nothing in them convinces, from the casting of the gun hundreds of feet long, to the returning projectile's final splash which breaks the bowsprit of the *Susquehanna*. They do not convince; they divert. When we look back upon the books, it is episodes such as Barbicane's acceptance of the wager, or the wrecking of the Baltimore theatre where a foolish manager had put on *Much Ado about Nothing*, that we recollect, not the scientific descriptions of the moon.

The great difference between Jules Verne and Mr. Wells is that the latter was trained in scientific methods of thought, while the former was not. Before Jules Verne took to romances, he wrote operatic libretti. Before Mr. Wells took to romances, he was a pupil of Huxley's at the Royal College of Science; he graduated at London university with first-class honours in science; and his first literary production, if I mistake not, was a text-book of biology. Those who prefix "pseudo" to the scientific part of Mr. Wells's novels are not the men of science. On the contrary, one may pleasantly observe the experts of *Nature*, a scientific organ of unrivalled authority, discussing the gravitational phenomena of *The First*

Men in the Moon, with the aid of diagrams, and admitting that Mr. Wells has the law on his side. The qualities of *The First Men in the Moon* are fourfold. There is first the mere human psychology. We begin with two human beings, Mr. Cavor the inventor, and Mr. Bedford the narrator. They are real persons, realistically described, and whether Mr. Cavor stands abashed before the Grand Lunar, or Mr. Bedford floats alone in infinite space, neither of them once loses his individuality or ceases to act or think in a perfectly credible and convincing way. Secondly, there is the scientific machinery of the narrative, always brilliantly invented, lucidly set forth, and certainly not yet impugned by science. Thirdly, there is the graphic, picturesque side of the affair, as examples of which I may refer to the splendid sunrise on the moon, the terrible lunar night, and that really wonderful instance of close creative thought, the exposition of the air-currents through the caverns of the moon. Fourthly, and to my mind most important, there is what I must call, for lack of a better term, the philosophic quality, that quality which is fundamental in all Mr. Wells's work, and which here is principally active in the invention of the natural history and the social organization of the moon. "Naturally," says Bedford—and we should mark that "naturally," for it discloses the true bent of Mr. Wells's mind—"naturally, as living beings our interest centres far more upon the strange community of lunar insects in which Cavor was living than upon the mere physical condition of their world."

It is impossible not to perceive in Mr. Wells's powerful and sinister projection of the lunar world a deeply satiric comment upon this our earthly epoch of specialization. Among the Selenites, it will be remembered, a race distantly resembling mankind, specialization was carried to the final degree. "Every citizen knows his place. He is born to that place, and the elaborate discipline of training and education and surgery he undergoes fits him at last so completely to it that he has neither ideas nor organs for any purpose beyond it." Some Selenites were all brain, others all limbs. Some could do nothing but remember (living histories and encyclopedias); others could only carry; others could only analogize; still others could only draw. Thus Phi-oo's broken-English description of the artist: "Eat little—drink little—draw. Love draw. No other thing. Hate all who not draw like him. Angry. Hate all who draw like him better. Hate most people. Hate all who not think all world for to draw. Angry. M'm. All things mean nothing to him—only draw. He like you . . . if you understand. . . . New thing to draw. Ugly—striking. Eh?" And this more awesome and pathetic passage from Cavor's Marconi message to earth: "I came upon a number of young Selenites confined in jars from which only the fore-limbs protruded, who were being compressed to become machine-minders of a special sort. The extended 'hand' in this highly developed system of technical education is stimulated by irritants and nourished by injection, while the rest of the body is starved. . . . It is quite unreasonable, I know, but such glimpses of the educational methods of these beings affected me disagreeably. I hope, however, that may pass off, and I may be able to see more of this aspect of their wonderful social order. That wretched-looking hand-tentacle sticking out of its jar seemed to have a sort of limp appeal for lost possibilities; it haunts me still, although, of course, it is really in the end a far more humane proceeding than our earthly method of leaving children to grow into human beings and then making machines of them."

Here, in the guise of romance, is a serious criticism of life, and this sober philosophic spirit decked in the picturesque colours of fantasy pervades all the latter part of the book, growing more and more impressive until it reaches its culmination in the sublime apparition of the Grand Lunar, that calm and supreme pure Intelligence who was so disturbed by Cavor's account of our incredibly ridiculous Earth that he killed the traveller, in order to prevent any organized invasion of the moon from this terrene ball of lust, bloodshed and the Absurd.

Having dissipated, I hope, the Jules Verne theory of Mr. Wells's ancestry, and incidentally examined his latest and best "scientific romance," I may proceed to a more general consideration of his work. In the year 1895, besides *The Time Machine*, which made his reputation, Mr. Wells, as if to indicate at once the various lines on which he would develop, published a volume of sketches, a volume of short stories, and that extraordinary fantastic irony, *The Wonderful Visit*, which many people regard as the most perfect and delightful thing he has yet accomplished. Touching the last first, it may be said that *The Wonderful Visit*, together with its successor in the same kind, *The Sea Lady*, stands a little apart from the main body of the author's productions. But in the record of the sojourn of the angel in the convention-ridden village, and of the mermaid in the convention-ridden seaside resort, are apparent the moral and imaginative qualities which have enabled Mr. Wells to deal so effectively with themes conceived on a much grander scale. This moral and this imaginative quality are really two sides of one gift—the gift of seeing things afresh, as though no one had ever seen them before, a gift of being able to forget all labels, preconceptions and formulae devised and invented by other people, of approaching the investigation of phenomena with senses absolutely virginal. It is the peculiar attribute of the artist; it should be, but often is not, the peculiar attribute of the moralist. Mr. Wells the artist and Mr. Wells the moralist (I scarcely know which is paramount) possess it in an abnormal degree. Once the angel arrives in the village, that village ceases to be a village and becomes a concatenation of inexplicable phenomena—inexplicable not only to the angel, but also to the good vicar who endeavours to explain them. To the angel's reiterated "Why? why? why?" there is no answer save the irrational, "Because it has always been so," "Because people have agreed that it shall be so," "Because it would never do to alter it." After the angel has perambulated the village, and especially after he has played the violin at Lady Hammergallow's party, the reader is overcome with a disconcerting and blinding vision of things as they actually are, and he see suddenly how much of beauty and joy and sweet reasonableness humanity loses by its habit of clinging to the past instead of reaching forward to the future. The most illuminating part of the book is the vicar's long and poignant reply to the angel's remark: "This life of yours—I'm still in the dark about it. How do you begin?" I will quote briefly from the end of it:—

"And the other people here—how and why is too long a story— have made me a kind of chorus to their lives. They bring their little pink babies to me and I have to say a name and some other things over each new pink baby. And when the children have grown to be youths and maidens, they come again and are confirmed. You

will understand that better later. Then before they may join in
couples and have little pink babies of their own, they must come
again and hear me read out of a book. They would be outcast, and
no other maiden would speak to the maiden who had a little pink
baby without I had read over her for twenty minutes out of my
book. It's a necessary thing, as you will see, odd as it may seem to you.
And afterward when they are falling to pieces, I try and persuade
them of a strange world in which I scarcely believe myself, where life
is altogether different from what they have had—or desire. And in
the end, I bury them, and read out of my book to those who will
presently follow into the unknown land. I stand at the beginning,
and at the zenith, and at the setting of their lives. And on every
seventh day, I who am a man myself, I who see no further than they
do, talk to them of the life to come—the life of which we know
nothing, if such a life there be. And slowly I drop to pieces amidst
my prophesying."

"What a strange life!" said the angel.

"Yes," said the vicar, "what a strange life! But the thing that
makes it strange to me is new. I had taken it as a matter of course
until you came into my life."

I had taken it as a matter of course! That is precisely the attitude of
which Mr. Wells's attitude is the antipodes. With him, nothing is
of course, and every one who converses with him at any length
finds this out first. Under all the wit, the humour, the pathos, the
wayward beauty of *The Wonderful Visit* may be perceived this firm
and continuous intention—to criticize the social fabric, to demand
of each part of it the reason for its existence, and in default of a
reply, to laugh it out of existence.

The Wheels of Chance is a quasi-satiric romance from which the
supernatural element is excluded. Its hero, Mr. Hoopdriver, the
draper's assistant who issued forth on a bicycle tour, fell in with a
maid, stole a bicycle, and duly returned to his counter, is the best-
loved of all Mr. Wells's creations. But I can merely mention the
book here as the precursor of the realistic novel, *Love and Mr.
Lewisham*, the only novel, in the usual meaning of the term, which
Mr. Wells has yet written, but which is surely to be followed by
others. In it we have the history of a student of science with lofty
ideals who got into the toils of that blind force of nature which we

call love, and was, in a worldly sense, thereby utterly ruined. The
sayings of Mr. Chaffery, that audacious and unmoral spirit who
saw things as they are and gained a livelihood by deceiving the
fools who wanted to be deceived, are the memorable utterances
in the book. Here, for example, is Mr. Chaffery's recipe for a happy
life: "In youth, exercise and learning; in adolescence, ambition,
and in early manhood, love—no footlight passion. Then marriage,
young and decent, and then children and stout honest work for
themselves and for the State in which they live; a life of self-
devotion, indeed, and for sunset a decent pride—that is the happy
life . . . the life Natural Selection has been shaping for man since
life began. So a man may go happy from the cradle to the grave—
at least passably happy. And to do this needs just three things—a
sound body, a sound intelligence, and a sound will. . . . A sound
will. No other happiness endures. And when all men are wise, all
men will seek that life. Fame! Wealth! Art! The Red Indians
worship lunatics, and we are still by way of respecting the milder
sorts. But I say that all men who do not lead that happy life are
knaves and fools." So that only in the worldly sense was Lewisham
ruined. At the end of the book, as he stands staring through the
window, thinking of his career perforce abandoned and of the
prospect of immediate fatherhood ("the most important career in
the world"), his feelings are symbolized for us in an image of really
exquisite beauty—"The dwindling light gathered itself together
and became a star."

Here, therefore, even in the realistic novel of modern matter-of-
fact, we are not allowed to get away from the scientific principles
that man is a part of nature, that he is a creature of imperious natural
forces, that he is only one link in the chain of eternal evolution.

In the "scientific romances," to which we may now at last come,
the principle of evolution and a conception of "man's place in
nature" are Mr. Wells's great basic facts.

In his lecture on "The Discovery of the Future," delivered at the
Royal Institution on January 24th last,[2] Mr. Wells contrasted two

2. The lecture was first printed in *Nature*, LXV (February 6, 1902), 326–331.
It was published as a booklet by Fisher Unwin (London, 1902), and was reprinted
in the *Annual Report* of the Smithsonian Institution for 1902 (Washington: G.P.O.,
1903), I, 375–392.

divergent types of mind, distinguishable "chiefly by their attitude toward time and more particularly by the relative importance they attach, and the relative amount of importance they give, to the future of things." The first type of mind, he continued, interprets the things of the present, and gives value to this and denies it to that, entirely with relation to the past. The second type is constructive in habit; it interprets the things of the present, and gives value to this or that, entirely in relation to things designed or foreseen. "While from that former point of view our life is simply to reap the consequences of the past, from this our life is to prepare the future." And he said further: "The former type one might speak of as the legal or submissive type of mind, because the business, the practice and the training of a lawyer dispose him toward it; he of all men must most constantly refer to the law made, the right established, the precedent set, and most consistently ignore or condemn the thing that is only seeking to establish itself. The latter type of mind I might for contrast call the legislative, organizing or masterful type, because it is perpetually attacking and altering the established order of things, perpetually falling away from respect for what the past has given us. *It sees the world as one great workshop and the present as no more than material for the future, for the thing that is destined yet to be.* It is in the active mood of thought, while the former is in the passive; it is the mind of youth, it is the mind more manifest among the Western nations; while the former is the mind of age—the mind of the Oriental. Things have been, says the legal mind, and so we are here. *And the creative mind says, we are here because things have yet to be.*"

The sentences which I have italicized contain the key to Mr. Wells's philosophy of life. He has no use for precedents and conventions. The past may survive only so long as it can pass the tests of reason. The present must look, never back at death, but always forward toward life. Among all Mr. Wells's tales I remember but one, "A Story of the Stone Age," which deals with the past. It is the future, it is evolution, it is innovation, which he preaches and will always preach.

He said in that same lecture: "The essential thing in the scientific process is not the collection of facts, but the analysis of facts; facts are the raw material not the substance of science; the aim and the test and the justification of the scientific process is not a marketable conjuring-trick, but prophecy. Until a scientific theory yields confident forecasts it is unsound and tentative; it is mere theorizing." So science is, ultimately, prophecy—something to help us to shape our ends. And Mr. Wells is a man of science in order, first and foremost, that he may be a prophet and map out the path so that humanity shall avoid détours. And prophecy is really what he has always been at when he has touched science. He may juggle with our ideas of time and space, as in *The Time Machine*, "The Plattner Story," "The Crystal Egg," and "The Accelerator"; he may startle or shock us by the artistic presentation of a scientific "conjuring-trick," as in *The Invisible Man* and *The Island of Doctor Moreau*; he may awe us by sheer force of an original imaginative conception, as in "The Star," "Under the Knife," and "The Man Who Could Work Miracles." But his real, preferred business has been to prophesy, to peer into the future. In *The Time Machine*, the Time-Traveller goes forward, not into "the dark backward and abysm." Mr. Wells's fancy was youthful in those days, and the Time-Traveller journeyed through a million years or so; he saw a grim and terrible vision of the evolution of the "submerged tenth" and the "upper classes," a world murderously divided against itself, a world in which it seemed that the aspirations and sacrifices and sufferings of mankind had come to nothing at all, had ended in utter moral disaster. He went further and witnessed the more fatigued revolution of a planet occupied by monsters round a sun dying of radiation. He watched what was the apparent final stultification of a Supreme Purpose. Then he came back and with a sublime and justifiable audacity remarked to his friends: "No. I cannot expect you to believe it. Take it as a lie—or a prophecy. Say I dreamed it in the workshop. Consider I have been speculating upon the destinies of our race, until I have hatched this fiction. Treat my assertion of its truth as a mere stroke of art to enhance its interest. And taking it as a story, what do you think of it?"

The War of the Worlds was not a prophecy, but it was in the nature of a prophecy, a speculative, warning criticism, so far as it described an organization of intelligent beings more advanced than our own. And the same is to be said of *The First Men in the Moon*. In *When the*

Sleeper Wakes and "A Story of the Days to Come," Mr. Wells returned to prophecy in fiction. But it was a much quieter, soberer, humbler, and an infinitely more useful prophecy than that of *The Time Machine*. Instead of dealing with thousands and millions of years, he dealt with a century or so. And in *Anticipations of the Reaction of Mechanical and Scientific Progress upon Human Life and Thought*, he has abandoned the garb of fiction, and he definitely stands forth naked and unashamed as a prophet of the real. My personal opinion is that he will work still more strenuously in this field, and that in the course of a few years, passing down toward the present through a series of futures less and less remote (he has already retreated from thirty millions years hence to a hundred hence), he may develop, still flying all his flags of imagination, fancy, humour, satire and irony, into an actual, prevalent political force. His strongest points are his clear vision and his intellectual honesty and courage; his weakest point is his instinctive antipathy to any static condition.

And his forecast of the more immediate future, his creed? You may see it set out with surprisingly close texture of detail in *Anticipations*; and in a forthcoming series of essays, possibly more boldly creative in character than *Anticipations*, the instant means to the Great End may be shadowed forth as they present themselves to his mind. Suffice it to say here that Mr. Wells firmly believes in universal peace and in the high destiny of nature, *The Time Machine* of seven years ago notwithstanding. "It it not difficult," he has said, "to collect reasons for supposing that humanity will be definitely and consciously organizing itself as a great world-state—a great world-state that will purge itself from much that is mean, much that is bestial, and much that makes for individual dullness and dreariness, greyness and wretchedness in the world of to-day."

"And finally," he added, "there is the reasonable certainty that . . . this earth of ours, tideless and slow-moving, will be dead and frozen, and all that has lived upon it will be frozen out and done with. There surely man must end. That of all such nightmares is the most insistently convincing. And yet one doesn't believe it. At least I do not. And I do not believe in these things because I have come to believe in certain other things—in the coherency and purpose in the world and in the greatness of human destiny. Worlds may freeze and suns may perish, but there stirs something within us now that can never die again."

And this by way of postscript: "The most persistently fascinating and the most insoluble question in the whole world is—what is to come *after* man?"

Cosmopolitan Magazine, XXXIII (August, 1902), 465–471.

Wells' *Tono-Bungay* (1909)

Wells! I have heard that significant monosyllable pronounced in various European countries, and with various bizarre accents. And always there was admiration, passionate or astonished, in the tone. But the occasion of its utterance which remains historic in my mind was in England. I was indeed in Frank Richardson's Bayswater.[1] "Wells?" exclaimed a smart, positive, little woman—one of those creatures that have settled every question once and for all beyond re-opening—"Wells? No! I draw the line at Wells. He stirs up the dregs. I don't mind the froth, but dregs I—will—not—have!" And silence reigned as we stared at the reputation of Wells lying dead on the carpet. When, with the thrill of emotion that a great work communicates, I finished reading "Tono-Bungay," I thought of the smart little woman in the Bayswater drawing-room. I was filled with a holy joy because Wells had stirred up the dregs again, and more violently than ever. I rapturously reflected, "How angry this will make them!" "Them" being the whole innumerable tribe of persons, inane or chumpish (this adjective I give to the world), who don't mind froth, but won't have dregs. Human nature—you get it pretty complete in "Tono-Bungay," the entire tableau! If you don't like the spectacle of man whole, if you are afraid of humanity, if humanity isn't good enough for you, then you had better look out for squalls in the perusal of "Tono-Bungay." For me, human nature is good enough. I love to bathe deep in it. And of "Tono-Bungay" I will say, with solemn heartiness, "By God! This is a book!"

You will have heard that it is the history of a patent medicine—the nostrum of the title. But the rise and fall of Tono-Bungay and its inventor make only a small part of the book. It is rather the history of the collision of the soul of George Ponderevo (narrator,

---

1. Frank Richardson (1870–1917), lawyer and novelist. His books included *The Bayswater Miracle* (1903).

and nephew of the medicine-man) with his epoch. It is the arraignment of a whole epoch at the bar of the conscience of a man who is
intellectually honest and powerfully intellectual. George Ponderevo
transgresses most of the current codes, but he also shatters them.
The entire system of sanctions tumbles down with a clatter like the
fall of a corrugated iron church. I do not know what is left standing,
unless it be George Ponderevo. I would not call him a lovable,
but he is an admirable, man. He is too ruthless, rude, and bitter
to be anything but solitary. His harshness is his fault, his one real
fault; and his harshness also marks the point where his attitude
towards his environment becomes unscientific. The savagery of his
description of the family of Frapp, the little Nonconformist baker,
and of the tea-drinkers in the housekeeper's room at Bladesover,
somewhat impairs even the astounding force of this, George's
first and only novel—not because he exaggerates the offensiveness
of the phenomena, but because he unscientifically fails to perceive
that these people are just as deserving of compassion as he is
himself. He seems to think that, in their deafness to the call of the
noble in life, these people are guilty of a crime; whereas they are
only guilty of a misfortune. The one other slip that George Ponderevo has made is a slight yielding to the temptation of caricature,
out of place in a realistic book. Thus he names a halfpenny paper,
"The Daily Decorator," and a journalistic peer, "Lord Boom." Yet
the few lines in which he hints at the tactics and the psychology of
his Lord Boom are masterly. So much for the narrator, whose "I"
writes the book. I assume that Wells purposely left these matters
uncorrected, as being essential to the completeness of George's
self-relevation.

I do not think that any novelist ever more audaciously tried, or
failed with more honour, to render in the limits of one book the
enormous and confusing complexity of a nation's racial existence.
The measure of success attained is marvellous. Complete success
was, of course, impossible. And, in the terrific rout, Ponderevo
never touches a problem save to grip it firmly. He leaves nothing
alone, and everything is handled—handled! His fine detachment,
and his sublime common sense, never desert him in the hour when
he judges. Naturally his chief weapon in the collision is just common

sense; it is at the impact of mere common sense that the current system crumbles. It is simply unanswerable common sense which will infuriate those who do not like the book. When common sense rises to the lyric, as it does in the latter half of the tale, you have something formidable. Here Wells has united the daily verifiable actualism of novels like "Love and Mr. Lewisham" and "Kipps," with the large manner of the paramount synthetic scenes in (what general usage compels me to term) his "scientific romances." In the scientific romance he achieved, by means of parables (I employ the word roughly) a criticism of tendencies and institutions which is on the plane of epic poetry. For example, the criticism of specialisation in "The First Men in the Moon"; the mighty ridicule of the institution of sovereignty in "When the Sleeper Wakes," and the exquisite blighting of human narrow-mindedness in "The Country of the Blind"—this last one of the radiant gems of contemporary literature, and printed in "The Strand Magazine"! In "Tono-Bungay" he has achieved the same feat, magnified by ten—or a hundred, without the aid of symbolic artifice. I have used the word "epic," and I insist on it. There are passages toward the close of the book which may fitly be compared with the lyrical freedoms of no matter what epic, and which display an unsurpassable dexterity of hand. Such is the scene in which George deflects his flying-machine so as to avoid Beatrice and her horse by sweeping over them. A new thrill, there, in the sexual vibrations! One thinks of it afterwards. And yet such flashes are lost when one contemplates the steady shining of the whole. "Tono-Bungay," to my mind, marks the junction of the two paths which the variety of Wells's gift has enabled him to follow simultaneously. And at the same time, it is his most distinguished and most powerful book.

I have spoken of the angry and the infuriated. Fury can be hot or cold. Of the cold variety is Claudius Clear's in the "British Weekly."[2] Extremely clever," says Claudius Clear. "There is, however, no sign of any new power." But, by way of further praise: "The

2. "Claudius Clear" was Sir William Robertson Nicoll (1851–1923), editor of the *British Weekly*. For an account of Bennett's feud with Nicoll, see James Hepburn (ed.), *Letters of Arnold Bennett*, I (London: Oxford University Press, 1966), 140 n.

episodes are carefully selected and put together with skill, and there are few really dull passages." This about the man of whom Maeterlinck has written that he has "the most complete and the most logical imagination of the age." (I think Claudius Clear may have been under the impression that he was reviewing a two hundred and fifty guinea prize novel, selected by Messrs. Lang and Shorter.) Further, "He writes always from the point of a B.Sc." But the most humorous part of the criticism is this. After stating that Ponderevo acknowledges himself to be a liar, a swindler, a thief, an adulterer, and a murderer, Claudius then proceeds: "He is not in the least ashamed of these things. He explains them away with the utmost facility, and we find him at the age of forty-five, *not unhappy, and successfully engaged in problems of aerial navigation*" (my italics). Oh! candid simplicity of soul! Wells, why did you not bring down the wrath of God, or at least make the adulterer fail in the problems of flight? In quoting a description of the Frapps, Claudius Clear says: "I must earnestly apologise for extracting the following passage." Why? As Claudius Clear gets into his third column his fury turns from cold to hot: "It is impossible for me in these columns to reproduce or to describe the amorous episodes in 'Tono-Bungay.' I cannot copy and I cannot summarise the loathsome tale of George Ponderevo's engagement and marriage and divorce. Nor can I speak of his intrigue with a typist, and of the orgy of lust described at the close of the book . . . ." Now, there is not a line in the book that could not be printed in the "British Weekly." There is not a line which fails in that sober decency which is indispensable to the dignity of a masterpiece. As for George's engagement and marriage, it is precisely typical of legions such in England and Scotland. As for the intrigue with a typist, has Claudius Clear never heard of an intrigue with a typist before? In faithfully and decently describing an intrigue with a typist, has one necessarily written a "Justine"? And why "orgy of lust"? Orgy of fiddlestick—if I am not being irreverent! The most correct honeymoon is an orgy of lust; and if it isn't, it ought to be. But some temperaments find a strange joy in using the word "lust." See the infuriating disquisition on "Mrs. Grundy" in "Tono-Bungay." The odd thing is, having regard to the thunders of Claudius Clear, that George Ponderevo is decidedly more chaste than nine men out of every ten, and than ninety-nine married men out of every hundred. And the book emanates an austerity and a self-control which are quite conspicuous at the present stage of fiction, and which one would in vain search for amid the veiled concupiscence of at least one author whom Claudius Clear has praised, and, I think, never blamed, at least on that score. I leave him to guess the author.

New Age, IV (March 4, 1909), 384–385. Reprinted under the title "H. G. Wells," *Books and Persons* (New York: George H. Doran Co., 1917), pp. 109–116.

Galsworthy's *A Commentary* (1908)

Mr. John Galsworthy's new book "A Commentary" (Grant Richards, 3*s*. 6*d*.) was published for Whitsuntide, and as I write this the chams, lamas, and mandarins of London letters are doubtless devising adjectives for it in the laborious leisure of their holiday. Among people who can distinguish between a real book and "The Historian's History of the World," Mr. Galsworthy was heavily prejudiced by the praise which was plastered over him by the master-plasterers of Fleet Street. There are a few critics whose approval would damn almost any book in the eyes of an intelligent bookman. Nearly all these chams, etc., conspired to assert that "The Man of Property" was the greatest modern novel, except "The Country House." The inordinate laudation poured out upon "The Silver Box," an ingenious but very slight and naif dramatic sketch, almost achieved the ruin of Mr. Galsworthy among bibliophiles. By the way, "The Silver Box" was not inspired by Anatole France's "Crainquebille"; it ought to have been. But when the lamas, etc., announced that "Joy," the successor to "The Silver Box," was a failure, then there began to be hope for Mr. Galsworthy. I at once felt instinctively that "Joy" must be pretty good. And it was. It was a misunderstood play, as H. G. Wells's "Island of Dr. Moreau" is a misunderstood novel.

Personally, I do not consider that either of Mr. Galsworthy's novels comes within the four-mile radius of the first-rate. They both lack a sense of beauty. They are as hard and hostile, and as harsh in colour, as a portrait by Sargent. They are also almost entirely deficient in individual characterisation, being crowded with types, not with persons. Now, "A Commentary" is frankly a collection of "characters," and it shows very clearly the qualities and defects of the author. The general effect of the book is one of monotony. It is chiefly governed by a strong prejudice against its own subjects.

It is as inflexible as a cocoanut, without the milk. All this is bad, and will assuredly debar Mr. Galsworthy from the immortality so kindly mapped out for him by mandarins, etc. I should say that Mr. Galsworthy will last about as long as Sargent, whose half-brother he is (in the arts). I read most of "A Commentary" as it appeared, once a fortnight or so, in the "Nation," and that was the safest way to appreciate it. Some of the sketches are exceedingly and dazzlingly brilliant, while others are imitations of Mr. Galsworthy written by a kind of astral Andrew Lang. The best of them reveal a writer. And when I say a writer, I signify one who can *write*. I mean this for high praise. There is a study of a barrister who, without knowing it, is always meeting himself. It is a pretty bit of work.

What Mr. Galsworthy has to do is to go out and buy some milk. Milk is a very difficult thing to buy, but if he can meet with some in his walks abroad, there is hope for him. For he has a soul, a mind, and an eye of his own. He must also contrive to take a walk with his prejudice against the successful classes, and lose it. First-rate writers have no business with hostilities. First-class writers ought to be aware that one kind of man is just as deserving of sympathy as another, and that to shed tears over the weak and the oppressed is a sign of facile emotionalism rather than of an ordered and powerful imagination. It is not morally reprehensible to live in Bedford Court Mansions.[1]

New Age, III (June 6, 1908), 112.

1. A block of flats, then quite new, on Bloomsbury Street, London, near the British Museum, and thus upper-middle-class.

A Few Words on Galsworthy (1909)

It is over nine years since I ceased to be a dramatic critic. I had no prejudices then. I was the proverbial photographic plate, highly sensitised, and utterly unspotted. I always went to a play prepared to like it. But in nine years I have quite gone to the bad, and I allow myself to be influenced by the most absurd, the most infantile considerations. For instance, on the morning after the original production of Mr. John Galsworthy's "Strife," I saw on the contents-bill of a London morning paper, "'Strife': a great play!" And I at once said to myself: "It must be pretty bad, then." For I could not conceive that it would ever occur to a daily paper to call a great play great within ten hours of its production. A daily paper usually wants about a quarter of a century in which to persuade itself to call a great play great. Then when I read that Mr. J. Galsworthy had dramatically presented the titanic struggle between capital and labour, and that he had held the balance evenly between them with masterly impartiality, and that he had shown himself keenly alive to the larger issues of his epoch—then I said to myself: "This thing is certain to be an awful bore." For I wondered what would have happened to his story while he was engaged in being alive to larger issues and fiddling with a pair of scales. In such a wrong frame of mind I went to see Mr. Galsworthy's play.

I thought the first act very dull. It consisted of a directors' meeting. The directors of the Trevartha Tinplate Company were discussing how not to bring to an end a strike which had already cost them fifty thousand pounds. They all desired peace except old John Anthony, the Chairman—one of your taciturn, Napoleonic men—who had never been beaten, who answered arguments by growls, and who on learning that his co-directors were plotting against him, merely ordered a whisky and soda. As I watched this directors' meeting I wondered whether Mr. Galsworthy or Mr.

Granville-Barker (who produced the play), or any of the actors, had ever seen a directors' meeting—it was so stagey, so subtly stagey and so minutely untrue to life. The mere genius of Mr. Dennis Eadie gave reality to one figure, but the rest, when they were not tedious, were caricatures; fairly good caricatures perhaps, yet out of place in a realistic piece. The faithful secretary of the company, with his dog-like attitude to old Anthony, and his singular clothes, was precisely the devoted retainer who has haunted the stage for fifty years: similarly the butler. Then came workmen, including David Roberts, the men's leader. They entered with the same comic mixture of timidity and brusquerie which has marked the entrance of bold, free workmen on the scene since everlasting. The one thing about them that had been studied was their Welsh accent. This realism of accent seemed monstrous in its environment of conventionality. There was a Trade Union official who spoke exactly as if he had been at Eton and Balliol and controlled the fortunes of his Union from the Carlton Club. You see how prejudiced I was.

In the second act I saw how the strike affected the private life of David Roberts. His exhausted wife was ailing by the expiring fire, and I instantly knew that that suffering woman had got to die just when David had flogged his tired men into new resistance, so as to put David into a theatrical hole. There was also a wild Welsh girl of noble and frenzied gesture who wanted the strike to end, and who without argument forced her lover to act against David, for love of her. I could not relate this picturesque creature to anything in real life. She was a figure of melodrama, and Miss Lillah McCarthy rightly played the part as such. The next scene was a men's meeting; and here again (though the stage management was good) I wondered if Mr. Galsworthy had ever attended a meeting of employees on strike. There were three principal speakers, representing the point of view of the Union, the extremist point of view, and the point of view of the old workman. They were all admirable—full of reasoned eloquence, and fit to be printed. The old workman's speech showed the most extraordinary psychological insight. I could just conceive the utterance of such speeches, but that they should have swayed the meeting, as they did, seemed to me grossly untrue to life. No general meeting, whether of employees, employers, statesmen, Socialists—what you like—is ever swayed by anything but clap-trap. And anybody who has followed any campaign, social or political, must be aware of this fact, which is the despair of the weak-stomached. The meeting ended with the news of the death of Mrs. Roberts, which, after all, had a genuine dramatic quality. It moved me.

All the second act was offensive to the eye. I understand, though I do not sympathise with, the general demand for luxurious splendour in stage-setting. Luxurious splendour is the crowd's sole notion of beauty. The crowd is wrong in thinking that beauty can only consist in luxurious splendour, but it is right in demanding a continuous pleasure to the eye on the stage. The interior of a workman's cottage, and the exterior of a works, are liable to strike the observer as ugly. But it is the artist's business to present everything beautifully, without distorting it from the truth. Novelists present superficial ugliness in such a way as to give the pleasure of beauty; so do painters. And Mr. Galsworthy, with Mr. Granville-Barker and the scene painter, ought to have achieved this result in the second act. He did not. And I am quite sure the failure was a grave fault in the play.

In the third act we saw the strike as it affected the private life of the masters. John Anthony's daughter didn't want the men to win because a defeat would be such a terrible blow for her father. She destroyed all her husband's arguments by simply repeating that her father's pride would never survive the triumph of the men. An excellent woman, she had been among the men's women-folk that afternoon, and had returned antipathetic to them, despite their misery. This trait was good; it was very true. All of us know that angry, instinctive feeling of repulsion that comes from contact. It is, for me, really one of the most shocking things in life. But there it is, and Mr. Galsworthy had got hold of it, and he used it well. He must have used it as a hammer to smash my prejudices. For I was impressed by the remainder of the play. Throughout the play he had been ardently alive to the larger issues of his epoch, and he had spilled a good deal of his cruel and bitter humour, and he had used his intellectual power of detachment to the end of impartiality, but he had not interested me in the concrete people on the stage, or even convinced me that they were people. He had appealed to the publicist in me. But in the third act he appealed to the child in me, and with much success. The figures became people, and I was glad to know what was going to happen to them. And I was sorry that things went wrong with them, and that ideals were shattered and efforts wasted, and ignoble compromises the final end. And it was beautiful. Here I ought to say that the performances of Mr. Norman McKinnel as the Chairman, and of Mr. Fisher White as the men's leader, were what is called "fine." They were quite as realistic as Mr. Galsworthy's drawing of the characters—and yet I dream of something much truer to life while just as "fine." "Strife" has survived its matinées, and its week of trial evening performances, and is now in the regular bill at the Adelphi. Its success pleases. It is not the work of a writer abounding in the dramatic sense; it is miles behind the quality of a good novel; it is mostly conventional; it is starved for want of first-hand observation (I wouldn't with-draw this even if I was told that Mr. Galsworthy has lived at Penrhyn for ten years); it consists largely of good intentions (which are worth naught in a work of art). But it is nourished on genuine ideas; it is scornfully honest; it despises the digesting playgoer; it is free from sentimentality; and it has a quarter of an hour's real emotion and vitality. I want to see Mr. Galsworthy's next play.

New Age, IV (April 1, 1909), 461. This is one of Bennett's few signed con-tributions to the *New Age*.

Galsworthy's *The Man of Property* (1910)

Mr. John Galsworthy, whose volume of sketches, 'A Motley,' is now in process of being reviewed, is just finishing another novel, which will no doubt be published in the autumn. That novels have to be finished is the great disadvantage of the novelist's career— otherwise, as everyone knows, a bed of roses, a velvet cushion, a hammock under a ripe pear tree. To begin a novel is delightful. To finish it is the devil. Not because, on parting with his characters, the novelist's heart is torn by the grief which Thackeray described with such characteristically false sentimentality. (The novelist who has put his back into a novel will be ready to kick the whole crowd of his characters down the front door steps.) But because the strain of keeping a long book at the proper emotional level through page after page and chapter after chapter is simply appalling, and as the end approaches becomes almost intolerable. I have just finished a novel myself; my nineteenth, I think. So I know the rudiments of the experience. For those in peril on the sea, and for novelists finishing novels, prayers ought to be offered up.

In accordance with my habit of re-reading books which have uncommonly interested me on first perusal, I have recently read again "The Man of Property." Well, it stands the test. It is certainly the most perfect of Mr. Galsworthy's novels up to now. Except for the confused impression caused by the too rapid presentation of all the numerous members of the Forsyte family at the opening, it has practically no faults. In construction it is unlike any other novel that I know, but that is not to say that it has no constructive design— as some critics have said. It is merely to say that it is original. There are no weak parts in the book, no places where the author has stopped to take his breath and wipe his brow. The tension is never relaxed. This is one of the two qualities without which a novel cannot be first class and great. The other is the quality of sound, harmonious design. Both qualities are exceedingly rare, and I do not know which is the rarer. In the actual material of the book, the finest quality is its extraordinary passionate cruelty towards the oppressors as distinguished from the oppressed. That oppressors should be treated with less sympathy than oppressed is contrary to my notion of the ethics of creative art, but the result in Mr. Galsworthy's work is something very pleasing. Since 'The Man of Property,' the idea that the creator of the universe, or the Original Will, or whatever you like to call it or him, made a grotesque fundamental mistake in the conception of our particular planet, has apparently gained much ground in Mr. Galsworthy's mind. I hope that this ground may slowly be recovered by the opposite idea. Anyhow, the Forsyte is universal. We are all Forsytes, just as we are all Willoughby Patternes, and this incontrovertible statement implies inevitably that Mr. Galsworthy is a writer of the highest rank. I re-read 'The Man of Property' immediately after re-reading Dostoievsky's 'Crime and Punishment' and immediately before re-reading Björnson's 'Arne.' It ranks well with these European masterpieces.

New Age, VII (July 14, 1910), 253. Reprinted under the title "John Galsworthy," *Books and Persons* (New York: George H. Doran Co., 1917), pp. 214–216.

James Joyce's *Ulysses* (1922)

The fame of James Joyce was founded in this country mainly by H. G. Wells, whose praise of *A Portrait of the Artist as a Young Man* had very considerable influence upon the young.[1] For although the severe young spend much time, seated upon the floor, in explaining to each other that H. G. Wells is and must be a back number, he can do almost what he likes with them. I read *A Portrait of the Artist as a Young Man* under the hypnotic influence of H. G. Wells. Indeed, he commanded me to read it and to admire it extremely. I did both. I said: "Yes, it is great stuff." But in the horrid inaccessible thickets of my mind I heard a voice saying: "On the whole, the book has bored you." And on the whole it had; and with the efflux of time I began to announce this truth. There are scenes of genius in the novel; from end to end it shows a sense of style; but large portions of it are dull, pompous, absurd, confused, and undirected. The author had not quite decided what he was after, and even if he had decided he would not have known how to get it. He had resources, but could not use them. He bungled the affair, and then threw his chin up and defied anyone to assert that he had not done what he did in the way he did solely because he wanted to do precisely that thing in precisely that way. A *post facto* pose with which all creative artists, and some others, are experientially acquainted.

A year or two later one of the intellectual young exhibited to me a copy of *The Little Review*, which monthly was then being mentioned in the best circles. I think this must have been in the period when even Mr. Middleton Murry was young. *The Little Review* contained an instalment of James Joyce's *Ulysses*. I obediently glanced through the instalment and concluded that it was an affected triviality which must have been planned in what the French so delicately

1. Wells' essay on *A Portrait of the Artist as a Young Man* appeared in the *Nation*, February 24, 1917, pp. 410–412. He praised the book as "great writing," and compared Joyce favorably with Swift and Sterne.

call a *chalet de nécessité*. I expressed this view, and the intellectual young concurred therein; but I seemed to detect in the concurrence a note of mere politeness to the grey-haired. Hence, recalling the time when I laughed at Cézanne's pictures, I wondered whether there might not be something real in the pages after all.

And then the other day, opening *La Nouvelle Revue Française*, I beheld blazing on its brow an article by Valery Larbaud entitled "James Joyce." [2] I was shaken. *La Nouvelle Revue Française* is in my opinion the finest literary periodical in the world. Valery Larbaud is a critic whom it is impossible to ignore. He is neither old nor young. He is immensely experienced in imaginative literature, and a novelist himself. He has taste. His knowledge of the English language and English literature is only less peculiar and profound than his knowledge of the French language and French literature. He is, indeed, a devil of a fellow. He probably knows more about Walter Savage Landor and Samuel Butler than anybody else on earth. He and Léon Paul Fargue [3] are the only persons on earth who understand the verse of St. Léger Léger. [4] He once amazed and delighted me by stating, quite on his own, that the most accomplished of all the younger British poets was Edith Sitwell: a true saying, though I had said it before him. And here was Valery Larbaud producing a long article on James Joyce, and *La Nouvelle Revue Française* giving it the place of honour! At this point, if I was A. B. Walkley, [5] I should interject that that *m'avait donné furieusement à penser*, and, if I were Mr. Clive Bell, [6] that that had made me exclaim (in French) *Mon Dieu!* What I actually did say was something other.

Valery Larbaud's article was, according to his wont, exhaustive. It contains a comprehensive account of James Joyce from the

2. Larbaud's essay appeared in the *Nouvelle Revue Française*, XVIII (April 1, 1922), 385–409.

3. Leon Paul Fargue (1876–1947), French poet and critic.

4. Marie Réné Auguste Alexis Saint-Léger Léger, French poet and diplomat (1887–   ), published as Saint-John Perse. He was awarded the Nobel Prize for literature in 1960.

5. Arthur Bingham Walkley (1855–1926), drama critic of the London *Times* from 1900 until his death.

6. Clive Bell (1881–   ), art critic and member of the Bloomsbury set.

creation to the present day, and in particular a full analysis and
final estimate of *Ulysses*. And the conclusion of it is that *Ulysses*
is a masterpiece, considered, shapely, and thoroughly achieved.
I was left with no alternative but to read the thing. I saw the
book at the house of a friend and I said: "You have just got to lend
me this." She lent it to me. It looks like a quarto, but it is an octavo:
over two inches thick; 730 pages, each of a superficies of seventy
square inches; over half a million words; and so precariously
broché that when you begin to read it in bed it at once disintegrates
into leaves, largely Sybilline. However, I read it. Perhaps some
pages here and there I only inspected, but roughly speaking I
did read it. And as I finished it I had the sensation of a general who
has just put down an insurrection.

Much has been made of the fact that the author takes more than
seven hundred big pages to describe the passage of less than twenty
hours. But I see nothing very wonderful in this. Given sufficient
time, paper, childish caprice, and obstinacy, one might easily write
over seven thousand pages about twenty hours of life. A young
French author once dreamed of a prose epic in many volumes,
of which the first one was to be entirely devoted to the hero's
journey in a cab from his home to the railway terminus. And why
not? Certainly a book to a day need not be excessive. But it all
depends on the day chosen. There is no clear proof that James
Joyce chose for his theme any particular day. He is evidently of a
sardonic temper, and I expect that he found malicious pleasure in
picking up the first common day that came to hand. It happened
to be nearly the dailiest day possible. (If he had thought of it he
would have chosen a day on which the hero was confined to his bed
with a *colique sèche*.) The uninstructed reader can perceive no form,
no artistic plan, no "organisation" (Henry James's excellent word)
in the chosen day.

But the uninstructed reader is blind. According to Valery Larbaud
the day was very elaborately planned and organised. James Joyce
loved the *Odyssey* in his youth, and the spirit of Homer presided
over the shaping of the present work, which is alleged to be full of
Homeric parallels. It may be so. Obviously Valery Larbaud has
discussed the work at length with the author. I should suspect the

author of pulling Valery Larbaud's leg, were it not that Larbaud has seen with his own eyes the author's drafts. They consist of notes of phrases meant to remind the author of complete phrases; the notes are crossed out by pencil marks of different colours; and the colour indicates the particular episode into which the phrase has been inserted. This method of composing a novel recalls Walter Pater's celebrated mosaics of bits of paper each holding a preciosity. It is weird, but it does demonstrate that the author laboured on some sort of an organised plan.

I therefore concede him a plan, successful or unsuccessful. And in doing so I must animadvert upon his lamentable lack of manners. For he gives absolutely no help to the reader. He behaves like a salesman in an old-fashioned, well-established small West-End shop, whose demeanour seems to say to you as you enter: "What! Here's another of 'em. I'll soon put him off. Now what in hell do *you* want, sir?" Nothing is easier than for an author to help his reader; to do so involves no sacrifice of principle, nor can it impair the value of the book. A writer writes not merely because he is interested, but also because he desires to interest. A sound book ought to be a fair compromise between author and reader. James Joyce, however, does not view the matter thus. He apparently thinks that there is something truly artistic and high-minded in playing the lout to the innocent and defenceless reader. As a matter of fact, there isn't. In playing the lout there is something low-minded and inartistic. *Ulysses* would have been a better book and a much better appreciated book, if the author had extended to his public the common courtesies of literature. After all, to comprehend *Ulysses* is not among the recognised learned professions, and nobody should give his entire existence to the job.

A more serious objection to the novel is its pervading difficult dullness. There is always a danger that short quotations may give a misleading and unfair impression of a work, or even of a chapter in a work; but I must risk the following extract, which I have conscientiously chosen as representative:

> Making for the museum gate with long windy strides he lifted his eyes. Handsome building. Sir Thomas Deane designed. Not following me?
>
> Didn't see me perhaps. Light in his eyes.

The flutter of his breath came forth in short sighs. Quick. Cold statues; quiet there. Safe in a minute.

No, he didn't see me. After two. Just at the gate.

My heart!

His eyes beating looked steadfastly at cream curves of stone. Sir Thomas Deane was the Greek architecture.

Looking for something I.

Scores and hundreds of pages are filled with this kind of composition. Of course, the author is trying to reproduce the thoughts of the personage, and his verbal method can be justified—does, indeed, richly justify itself here and there in the story. But upon the whole, though the reproduction is successful, the things reproduced appear too often to be trivial and perfectly futile in the narrative. I would not accuse him of what is absurdly called "photographic realism." But I would say that much of the book is more like an official shorthand-writer's "note" than a novel. In some of his moods the author is resolved at any price not to select, nor to make even the shortest leap from one point of interest to another. He has taken oath with himself to put it all down and be hanged to it. He would scorn the selective skill in such a masterpiece of narrative technique as *Esther Waters* (whose brilliance only experts can fully appreciate). He would probably defend himself, and find disciples to defend him. But unless the experience of creative artists since the recorded beginning of art is quite worthless, James Joyce is quite wrong-headed. Anyhow, with his wilfulness, he has made novel-reading into a fair imitation of penal servitude. It is not as if his rendering of life was exhaustive, or had the slightest pretension to be exhaustive. The rendering is extremely and ostentatiously partial. The author seems to have no geographical sense, little sense of environment, no sense of the general kindness of human nature, and not much poetical sense. Worse than all, he has positively no sense of perspective. But my criticism of the artist in him goes deeper. His vision of the world and its inhabitants is mean, hostile, and uncharitable. He has a colossal "down" on humanity. Now, Christ in his all-embracing charity might have written a supreme novel. Beelzebub could not.

Withal, James Joyce is a very astonishing phenomenon in letters. He is sometimes dazzlingly original. If he does not see life whole he sees it piercingly. His ingenuity is marvellous. He has wit. He has a prodigious humour. He is afraid of naught. And had heaven in its wisdom thought fit not to deprive him of that basic sagacity and that moral self-dominion which alone enable an artist to assemble and control and fully utilise his powers, he would have stood a chance of being one of the greatest novelists that ever lived.

The best portions of the novel (unfortunately they constitute only a fraction of the whole) are superb. I single out the long orgiastic scene, and the long unspoken monologue of Mrs. Bloom which closes the book. The former will easily bear comparison with Rabelais at his fantastical finest; it leaves Petronius out of sight. It has plenary inspiration. It is the richest stuff, handled with a virtuosity to match the quality of the material. The latter (forty difficult pages, some twenty-five thousand words without any punctuation at all) might in its utterly convincing realism be an actual document, the magical record of inmost thoughts thought by a woman that existed. Talk about understanding "feminine psychology" . . . I have never read anything to surpass it, and I doubt if I have ever read anything to equal it. My blame may have seemed extravagant, and my praise may seem extravagant; but that is how I feel about James Joyce.

It would be unfair to the public not to refer to the indecency of *Ulysses*. The book is not pornographic, and can produce on nobody the effects of a pornographic book. But it is more indecent, obscene, scatological, and licentious than the majority of professedly porno-graphical books. James Joyce sticks at nothing, literally. He forbids himself no word. He says everything—everything. The code is smashed to bits. Many persons could not continue reading *Ulysses*; they would be obliged, by mere shock, to drop it. It is published in France, but not in French, and I imagine that if it had been published in French there would have been trouble about it even in Paris. It must cause reflection in the minds of all those of us who have hitherto held and preached that honest works of art ought to be exempt from police interference. Is the staggering indecency justified by results obtained? The great majority of Britons would say that nothing could justify it. For myself I think that in the main it is not justified by results obtained; but I must plainly add, at the risk of opprobrium, that in the finest passages it is in my opinion justified.

Outlook, XLIX (April 29, 1922), 337–339. Reprinted, *Things That Have Interested Me, Second Series* (New York: George H. Doran Co., 1923), pp. 185–194.

Young Authors (1926)

I am very interested in young writers—and rather gloomy about them. Nor am I alone in gloominess. I find, when conversation on the subject has grown frank and intimate, that the young themselves are gloomy about their writers. I know that the war killed about 50 per cent. of potential talents. But the other 50 per cent. promise too little, and have performed almost nothing so far.

When I was young I wrote what I thought about literature current then, and I see no reason why advancing age should preclude me from writing what I think about current literature now. The new generation of writers is disappointing; it forces us to defer hope. Perhaps at all times elder writers have said this, but to-day the elder writers who say it are not contradicted by their fiery juniors.

When Kipling published 'The Story of the Gadsbys' everybody, old and young, save a few petrified mandarins, agreed that here was a man. Ditto when H. G. Wells published 'The Time Machine.' Ditto even when James Joyce published 'Portrait of the Artist as a Young Man.'

But to-day? . . . The elders and their immediate successors (such as E. M. Forster and D. H. Lawrence) can and do, when up to their form, knock the stuffing out of the boys and girls. There may be—there must be—one or two semi-exceptions; but not one who has caught and vanquished the general imagination of the educated public. We are concerned, and justifiably so. More can be said about this important matter. To be continued next week.

My remarks last week about the younger novelists have aroused some complaint, and it has been said to be odd that I, for years the champion of the young, should turn and rend them. I will therefore proceed further. What I have already written is nothing compared to what I will now write.

The real champion of the younger school is Mrs. Virginia Woolf. She is almost a senior; but she was the inventor, years ago, of a half-new technique, and she alone, so far as I know, came forward and attacked the old. She has written a small book about me, which through a culpable neglect I have not read. I do, however, remember an article of hers in which she asserted that I and my kind could not create character. This was in answer to an article of mine in which I said that the sound drawing of character was the foundation of good fiction, and in which incidentally I gave my opinion that Mrs. Woolf and her kind could not create character.[1]

I have read two and a half of Mrs. Woolf's books. First, 'The Common Reader,' which is an agreeable collection of elegant essays on literary subjects. Second, 'Jacob's Room,' which I achieved with great difficulty. Third, 'Mrs. Dalloway,' which beat me. I could not finish it, because I could not discover what it was really about, what was its direction and what Mrs. Woolf intended to demonstrate by it.

To express myself differently, I failed to discern what was its moral basis. As regards character-drawing, Mrs. Woolf (in my opinion) told us ten thousand things about Mrs. Dalloway, but did not show us Mrs. Dalloway. I got from the novel no coherent picture of Mrs. Dalloway. Nor could I see much trace of construction, or ordered movement towards a climax, in either 'Jacob's Room' or 'Mrs. Dalloway.' Further, I thought that both books seriously lacked vitality.

These three defects, I maintain, are the characteristic defects of the new school of which Mrs. Woolf is the leader. The people in them do not sufficiently live, and hence they cannot claim our sympathy or even our hatred; they leave us indifferent. Logical construction is absent, concentration on the theme (if any) is absent, the interest is dissipated; material is wantonly or clumsily wasted, instead of being employed economically as in great masterpieces. Problems are neither clearly stated nor clearly solved.

The new practitioners have simply returned to the facile go-as-you-please methods of the eighteenth century, ignoring the

1. See page 87 above for Bennett's article, and page 269 below for Mrs. Woolf's reply.

important discoveries and innovations of Balzac and later novelists. How different is the new school of fiction from the new school of painting, with its intense regard for logical design!

Lastly, there is absence of vital inspiration. Some novelists appear to have no zest; they loll through their work as though they were taking a stroll in the Park. I admit that I may be wrong on the second count; I may be blind to evidences of a design which is too subtle for my perception. But I do not think that I can be wrong on the first and third counts.

And I admit that some of the younger school can write very well. In the novels of Mrs. Woolf some brief passages are so exquisitely done that nothing could be done better. But to be fine for a few minutes is not enough. The chief proof of first-rateness is sustained power.∗∗∗

Evening Standard, November 25, 1926, p. 5, and December 2, 1926, p. 5. Reprinted, *The Savour of Life* (New York: Doubleday, 1928), pp. 53–59.

Virginia Woolf's *To the Lighthouse* (1927)

∗∗∗ I must say, despite my grave reservations concerning Virginia Woolf, that the most original of the bunch [of novels for review] is 'To the Lighthouse' (Hogarth Press). It is the best book of hers that I know. Her character drawing has improved. Mrs. Ramsay almost amounts to a complete person. Unfortunately she goes and dies, and her decease cuts the book in two. Also there are some pleasing records of interesting sensations outside the range of the ordinary novelist. The scheme of the story is rather wilful—designed, seemingly, but perhaps not really, to exhibit virtuosity. A group of people plan to sail in a small boat to a lighthouse. At the end some of them reach the lighthouse in a small boat. That is the externality of the plot.

The middle part, entitled 'Time Passes,' shows a novel device to give the reader the impression of the passing of time—a sort of cataloguing of intermediate events. In my opinion it does not succeed. It is a short cut, but a short cut that does not get you anywhere. To convey the idea of the passage of a considerable length of time is an extremely difficult business, and I doubt if it can be accomplished by means of a device, except the device of simply saying 'Time passes,' and leaving the effort of imagination to the reader. Apart from this honest shirking of the difficulty, there is no alternative but to convey the impression very gradually, without any direct insistence—in the manner of life itself.

I have heard a good deal about the wonders of Mrs. Woolf's style. She sometimes discovers a truly brilliant simile. She often chooses her adjectives and adverbs with beautiful felicity. But there is more in style than this. The form of her sentences is rather tryingly monotonous, and the distance between her nominatives and her verbs is steadily increasing. Still, 'To the Lighthouse' has stuff in it strong enough to withstand quite a lot of adverse criticism.

Evening Standard, June 23, 1927, p. 5.

Virginia Woolf's *Orlando* (1928)

You cannot keep your end up at a London dinner-party in these weeks unless you have read Mrs. Virginia Woolf's *Orlando* (Hogarth Press, 9*s.*).

For about a fortnight I succeeded in not reading it—partly from obstinacy and partly from a natural desire for altercation at table about what ought and ought not to be read. Then I saw that Hugh Walpole had described it as "another masterpiece," and that Desmond MacCarthy had given it very high praise.

I have a great opinion of the literary opinions of these two critics. So I bought the book and read it. I now know exactly what I think of it, and I can predict the most formidable rumpuses at future parties.

It is a very odd volume. It has a preface, in which Mrs. Woolf names the names of 53 people who have helped her with it. It has, too, an index. I admit some justification for the preface, but none for the index.

Further, the novel, which is a play of fancy, a wild fantasia, a romance, a high-brow lark, is illustrated with ordinary realistic photographs, including several of Vita Sackville-West (a Hawthornden prize-winner),[1] to whom the book is dedicated. The portraits of Miss Sackville-West are labelled "Orlando."

This is the oddest of all the book's oddities, and I commend it to Mr. H. M. Paull who has just published a rather comprehensive volume entitled *Literary Ethics: a Study in the growth of the literary conscience* (Butterworth, 15*s.*).

Mr. Paull has a chapter on "Actual Persons in Fiction and Drama." True, the numerous instances which Mr. Paull cites were

1. The Hawthornden Prize is given annually to an English writer under forty-two, for the best work of imaginative literature. V. Sackville-West won it for 1926 with her book of "British Georgics," *The Land*.

not done with the consent of the "actual persons" concerned. Mrs. Woolf's obviously was.

Orlando at the end of the book has achieved an age of some four centuries. Which reminds one of the Wandering Jew and the Flying Dutchman. Half-way through the story he changes into a woman—and "stays put." Which reminds one of *Seraphita*, the dullest book that Balzac ever wrote.

I surmise that Orlando is intended to be the incarnation of something or other—say, the mustang spirit of the joy of life, but this is not quite clear to me.

The first chapter is goodish. It contains vivacious descriptions of spectacular matters—such as a big frost, royal courts, and the love-making of Orlando and a Muscovite girl in furs and in the open air amid the fiercest frost since the ice-age. Mrs. Woolf almost convinces us of the possibility of this surely very difficult dalliance.

The second chapter shows a startling decline and fall-off. Fanciful embroidery, wordy, and naught else!

The succeeding chapters are still more tedious in their romp of fancy. Mrs. Woolf does not seem to have understood that fancy must have something to play *on*. She has left out the basic substance. For example, Orlando, both as man and as woman, is said to have had many lovers, but details are given of only one love.

I shall no doubt be told that I have missed the magic of the work. The magic is precisely what I indeed have missed.

The writing is good at the beginning, but it goes to pieces; it even skids into bad grammar (e.g. on p. 262).[2] Mrs. Woolf has accomplished some of the most beautiful writing of the modern age, including paragraphs that Nathaniel Hawthorne himself might have signed. *Orlando*, however, has nothing anywhere near as good as her best.

The theme is a great one. But it is a theme for a Victor Hugo, not for Mrs. Woolf, who, while sometimes excelling in fancy and in delicate realistic observation, has never yet shown the mighty

2. Page 262 (page 291 of the Harcourt, Brace edition) includes the latter part of a twenty-six-line sentence containing six parentheses; it is not, however, ungrammatical—it is only interminable.

imaginative power which the theme clearly demands. Her best novel, *To the Lighthouse*, raised my hopes of her. *Orlando* has dashed them, and they lie in iridescent fragments at my feet.

Evening Standard, November 8, 1928, p. 5.

Virginia Woolf's
A Room of One's Own (1929)

⋆⋆⋆ Another book about writing, but a far better one, is Virginia Woolf's *A Room of One's Own* (Hogarth Press, 5*s*). I have often been informed by the elect that a feud exists between Virginia Woolf and myself, and I dare say that she has received the same tidings. Possibly she and I are the only two lettered persons unaware of this feud. True, she has written a book about me and a mythical Mrs. Brown. But I have not read the book (I don't know why). True, I always said, until she wrote *To the Lighthouse*, that she had not written a good novel. But I have said the same of lots of my novelist friends. True, she is the queen of the high-brows; and I am a low-brow. But it takes all sorts of brows to make a world, and without a large admixture of low-brows even Bloomsbury would be uninhabitable.

One thing I have said of her: she can write. *A Room of One's Own* is a further demonstration of this truth. (She has her private notions about grammar. See p. 50.)[1] And I have said that you never know where you are in a book of hers. *A Room of One's Own* is a further demonstration of this truth also. It is stated to be based on two papers read to the Arts Society of Newnham and the One-Damned-Thing-After-Another Society at Girton. On p. 6 she refers to herself as a lecturer. On p. 7 she suggests that you may throw "it" into the waste-paper basket. Well, you can't throw a lecture into the waste-paper basket. You can only walk out from a lecture, or treat your ears as Ulysses treated the ears of his fellow-mariners.

The book has a thesis: namely, that "it is necessary to have five hundred a year and a room with a lock on it if you are to write

1. Page 50 (page 56 in the Harcourt, Brace edition) contains no glaring example of "bad grammar." Perhaps Bennett objected to the following awkward sentence: "What is the real nature of what I call for the moment their anger? I asked."

fiction or poetry." With the implied corollary that women, being usually without five hundred a year of their very own, and liable to everlasting interruption, are at a serious disadvantage as novelists and poets.

The thesis is disputable. Dostoievsky wrote some of the greatest novels in the world while he was continually distracted by terrible extra-artistic anxieties. And I beg to state that I have myself written long and formidable novels in bedrooms whose doors certainly had no locks, and in the full dreadful knowledge that I had not five hundred a year of my own—nor fifty. And I beg to state further that from the moment when I obtained possession of both money and a lockable door all the high-brows in London conspired together to assert that I could no longer write.

However, Virginia Woolf's thesis is not apparently important to her, since she talks about everything but the thesis. If her mind was not what it is I should accuse her of wholesale padding. This would be unjust. She is not consciously guilty of padding. She is merely the victim of her extraordinary gift of fancy (not imagination). If I had to make one of those brilliant generalizations now so fashionable, defining the difference between men and women, I should say that whereas a woman cannot walk through a meadow in June without wandering all over the place to pick attractive blossoms, a man can. Virginia Woolf cannot resist the floral enticement.

Some will describe her book as a feminist tract. It is no such thing. It is a book a little about men and a great deal about women. But it is not "feminist." It is non-partisan. The author writes: "Women are hard on women. Women dislike women. Women—but are you not sick to death of the word? I can assure you that I am." Admirable attitude! And she comes to no satisfactory conclusion about the disparateness of men and women. Because nobody ever has and nobody could.

You may walk along Prince Consort Road, and through the open windows of the Royal College of Music hear the scrapings, the tinklings and the trillings of a thousand young people trying to make themselves professional musicians. And you may reflect that ten years hence nine-tenths of the girls among them will have abandoned all scraping, tinkling and trilling for love, domesticity and (perhaps) cradles. And you may think that you have discovered the origin and explanation of the great disparateness of men and women. Not so! Great opera-singers have borne child after child, and remained great opera-singers.

Evening Standard, November 28, 1929, p. 5.

III.   HERESIES

My Literary Heresies (1904)

I. Preliminary and Poetical

I shall define heresy as a difference from the general body of expert opinion. But I add to that definition something from the legal definition of heresy, which said that heresy, before it really became heresy, must be "publicly avowed and obstinately maintained." I am about to make my heresies heresies in the legal sense of the term. A little frank heresy never does any harm. It affords innocent delight to the other heretics, annoys those of the orthodox who cannot give reasons for the faith that is in them, and generally adds to the gaiety of the planet. But in literature there are two kinds of heresy, as there are two divisions of authors. There are the authors who have been dead, say, a couple of centuries, and whose reputations are finally decided by the secular verdict of Time (Time who is never wrong, in the end); and there are the authors about whom the Old Beggar (I refer to Time) has not yet quite come to an absolute conclusion. Now, the heretic who publicly avows and obstinately maintains heresies concerning the former division of authors may be dismissed as a crank, or as a humorist, or as unlettered. His heresies have no importance; he need not be burnt at the stake. Herbert Spencer's views on Homer and Mr. Bernard Shaw's views on Shakespeare have no literary interest; they have merely the interest of showing that Herbert Spencer was unlettered, and that Mr. Bernard Shaw is a singular amalgam of crank and humorist. Every great man, and most small ones, have similar aberrations. Horace Walpole and myself, for example, couldn't abide Spenser; the immortal phrase-maker spoke casually of "wading through Spenser's allegories and drawling stanzas." But we don't go and make a boast of it. We know we are wrong. Similarly, I confess to an undue regard for Crashaw, whose finest conceits are to me quite incomparable. But I never preach Crashaw.

On the other hand, concerning the authors round whom Time has not established a body of absolutely permanent and definite Doctrine, a man has the right to be heretical; there is always a chance that Time will one day say to him: "Come up higher, heretic; henceforth you are orthodox," while the whilom orthodox are cast into outer darkness. I reckon, for example, that a man has the right to be openly heretical about Scott; it is doubtful whether Time has finished with Scott. I am not heretical about Scott; but, having cleared the ground, let me out with my heresies, and let me say that I am very fervent about them. I write these heretical lines on my thirty-seventh birthday. I have lived solely in, by, and for literature for many years. I have collected a library; indeed, several. You may know a really horsey man by the way he handles a strange horse in a loose-box. Put me into a strange library, and—and—see! That is the test of the bookman! I have what Carlyle called "a strict taste in books." I was born with it. (I take no credit for that. It merely was so, and all is for the best in the best of all possible worlds, as you doubtless know.) I am not to be gulled, hoodwinked, bullied, or even blinded by glitter. My opinions are mature, informed, and settled. If, when I talk about books, I do not know what I am talking about, then I ought to be ashamed of myself. In brief, I am like all true bookmen. Other people call it cheek, but true bookmen know that it isn't.

I must begin with poetry, of course. If it is heresy to regard Wordsworth as the greatest poet since Milton, then I am ready for the thumb-screw. Also I think that Coleridge has got somewhat above himself, and that Keats's "Hyperion" is too much of a *tour de force* to be a masterpiece. But these are the fine shades. Tennyson and Browning are the great bones of contention. I am strongly anti-Tennysonian. Speaking with a heretic's licence, I would undertake to write on a five shilling-piece all of Tennyson that will be regarded as great poetry in 2104. I have never liked Tennyson's individuality. His education was extremely faulty. You could pick it up at Oxford any day—"that nursery of nonsense and bigotry." He did not seek to remedy its defects. He was admittedly a boor, and gorgeously egotistic. Still, he *was* Tennyson, and he wrote "The splendour falls on castle walls," and a few similar lovely trinkets. His renown was due to the applause of the most grossly inartistic generation that England has seen for over three centuries. He was a bad judge of literature. He said that the finest line he ever wrote was "The mellow ousel fluting in the elm."[1] (But perhaps it was.) Take the bulk of his work, "In Memoriam," "Princess," "Idylls," and the plays. Well, the "Idylls," which twenty years ago we adored, are as dead as a doornail. His keenest admirers have ceased to defend them. As for the plays, there has recently been an agreeable "scrap" in the "Times" between that champion lightweight Mr. A. B. Walkley and sundry others as to whether the supreme test of a play is in the reading or in the witnessing of it. The controversy would have been futile in respect to Tennyson's plays, for they will stand neither test. "In Memoriam"? How old-fashioned and early Victorian it seems! Fancy going to it for philosophic sustenance! Longfellow has been laughed at for "The Psalm of Life," but "The Psalm of Life" is worth fifty of the famous "stepping stones and dead selves" stanza. The songs in the "Princess" may live, by which I mean that they still have the power to charm me. These and some minor pieces show Tennyson as a distinguished minor poet, I think. But for a great poet, well, he simply didn't know enough—I mean about Life with a large L and that sort of thing, nor about Art with a large A. As to life, he was too vain and too petted ever to come to grips with it. And as to art, despite his classic lore, he never grasped the fundamental classic maxim that the first quality in a work of art is good construction. He had a pretty gift, but he belonged essentially to the half-educated. I speak on behalf of posterity, which cannot, at the moment, speak for itself.

Browning was a much finer man (read his love-letters). He was a greater man; he was truly educated; he was quite abreast of his time, which Tennyson was not. The pity is that Browning never learnt the elementary part of his craft. He could never *write* save by divine flukes, not even prose, to say nothing of verse. The first duty of a writer is to be readable, and Browning was seldom readable. In asserting this, I am not merely repeating a facile jibe. Browningites state that Browning is perfectly lucid to anyone who will take the trouble to understand him. Mr. Chesterton (that lightning-artist and

1. From "The Gardener's Daughter." Bennett slightly misquotes the line.

entertainer) has recently said as much. But Browning is not perfectly lucid. Tennyson could, at any rate, say beautifully and clearly what he meant. Browning couldn't. What "The Ring and the Book" might have been if Browning had learnt his trade I hesitate to guess. It might have been Shakespearean. As it is, I wouldn't undertake to read it again for twenty-five pounds. I would no more read it again than I would read "Festus."[2] It is useless to say: "Ah! But you shirk the intellectual labour!" Yes, I do, because the end of a work of art is to please the aesthetic sense, and it is impossible that the aesthetic sense should remain in a condition to be pleased while the intellectual faculty is at full stretch. One might as well try to enjoy a Beethoven sonata while playing a game of chess. The thing can't be done. As long as writers of the class of Shakespeare and Milton take the trouble to be limpid, sufficient people will not find sufficient time for the keeping alive of the reputation of a Browning. Without doubt Browning has superb moments. I would write "O Lyric Love" on the obverse of that five shilling-piece, and cast it into eternity sure that it would pass current for ever.

II. IN FICTION

Perhaps it is because I am "in the trade" that my leading heresies relate to fiction. It requires some screwing up of courage to say outright that between Scott and Meredith I regard no English novelist as really great. But this is what I mean—it is what I should say in the end, so I may as well say it plump and get the worst over. And between Scott and Meredith the only English novelist that I care to read at all is Jane Austen. The Tennysonian pleasantry of classing Jane with Shakespeare seems to me fatuous, but I certainly do look on "Persuasion" as the finest "minor novel" in our language. Dickens and Thackeray I cannot read with pleasure (of course I enjoyed Dickens as a boy); I have tried so often that I will try no more. So much the worse for me? You may think so, but I don't. Opinion is steadily coming round to me and the obstinate heretics with whom I class myself. Twenty years ago who would have dared

2. *Festus*, a vast dramatic poem by Philip James Bailey (1816–1902), was first published in 1839. It eventually ran to 40,000 lines, and earned for Bailey and his friends the nick-name of "Spasmodic Poets."

even to apologise for Dickens or Thackeray? They were as sacred as "Omar" is now, and twenty times more so. But to-day they both have their ardent apologists, especially Thackeray. It is not long since we had the spectacle of Mr. Andrew Lang[3] saying, in effect, that he should continue to adore Thackeray in spite of his reason. Good. I can understand that attitude. In the old days who would have dared to insinuate that Colonel Newcome is all fudge? To-day who will deny that the Colonel is fudge of the crassest sentimental kind? Times change. The existence of an anti-Thackeray-Dickens body of opinion is now admitted, and it continually makes the "Old Guard" of criticism very cross—which means a great deal.

My reason for objecting to Dickens is not that he constantly exaggerated nature into a grotesquerie. He was perfectly entitled to choose his own convention, as Scott or Fielding did. Nor would I deny that he had enormous inventive force (I use the word "inventive" rather than "imaginative"—he had not much imagination), nor that he possessed a virtuosity in some departments of his craft which has seldom been equalled. The counts of my indictment are: (1) That he was devoid of a feeling for beauty and a feeling for literature—the two first qualifications of a literary artist of the first rank. His constant search for ugliness abrades me as much as anything. (2) That he had no power of construction. The plots of all his most ambitious novels are wonderful but utterly infantile exercises in Coincidence. (3) That he was extremely ignorant of everything except the details of the daily life of bizarre persons. (4) That he had no natural distinction of mind. In Dickens there is nothing *fine*. (5) That his pathos is merely comic, and an absolute proof that his conception of pathos was the conception of a milliner's apprentice. (6) That his humour is monotonous. (7) That his style, while often vigorous, is nothing more. Such is my accusation. Do not suppose that I think he was not a most extraordinary man, or that he had not various admirable and rare qualities. My theory is that his defects outweigh his qualities, and that the vast mass of his work must perish. I am ready to admit, cautiously, that here and there in that row of volumes there may possibly be something that will survive; but I gravely doubt.

3. Andrew Lang (1844–1912), Scottish poet, critic, and man of letters. His essay on Thackeray is in *Essays in Little* (London, 1891).

Thackeray is a less considerable figure, a man of much less force than Dickens, and one whose vogue will die much sooner. "The Newcomes," "The Virginians," "Pendennis," have already fallen from their high estate. And "Vanity Fair" stands by no means where it did. Thackeray pretended to write about life as he found it; in other words, he pretended to set it forth seriously, truthfully, and realistically. But he never did any such thing. He never could look life steadily in the face, because he was a bit of a snob and wholly a sentimentalist. He lived at a time when the very greatest masterpieces of nineteenth century fiction were being produced—those of Balzac, Stendhal, Turgenev, &c.; and his ideas about them, when he had any, were the ideas of a bagman or of a curate. He had the effrontery to lecture on eighteenth century literature; but what did he know about it? He "got it up." I wonder whether it ever really struck him that in his novels he was doing over again—and feebly, timidly, and falsely—what Richardson had done perfectly in "Clarissa Harlowe." I cannot imagine how anyone can call Thackeray true to life after having read "Clarissa"—perhaps the greatest realistic novel in any language. And if "Vanity Fair" is first-class and great, I desire to be supplied with an adjective for "Clarissa." The fact is that "Vanity Fair" is not true to life, and everybody well knows that it is not. It dilutes truth, flatters human nature (as if human nature stood in need of flattery at the hands of a clubman), and sprinkles sugar over the mess. It appeals to the weakest in us, not to the sternest. As for "Esmond," it is a laborious and highly-wrought confection; it throbs with the warm, pulsating vitality of a stone statue. Further, Thackeray, like Dickens, wrote from hand to mouth—I mean from month to month (masterpieces are not so written)—and thought a great deal too much of his public. His style has not the positive badnesses of Dickens's, but it very seldom approaches anything like distinction. Read an essay of Lamb's, or a passage from Ruskin, and then turn up your favourite passages in Thackeray, and reconsider the style.

To sum up about Dickens and Thackeray. They are being read less and less by the handful of literary experts and enthusiasts who ultimately make and unmake reputations, who ultimately influence the general body of public opinion. Their works will enjoy a large circulation for many years to come, but death has already got them. Think what a really great novel is, a novel that faces life squarely, and continually appeals to the sense of sheer beauty. Think of "War and Peace," "Père Goriot," "Madame Bovary," and then think of "Vanity Fair." "Vanity Fair" is simply not in the same class with them. It isn't broad enough, or wide enough, or deep enough. It is second rate. As for "A Tale of Two Cities" or "Copperfield," what sort of a show would they make among the high gods of Olympus? Of course, "Pickwick," and things in "Nicholas Nickleby," and so on, have a flavour (something garlic) all their own, unique. . . . They may survive; they may, just! But when one meditates upon the great European names, the names that shed a radiance over a whole continent—Richardson, Scott, Balzac, Stendhal, Turgenev, Flaubert, Tolstoi—does one instinctively include Dickens and Thackeray in the mighty catalogue? Does not one instinctively put these two down a couple of pegs, as being insular, as being "local poets"?

There remain several ladies. The Brontës I can respect. Working under terrible disadvantages of environment, experience, and temperament, they certainly did work sincerely, and with a single aim. They certainly had a sense of beauty, a dim feeling for words, and a sort of spinsterish personal distinction. "Villette" is the best of their bundle. "Wuthering Heights" would have been the best if Emily had known about forty times as much as she did concerning life and her trade. The Brontë novels are worth reading, once. They are more ambitious and turbulent than "Persuasion," but they lack its perfection. They, too, are good "minor novels." I rate them higher than anything of George Eliot's. "Scenes from Clerical Life" is, of course, tedious, and the long-long novels are both tedious and pretentious. The three others—"Silas Marner," "Adam Bede," and "The Mill on the Floss"—have an unchastened power; but so unchastened, so fitful, so sprawling, and so unoriginal! I could not anticipate the business of reading these again with anything but alarm. They are several miles removed from the mediocre, but when I think of the strong, wide sweep; the masterly and restrained ease, the rich inspiration, the full knowledge, the noble and flawless style of a George Sand—well, I cease to think of George Eliot, and turn with a more assured patriotism to George Meredith.

III. CONCERNING THE LIVING

The last original trace of the great romantic movement which was born with the century vanished with Wordsworth. A new romantic movement began about the "sixties." It showed itself not only in George Meredith's novels and poems, and Rossetti's and Swinburne's poems, but also in the domain of the graphic arts. The outstanding characteristic of nearly all the so-called "great" early Victorian novelists was a lack of feeling for romantic beauty. Meredith reintroduced this quality into English fiction, and (such is my heresy) he wrote the first great novels since Scott. But I have my minor heresies concerning even Meredith. He is known as the author of one of his least satisfactory novels, "The Ordeal of Richard Feverel." Glorious as this book is in parts, it cannot survive criticism as an organic whole. It falls to pieces completely at the end, which is a melodrama based on sheer accidents. Indeed, from the moment when, in a sentimental and wholly mawkish way, he separated the young husband and wife, the author lost his grip of the story; and well he might, seeing that he had parted company with human nature. The relations between Richard and "Sir Julius" disclose Meredith's genius struggling against the influence of Charlotte M. Yonge. In my opinion it is a nice question whether "The Egoist" or "The Adventures of Harry Richmond" is the best Meredith. I incline to the latter, than which I know nothing in this world finer for pure romance. I may say that I cannot read "The Tale of Chloe." I never could understand it. I call it Browning without the amusing rhymes.

I come to Mr. Hardy. Three English novelists have invented three original sorts of novel. Richardson in "Clarissa" wrote the first realistic novel. Scott wrote the first romantic novel (as distinguished from the merely fanciful romance). These two men influenced, and are responsible for, all the French fiction of the nineteenth century, for Richardson fathered the Balzac side of it, while Scott fathered the Dumas side of it. Of course, they were responsible also for most English fiction of the nineteenth century, but that is a minor matter. The third inventor of an original sort of novel was Thomas Hardy.

If you take up a novel like "The Mayor of Casterbridge," and regard carefully its environment, its atmosphere, its construction, its characteristics, its curious emotion, and its equally curious humour, you will be obliged to admit that nothing like it existed in English fiction until Thomas Hardy came. It is a new thing. You can even find Dickens in Smollett, and moreover Dickens was quite divorced from beauty; but "The Mayor of Casterbridge" (or "Far from the Madding Crowd," which came earlier and is nearly as good) is as new as "Christabel" was new. It contains a new beauty, a new thrill for the amateurs of beauty: it does not "derive."

Meredith is more learned in human nature than Hardy; he has much more intellect than his younger rival; he is more lettered; his virtuosity is much greater. Meredith works consciously, Hardy unconsciously. Meredith is a critic, and a fine one; Hardy is not. Meredith, since his adolescence, never stumbles; Hardy frequently stumbles. But Hardy's stumbling is, all the same, divine. He is the child of pure genius. He discovered a whole world. I need not say that I consider "Tess" one of Hardy's least good books; its faults made its fortune. Many heretics think very highly of "Jude," but I belong to a little sect by myself which reckons "Jude" as a second sign of decadence, "Tess" being the first. The rank stupidity of the reception given to "The Well-beloved," that utterly charming conceit, irritates me. So much for these two giants, who inaugurated the modern golden age of English fiction, and who have atoned for the smugness, the ugliness, and the moral cowardice of the "great" early Victorian era, an era whose achievements in fiction were indeed little better than its achievements in painting. It will now be perceived that I have turned the nineteenth century upside down; heretics delight in such feats.

I approach the delicate ground of my own generation. Am I to publish the smallness of my esteem for certain of my contemporaries, men and women who practise the honourable calling of literature with dignity and success, but whose performances leave me quite cold? I cannot. I must employ the method of silence. I must name only those who seem to me to "count." The men whom I admire, whose new novels I anticipate with eagerness more or less acute, are nine in number. I give them in alphabetical order:—Joseph Conrad,

Murray Gilchrist, W. W. Jacobs, Henry James, Rudyard Kipling, George Moore, Arthur Morrison, Eden Phillpotts, and H. G. Wells. Please rest assured that it is not by accident that I have omitted ——— or ———. I really do not believe that ——— and ——— have done anything of permanent artistic value. I may have omitted one or two younger writers through carelessness, but the solid reputations which you are astonished not to find in my list are absent through unavoidable causes. You see, I am a heretic. Naturally, I do not hold all the sacred nine in equal regard. Concerning one or two, I am prevented by literary etiquette from expressing my admiration in detail, and hence I do not care to express a detailed admiration of the remainder.

I must be content with a few notes. For example, I regard Mr. George Moore as a greater novelist than our dear old Thackeray. If "A Mummer's Wife," "A Drama in Muslin," and "Sister Teresa," are not three of the greatest novels of their century, may Mudie desert me in my old age! Mr. Moore wrote the first realistic novel after "Clarissa." He anticipated De Maupassant's "Bel Ami" by two years. And in his time he has made mistakes. I think I would give about a peck and a half of early Victorian masterpieces for "Sister Teresa." As to Mr. H. G. Wells, it may surprise some people to know that in imaginative literature he "stands for" England to-day on the Continent. When an Englishman's novels are published simultaneously in London, New York, Paris, and Rome, it behoves Englishmen to stop in the street and meditate on the phenomenon. Mr. Wells is in danger of being mistaken both for a sensational serialist and a social reformer. As a fact, he has carried both professions to a tremendous height; but he happens to be chiefly a great novelist. "The First Men in the Moon," which had an extraordinary success in the "Strand Magazine" as a sensational serial, is a serious realistic novel, intimately critical of our political and social life. This remark is profoundly true, but the truth of it will perhaps occur to the general public in twenty years or so. The case of Mr. Kipling is very complicated. Unlike Mr. ——— he has genius, but like the same Mr. ——— he has never properly learnt his trade; he lacks the constructive power; and his feeling for beauty is but faint. I make these observations in order to show that I am not a whole-hearted admirer of Kipling; there is something in most of his work to which I am extremely antagonistic. I must mention that Mr. Arthur Morrison is for me the author of "Cunning Murrell."[4]

How I wish I could reckon Mr. Watts Dunton's strange and solitary work. "Aylwin," among my delights! I feel sorry whenever I think of that book, which has a soul of true romance strangled in the grip of an early-Victorian technique! It is a novel that refuses to be "classed," and though in the end I found it tedious, I willingly admit that I may be wrong about it. Heretics are incapable of being wrong; but I make an exception in this case. I have given nearly all my space to novels, and I do not regret having done so. The novel is certainly the monopoliser of modern literary creative energy. Compared to the novelists, the poets of the period, except Mr. Yeats, are, in my view, pigmies. They tower over the essayists, and with that triumph they must be satisfied.

T.P.'s Weekly, IV (September 9, 16, and 23, 1904), 328, 364, 392.

4. Arthur Morrison (1863–1946), best known for his realistic books about London's East End: *Tales of Mean Streets* (1894) and *A Child of the Jago* (1896). Morrison also wrote popular fiction, which Bennett evidently preferred (*Cunning Murrell* was published in 1900).

The First Post-Impressionist Show (1910)

The exhibition of the so-called "Neo-Impressionists" over which the culture of London is now laughing, has an interest which is perhaps not confined to the art of painting. For me, personally, it has a slight, vague repercussion upon literature. The attitude of the culture of London towards it is of course merely humiliating to any Englishman who has made an effort to cure himself of insularity. It is one more proof that the negligent disdain of Continental artists for English artistic opinion is fairly well founded. The mild tragedy of the thing is that London is infinitely too self-complacent even to suspect that it is London and not the exhibition which is making itself ridiculous. The laughter of London in this connection is just as silly, just as provincial, just as obtuse, as would be the laughter of a small provincial town were Strauss's "Salomé," or Debussy's "Pelléas et Mélisande" offered for its judgment. One can imagine the shocked, contemptuous resentment of a London musical amateur (one of those that arrived at Covent Garden box-office at 6 a.m. the other day to secure a seat for "Salomé") at the guffaw of a provincial town confronted by the spectacle and the noise of the famous "Salomé" osculation. But the amusement of that same amateur confronted by an uncompromising "Neo-Impressionist" picture amounts to exactly the same guffaw. The guffaw is legal. You may guffaw before Rembrandt (people do!), but in so doing you only add to the sum of human stupidity. London may be unaware that the value of the best work of this new school is permanently and definitely settled—outside London. So much the worse for London. For the movement has not only got past the guffaw stage; it has got past the arguing stage. Its authenticity is admitted by all those who have kept themselves fully awake. And in twenty years London will be signing an apology for its guffaw. It will be writing itself down an ass. The writing will consist of large cheques payable for Neo-

Impressionist pictures to Messrs. Christie, Manson and Woods. London is already familiar with this experience, and doesn't mind.

Who am I that I should take exception to the guffaw? Ten years ago I too guffawed, though I hope with not quite the Kensingtonian twang. The first Cézannes I ever saw seemed to me to be very funny. They did not disturb my dreams, because I was not in the business. But my notion about Cézanne was that he was a fond old man who distracted himself by daubing. I could not say how my conversion to Cézanne began. When one is not a practising expert in an art, a single word, a single intonation, uttered by an expert whom one esteems, may commence a process of change which afterwards seems to go on by itself. But I remember being very much impressed by a still-life—some fruit in a bowl—and on approaching it I saw Cézanne's clumsy signature in the corner. From that moment the revelation was swift. And before I had seen any Gauguins at all, I was prepared to consider him with sympathy. The others followed naturally. I now surround myself with large photographs of these pictures of which a dozen years ago I was certainly quite incapable of perceiving the beauty. The best still-life studies of Cézanne seem to me to have the grandiose quality of epics. And that picture by Gauguin, showing the back of a Tahitian young man with a Tahitian girl on either side of him, is an affair which I regard with acute pleasure every morning. There are compositions by Roussel which equally enchant me. Naturally I cannot accept the whole school—no more than the whole of any school. I have derived very little pleasure from Matisse, and the later developments of Félix Vallotton leave me in the main unmoved. But one of the very latest phenomena of the school—the water-colours of Pierre Laprade—I have found ravishing.[1]

It is in talking to several of these painters, in watching their familiar deportment, and particularly in listening to their conversations with others on subjects other than painting, that I have come to connect their ideas with literature. They are not good theorisers

1. Ker-Xavier Roussel (1867–1944) and Félix Vallotton (1865–1925) were painters in the "nabis" group of Bonnard and Maillol; Pierre Laprade (1875–1931) was a minor post-impressionist. Vallotton and Laprade were among the artists represented in the show; Roussel was not.

about art; and I am not myself a good theoriser about art; a creative artist rarely is. But they do ultimately put their ideas into words. You may receive one word one day and the next next week, but in the end an idea gets itself somehow stated. Whenever I have listened to Laprade criticising pictures, especially students' work, I have thought about literature; I have been forced to wonder whether I should not have to reconsider my ideals. The fact is that some of these men are persuasive in themselves. They disengage, in their talk, in their profound seriousness, in their sense of humour, in the sound organization of their industry, and in their calm assurance—they disengage a convincingness that is powerful beyond debate. An artist who is truly original cannot comment on bootlaces without illustrating his philosophy and consolidating his position. Noting in myself that a regular contemplation of these pictures inspires a weariness of all other pictures that are not absolutely first-rate, giving them a disconcerting affinity to the tops of chocolate-boxes or "art" photographs, I have permitted myself to suspect that supposing some writer were to come along and do in words what these men have done in paint, I might conceivably be disgusted with nearly the whole of modern fiction, and I might have to begin again. This awkward experience will in all probability not happen to me, but it might happen to a writer younger than me. At any rate it is a fine thought. The average critic always calls me, both in praise and dispraise, "photographic"; and I always rebut the epithet with disdain, because in the sense meant by the average critic I am not photographic. But supposing that in a deeper sense I were? Supposing a young writer turned up and forced me, and some of my contemporaries—us who fancy ourselves a bit—to admit that we had been concerning ourselves unduly with essentials, that we had been worrying ourselves to achieve infantile realisms? Well, that day would be a great and a disturbing day—for us. And we should see what we should see.

New Age, VIII (December 8, 1910), 135. Reprinted under the title "Neo-Impressionism and Literature," *Books and Persons* (New York: George H. Doran Co., 1917), pp. 280–285. The show, entitled "Manet and the Post-Impressionists," was the first exhibition of post-impressionist paintings in London. It was arranged by Roger Fry, and opened at the Grafton Gallery on November 8, 1910.

Chekhov's *Cherry Orchard* (1911)

At last, thanks to the Stage Society, we have had a good representative play of Anton Chekhov on the London stage.[1] Needless to say, Chekhov was done in the provinces long ago. "The Cherry Orchard," I have been told, is Chekhov's dramatic masterpiece, and I can well believe it. But it is a dangerous thing to present foreign masterpieces to a West End audience, and the directors of the Stage Society discovered, or re-discovered, this fact on Sunday night last. The reception of "The Cherry Orchard" was something like what the reception of Ibsen's plays used to be twenty years ago. It was scarcely even a mixed reception. There could be no mistake about the failure of the play to please the vast majority of the members of the Society. At the end of the second act signs of disapproval were very manifest indeed, and the exodus from the theatre began. A competent authority informed me that at the end of the third act half the audience had departed; but in the narrative fever of the moment the competent authority may have slightly exaggerated. Certain it is that multitudes preferred Aldwych and the restaurant-concerts, or even their own homes, to Chekhov's play. And as the evening was the Sabbath you may judge the extreme degree of their detestation of the play.

A director of the Stage Society said to me on the Monday: "If our people won't stand it, it has no chance, because we have the pick here." I didn't contradict him, but I by no means agreed that they had the pick there. The managing committee of the Society is a very enlightened body; but the mass of the members is just as stupid as any other mass. Its virtue is that it pays subscriptions, thus enabling the committee to make experiments and to place before the forty or fifty persons in London who really can judge a play the sort of play which is worthy of curiosity.

1. *The Cherry Orchard* was first performed in London on May 29, 1911. Both the public and the critics disliked the play.

In spite of the antipathy which it aroused, "The Cherry Orchard" is quite inoffensive. For example, there is nothing in it to which the Censor could possibly object. It does not deal specially with sex. It presents an average picture of Russian society. But it presents the picture with such exact, uncompromising truthfulness that the members of the Stage Society mistook nearly all the portraits for caricatures, and tedious caricatures. In naturalism the play is assuredly an advance on any other play that I have seen or that has been seen in England. Its naturalism is positively daring. The author never hesitates to make his personages as ridiculous as in life they would be. In this he differs from every other playwright that I know of. Ibsen, for instance; and Henri Becque.[2] He has carried an artistic convention much nearer to reality, and achieved another step in the evolution of the drama. The consequence is that he is accused of untruth and exaggeration, as Becque was, as Ibsen was. His truthfulness frightens, and causes resentment.

People say: "No such persons exist, or at any rate such persons are too exceptional to form proper material for a work of art." No such persons, I admit, exist in England; but then this play happens to be concerned with Russia, and even the men's costumes in it are appalling. Moreover, persons equally ridiculous and futile do exist in England, and by the hundred thousand; only they are ridiculous and futile in ways familiar to us. I guarantee that if any ten average members of the august Stage Society itself were faithfully portrayed on the stage, with all their mannerisms, absurdities and futilities, the resulting picture would be damned as a gross and offensive caricature. People never look properly at people; people take people for granted; they remain blind to the facts; and when an artist comes along and discloses more of these facts than it is usual to disclose, of course there is a row. This row is a fine thing; it means that something has been done. And I hope that the directors of the Stage Society are proud of the reception of "The Cherry Orchard." They ought to be.

I do not think it is a great play. But it is an intensely original and interesting play. I do not agree with any of the criticisms which

2. Henri Becque (1837–1899), French playwright, known for his portrayal of bourgeois life.

have been passed upon it. It has a theme, and a perfectly plain theme—the break-up of an estate and of a family. It has a plot, and the plot is handled throughout with masterly skill. It is simply crammed with character. Indeed, it has so much characterisation, and unfamiliar characterisation, that an unimaginative audience could not project itself beyond the confusing externalities of the characterisation into the heart of the play. The second act is the least diverting. The first, third and fourth have not a weak moment. The close (more generally praised than any other part of the play) is perhaps somewhat over-theatrical for my realistic taste.

I consider that very great credit is due to the producer, Mr. Kenelm Foss. His task was terrific, and—one or two slight roughnesses apart—he triumphed throughout. Much of the acting was admirable. Mr. Franklyn Dyall as the billiard-playing fool (the heroine's brother) was merely great. Miss Mary Jerrold as the adopted daughter provoked my enthusiasm. Mr. Nigel Playfair as the money-borrowing landowner could not have been surpassed. I did not think that Miss Katharine Pole as the widowed heroine quite ranked with these artists; she had the most difficult rôle of all. The minor parts were well done, some of them admirably done. Take the play in its entirety, and it is one of the most savage and convincing satires on a whole society that was ever seen in the theatre. It is a terrible play. It is a thoroughly unpleasant splendid play. And I am delighted that a fraction of London has had to swallow the pill.

New Age, IX (June 8, 1911), 132.

The Twelve Finest Novels (1927)

Some weeks ago in this place I made the statement that the twelve finest novels are all Russian. I first offered this affront to Western literary opinion fifteen years ago in New York. All the principal newspapers from New York to San Francisco instantly fell upon it, and much opposition was aroused. I have publicly offered it several times since, and trouble, characterised by vituperation, has always ensued—until the last occasion.

So far as I know, the glove has not yet been picked up: which seems to show that the work of Mr. Edward Garnett (the original introducer) and Mrs. Constance Garnett (translator in chief of Russian novels to the Anglo-Saxon publics) has at length produced some effect on a generation not wholly unwilling to learn. Indeed, my remark has been received with sympathy, and I have been asked for "guidance" on the matter.

Of course there is, really, no such dozen as "the twelve finest novels." I spoke "in a manner of speaking." It is impossible to say, for instance, that "The Charterhouse of Parma" is a finer novel than "Pride and Prejudice," or vice versa. Or that "Resurrection" is a finer novel than "The Woodlanders," or vice versa. When a work reaches a certain pitch of fineness, nothing human can with propriety be raised above it. It exists in splendour, and there it is, safe from any comparisons. You deeply enjoy it, you laud it, and you are content with that.

The Russians, however, have this advantage over the rest of the world: that though in breadth of interest and in artistic discipline they fall a little short of the greatest non-Russian achievements, they handsomely excel in the best sort of realism—namely, the realism which is combined with a comprehending charity of judgment. Also, in the main, their creations are more heroical in scale.

No Russian novelist working on a large canvas has yet equalled Balzac in breadth of interest. The curiosity of Chekov was every whit as inclusive as that of Balzac—perhaps even more inclusive. But Chekov never worked on a large canvas. Balzac wrote a novel one of whose chief themes is the French law of bankruptcy, and he made it enthralling. He, at any rate, saw life whole, even if he saw it over-romantically. (I will be courageous, and say outright over-sentimentally!)

The Russians were too absorbed in individual psychology to have time or inclination to worry about the large social problems from which Balzac never shrank. Moreover, in their excuse, it may be argued that the tragi-comic censorship effectively prevented a frank handling of large social problems by Russian writers. There are vast tracts of phenomena affecting the life of human beings which are merely left out of some of the top-notch masterpieces of Russia. I do not remember a single landscape worth mentioning in all Dostoievsky, though there are many in Chekov and some quite superlative ones in Tolstoi and Gogol, who in their turn had a blind eye, or a blinded eye, for other entrancing aspects of existence.

As for artistic discipline, Russian novelists are unquestionably deficient in it. They appear to despise form—except Turgenev, who could assuredly have taught even Henry James how to "organise" a novel. I reckon that Turgenev could say more in fewer words than any other novelist that ever lived. The Russians as a rule are far too prodigal of words, and far too excited about the particular page which they happen to be writing, to the neglect of the main outline of the work. The consequences are sometimes very exasperating to the impatient.

Russian realism stands unique. Probably because it does not occur to a Russian novelist not to be realistic. The unrealists are an enigma to him (and rightly). "Here are the facts," he seems to say. "Why hide them?" But Russian realism is never crude.

Zola was a realist; he gave a complete picture of an entire epoch; he strove to be impartial; his novels are epical. Unfortunately he lacked taste. He is frequently crude. His mind, high though it was, turned too often naturally to the obscene. Worse than this, he lacked sympathy. If he explained the weaknesses of human nature, he did so with a certain chill, disillusioned hostility towards human nature. The Russians are more generally sympathetic. They are not frightened by any manifestation of humanity, as, for example, Thackeray was.

Again and again in "Vanity Fair" you may see Thackeray approaching a difficulty whose solution will demand honesty and bravery, and you ask yourself: "How is he going to get through this?" Well, he doesn't get through it. He curves away from it, or he stops dead. He is a coward. Perhaps his cowardice springs from a good motive—the fear of disgusting you with human nature. But he is a coward all the same. He half-develops situations which at the critical moment he dares not to grapple with.

The Russians have no qualms about disgusting you with human nature, for they are not themselves disgusted with it. They understand; they forgive; they love. They compel you to do the same. There is a Christ-like quality in the finest Russian fiction.

Next week I will try to enumerate the twelve Russian novels which I would place at the head of the world's fiction.

Those twelve finest novels in the world, all Russian!

Details. Twenty-five years ago I would have begun with Turgenev; but in those days Dostoievsky had not been adequately or even decently translated. Now, whenever my mind dwells on the greatest achievements in fiction, I think, before any other novel, of "The Brothers Karamazov." I read this first in French, and though the translation was mediocre in quality and most grossly mutilated, I came immediately to a very definite conclusion about the book.

I had never met with anything so vast and comprehensive in scale, so consistently powerful, so profound, so beautiful, so tragic, so moral, so philosophical in intention and execution, so convincing, so enthralling. Later, I read it twice in the complete English translation, and my estimate of it was thereby only raised.

I am willing to concede arguments to the effect that Einstein is endowed with the most prodigious intellect in the history of the race, that Shakespeare stands alone, and that Abraham Lincoln stands alone; but I implacably affirm that a greater novel (in our modern sense of the word "novel") than "The Brothers Karamazov" has yet to be written. It will be written—I doubt not, for I have a dogmatic belief in progress.

Further, I rate "The Idiot" little lower than "The Brothers." "The Idiot" is lovely; its closing pages are the summit of simple majesty. A still lovelier book, and a much shorter, is "The House of the Dead." "The House of the Dead" is chiefly a record of experiences. If you choose you may decline to class it as a novel. It is, in my opinion, the most celestial restorative of damaged faith in human nature that any artist ever produced. The most successful and touching demonstration of the truth that man is not vile.

Fourthly, "Crime and Punishment," the best-known of the four, a novel which cannot possibly be omitted from the dozen. The objectors to Dostoievsky say that he was an epileptic. Well, he was. And what of it? They say also that he was morbid. This I deny. He was an imperfect person; he made a mess of his life; he suffered terrible trials; he was continuously hard up for a hundred roubles. But none of these things made him morbid; his outlook upon the world was always sane, undistorted, and kindly. He loved men.

Now Tolstoi. He wrote three terrific novels: "Anna Karenina" and "War and Peace" when he was young, and "Resurrection" when he had passed the climacteric. All three took Europe and America by the neck, and they have never in the slightest degree relaxed their hold on the imagination of the Western world—"Anna Karenina" by its pathos, "War and Peace" by its sweeping grandeur, "Resurrection" by its overpowering moral lesson, and all by their sheer mighty force.

You cannot get away from these books. They force themselves instantly into any general discussion of the novel. Everybody who has read them remembers them, and admits their sway; and those who haven't read them must either pretend to have read them or submit to being thrown out of the argument with contumely.

The mind of Tolstoi is harder, less sympathetic, less exquisitely compassionate than that of Dostoievsky. But his regard for truth was not inferior; the general level of his creative power was perhaps slightly higher—at any rate, his methods of presentation are more readily effective, because less subtle and indirect; also, he had a better sense of form, and far more discipline, than Dostoievsky. After a course of Dostoievsky you may be inclined to think that Tolstoi is relatively commonplace, banal, vulgar, material. But go back to Tolstoi, and you will once more be his helpless and contented victim.

I have now already mentioned seven books. Exclude any one of them from the dozen and what non-Russian work could you have the effrontery to put in its place? I cannot guess, unless it be a Stendhal. Would you dare to oust any one of them in favour of a Dickens?

Turgenev. He no longer has the vogue of twenty-five years ago among the British intelligentsia. Russians never admired him as they admired Dostoievsky and Tolstoi, or even Gogol. I think that as a rule the compatriots of a writer are his best judges. (The exception to the rule is America, which for quite irrelevant reasons seriously under-rates Poe and Whitman, and which respects Hawthorne for his secondary qualities. No finer prose than Hawthorne's was written in the nineteenth century. George Moore first made me see this, by quotations.)

I accept the verdict of Russia on Turgenev, but I imagine that it may be somewhat vitiated by a political or social prejudice. Still, no Russian would contend that Turgenev was not among the world's greatest. He cannot so powerfully move me as Dostoievsky and Tolstoi, but he was certainly a more finished artist than either of his contemporaries. Everything that he did shows a superb perfection— even in English. What form, what control of the vehicle, what grace, what tenderness!

I would name "Torrents of Spring" (better entitled "Spring Floods"), "Virgin Soil," "On the Eve," and "Fathers and Children." They are all short. The longest, "Virgin Soil," is, I fancy, shorter than the shortest Tolstoi or Dostoievsky, except "The House of the Dead." "Torrents of Spring" is youthful—the most romantic expression of young love. "Virgin Soil" and "Fathers and Children" mark an epoch in the sociological development of the novel. "On the Eve" is the quietest, most insinuating, most beautiful thing ever done.

All these books are classics. They do not take you by the neck. They steal around you, envelop you; they impregnate you.

Gogol.—He wrote only one novel (unless "Taras Bulba" is long enough to count as a novel)—and even that he left very far from finished—"Dead Souls." Despite the indignities which it has suffered in various translations (not the latest English translation), and at the hands of misguided individuals who had the impudence to finish it, "Dead Souls" has taken its place in all Europe as a comic, ironic masterpiece of the first order.

It is a rollicking and murderous satire, and must have directly or indirectly influenced all later novelists who have castigated their country because they loved it—yes, down the decades of a century as far as Sinclair Lewis! "Dead Souls" is gorgeous reading. It is the greatest lark imaginable, and withal deadly. Nothing better of its kind exists. (I do not, however, rank it as Gogol's very best. I would give that place to his long-short story, "The Overcoat.")

That makes twelve.

Evening Standard, March 10, 1927, p. 5; March 27, 1927, p. 5. Reprinted under the title "Russian Fiction," *The Savour of Life* (New York: Doubleday, 1928), pp. 127–135.

On Re-reading the English Novelists (1927)

I

A journalist of the first importance, and of mature years, said to me the other day that when he went for a holiday he usually took with him novels that he had read before, and read them again. He mentioned no titles, but I believe that he confined himself to English novels. The remark made me realise how heterodox I am in these grave matters. I can read certain English poems over again. But if I went away with only English novels I should feel that I was terribly cut off from the great world. In the frightful, but fortunately rare, ordeal of a holiday, I insist on having foreign novels as an aid to keeping my reason.

I have read the following novels three times, and I may well read them again: Balzac's "Cousin Bette" and "The Curé of Tours," Zola's "Nana," Charles Louis Philippe's "Bubu de Montparnasse," de Maupassant's "Pierre and Jean," Dostoievsky's "The Brothers Karamazov." These titles occur to me at once. There are other foreign novels which I may have read twice or thrice. And, among English novels, I have read some Hardy and some George Moore twice. But as for English novels in general, even the masterpieces are rendered insular for me by our racial sentimentality and prudery, and few of them indeed would I read again except for a cash payment.

Our pre-nineteenth century novels, like those of other countries, are too old-fashioned to be enjoyable. The novel as we know it only began in 1830, when Balzac began "The Human Comedy" series. Defoe? Defoe was wonderful—for his time. I have not read "Robinson Crusoe" since boyhood's omnivorous, gluttonous days, and I doubt if I shall re-open it. The other Defoe novels, such as "Moll Flanders" and "Roxana," are too bald and bony to be attractive reading. They are neither sentimental nor prudish, but they have the aridity of reporting. They leave too much out. They lack warmth.

Richardson? No; Richardson is 75 per cent. boring. Life is far longer than it used to be, but it is still far too short for "Clarissa." Smollett? Certainly not. Too rough-and-tumble. Amusing only in spots. Fielding? Yes. His three principal novels have the wide-world quality, and "Tom Jones" is not much superior to the other two.

Sterne? Yes. I might get through "Tristram Shandy" once more; but it is too individual and capricious an expression of its author to count seriously as a picture of any world. Swift? Well, "Gulliver's Travels" is mighty stuff, but not in our sense a novel. For that it is too fantastic, and its aim too exclusively and ferociously satiric. Goldsmith? Not primarily a novelist; but "The Vicar of Wakefield," innocent of all construction though it be, is a pleasing enough piece of sentimentality.

Scott I will not now read. He was an original force; he brought something that was almost new into the novel. He changed the novel. He deserved his immense vogue. But his importance has now dwindled to the historic. The trouble with Scott is that he had the country-gentleman mind, which is admirable in its proper sphere, but unsuited to a creative artist. If he knew anything about women (which I doubt) he took care to keep the knowledge out of his novels. His ingenuousness is touching, but it is also tiresome. And he was long-winded as nobody ever was since the interminable author of "The Grand Cyrus."[1] I once read "Waverley," because I was determined to read it—being in those days young and strong and obstinate. But during the last pages I was still asking myself: "When is this book going to begin?" Yet there are people of my age who, I am informed, read all Scott every year. Their scant spare time must be given almost exclusively to snatching hasty meals and getting a wink of sleep. I admit that about two-thirds of "The Heart of Midlothian" is extremely powerful; but the remaining third declines and falls off like the Roman Empire—only much less excitingly.

Maria Edgeworth? Certainly not. She merely cannot be read.

1. *Artamène, ou le Grand Cyrus*, a ten-volume romance (pub. 1649–1653) by Madeleine de Scudéry (1607–1701).

Fanny Burney? Bright in parts. Unreadable in the mass. But what could you expect from the astounding foolishness of a young woman who ruined her whole life in order to be a functionary and slave at the dullest court since the court of the singular Spaniard who built the Escurial? The poor thing had no sense and no sense of proportion. She had a sharp eye for the minor comicalities of existence. But the full equipment of the first-rate novelist she did not possess. More, she had, I imagine, no conception of what the full equipment must be.

Jane Austen? I feel that I am approaching dangerous ground. The reputation of Jane Austen is surrounded by cohorts of defenders who are ready to do murder for their sacred cause. They are nearly all fanatics. They will not listen. If anybody "went for" Jane, anything might happen to him. He would assuredly be called on to resign from his clubs. I do not want to resign from my clubs. I would sooner perjure myself. On the other hand I do not want to "go for" Jane. I like Jane. I have read several Janes more than once. And in the reading of Jane's novels there happens to be that which can only happen in the work of a considerable author. I mean that first you prefer one novel, then you prefer another novel, and so on. Time was when I convinced myself that "Persuasion" was her master-piece, with "Emma" a good second. Now I am inclined to join the populace and put "Pride and Prejudice" in the front, with "Mans-field Park" a good second.

But listening to the more passionate Janeites (and among them are some truly redoubtable persons), one receives the impression that in their view Jane and Shakespeare are the only two English authors who rightly count, and that Shakespeare is joined with her chiefly as a concession to the opinion of centuries. I do not subscribe to this heated notion. I do not even agree that Jane was a great novelist. She was a great little novelist. She is marvellous, intoxicating: she has unique wit, vast quantities of common-sense, a most agreeable sense of proportion, much humanity, much narrative skill. And she is always readable.

But her world is a tiny world, and even of that tiny world she ignores, consciously or unconsciously, the fundamental factors. She did not know enough of the world to be a great novelist. She had not the ambition to be a great novelist. She knew her place; her present "fans" do not know her place, and their antics would without doubt have excited Jane's lethal irony. I should say that either Emily or Charlotte Brontë was a bigger novelist than Jane. The hallowed name of Brontë brings me into the Victorian era of fiction, concerning which I will, if I still survive, enrage the earnest orthodox next week.

II

Last week I threatened remarks on Victorian novelists. The moment has come. First I wish to correct an apparent misapprehension. I have no bias against the Victorians. I am a Victorian myself. I spent the twenty-four most impressive years of my life under influences which were mainly, if not exclusively, Victorian. I am a faithful admirer of the Victorian age. I think it one of the greatest, perhaps the greatest, age in English history. I am a faithful admirer of its finest poets, men of science, philosophers, historians. I think that some of them are still under-rated. Tennyson, for instance, Matthew Arnold, Huxley, Carlyle, and Stubbs.[2] Tennyson is now under-rated. Matthew Arnold was never put high enough; nor Huxley, nor Stubbs.

I also admire the finest Victorian novelists. And the fact that I upbraid them is no proof that I do not regard them as very considerable persons. I am capable of upbraiding Shakespeare. If I deal chiefly with novelists, the reason is that fiction happens to be my specialty. Of late I have largely occupied myself, in print, with modern novelists. But that does not prevent me from highly appreciating other kinds of modern work. I may mention Dr. and Mrs. Beard's "Rise of American Civilisation" (Cape), and Miss Mayo's "Mother India" (Cape, too), in my opinion books which are likely to be as influential, and valuable, as any novels written or to be written between 1907 and 1947.

Dickens. Dickens was a great creative genius. I admit it, while saying plainly that since I was less of a boy than I am to-day I have never been able to read a novel of Dickens from beginning to end. With one exception, "A Tale of Two Cities," which I undertook to

2. William Stubbs (1825–1901), English historian and author of *Constitutional History of England* (1874–1878).

read and write about for a monetary consideration. The task was desolating. My objections to Dickens are that he had a common mind and an inferior style, and that his novels are very patchy. And how should they not be patchy, seeing that he so often wrote against time?

His plots are childish, his sentimentality is nauseating. That he had a kind heart and a democratic passion for justice is quite beside the point. Many hundredth-rate novelists have had kind hearts and a passion for justice. On the other hand he was a superlatively successful creator of comic characters, and nobody but a genius could have written his best scenes of comedy. These scenes are rich; they are full of the juice of English humour. But in order to get at them, what a price you must pay in tedium! I will not pay the price. The purse of my patience is too shallow. Why should I spend my time on Dickens when I can derive a pleasure almost unmixed from reading Thomas Hardy or George Moore?

Thackeray. Now, Thackeray was very naughty. He had more education and more taste than Dickens. Dickens did not sin against the light. Thackeray did. "Vanity Fair" is a great novel. Yes, I think it is. But the compromises between falsity and truth which disfigure it, the evasions, the omissions, the shirkings of difficulties—these things are unworthy of any serious artist, much more of a great artist. The man knew what he was doing, and he did it deliberately. He wanted to be loved more than he wanted a clear artistic conscience. And he was cursed by a certain smugness.

As for his other chief works, "Pendennis" can assuredly be read. "Barry Lyndon" is perhaps his most satisfactory book. "Esmond" is a tour de force. After reading it I had to go away to recuperate; but I did read it. "The Newcomes" cannot be read. "The Virginians"—the thought of its dullness and deadness appals the spirit. Thackeray created brilliantly a few unsympathetic characters. But he was a Snowdon compared to Dickens's Ben Nevis. The Himalayas are not English.

The Brontës. I will leave out Anne, who was a mere sister. I would rank both Emily and Charlotte as bigger people than Thackeray. They had a fundamental power fully equal to Thackeray's. And in addition they had a sense of beauty which heaven denied to him, and a sense of the romantic quality of life which he could not approach. When I think of the Valkyrie Charlotte being nervous and tongue-tied in the presence of a prim warrior like Thackeray, with his fondness for armistices, I at once try to think of something else. I regard "Wuthering Heights" as the summit of feminine attainment in fiction. "La Princesse de Clèves" is marvellously distinguished, but seems slight after the colossal affair of Emily. "Wuthering Heights," by its beauty, grandeur, and romance holds me as no novel by Scott could.

As for Charlotte, "Jane Eyre," "Villette," and "Shirley" are all fine, extremely fine, and the first two come as near to Emily's lonely masterpiece as any work by any woman ever did. If the word genius is applicable to any writers it is applicable to Emily and Charlotte. What fire! What loveliness! What creative force! What invention! What style! Had destiny given them a fair chance, instead of installing them in an ecclesiastical drawing-room whose windows overlooked a country churchyard, what could they not have accomplished! Their trouble was that they knew not enough of the world. Charlotte learnt more of it than Emily; but both were inadequately furnished with external inspiration. They lacked perspective, and the fault was heaven's, not theirs. Miraculous creatures, however, they were. The other major Victorians must stand over for seven days.

III

I must now finish the chief Victorian novelists left over from last week. The Brontës ended my previous article.

George Eliot. The excellent and somewhat formidable creature, after basking—she and her ghost between them—in a prodigious popularity for many years, is now an exile among the Neglected. (But she may well one day be received again with bay-leaves and triumphal arches.) I have an idea that her temporary fate is the result of her most imposing books, "Romola " and "Daniel Deronda." She had built big houses, and she said to herself that she would build bigger and still bigger. But these were houses of the dead. Indeed, the inhabitants of the two tremendous edifices never came to life. They were born whole, born mature, but born dead.

Thus all the learning and the historical imagination and the philosophy and the invention which went to the making of the monuments were thrown away. Happily their author never learnt the sad fact; for both books had immense sales in their time. They are probably still bought, but my information about human nature prevents me from believing that they are still read.

The earlier books are a different matter. George Eliot began late and she began well. No woman novelist has had a better equipment for the grand enterprise of fiction. She was highly educated; she had a fine mind, which she both refined and broadened by study; her knowledge enabled her to correct her notions of the present by reference to the past: and throughout the years of ardent preparation she managed to preserve intact her sense of humour.

She was nearly forty when "Scenes of Clerical Life" appeared and was half-drowned in merited praise. You can enjoy even to-day "Scenes from Clerical Life," but only on one condition. You must abandon relatives and friends, and all ties, and all other interests, and yield yourself totally and utterly to the preliminary long-windedness of the author. If you can accomplish this feat of renunciation you will not arrive at the close of her first volume of fiction without being convinced that you have read something.

She then wrote three really admirable novels: "Adam Bede," "The Mill on the Floss," and "Silas Marner." What the faults of these books are I really don't know. They have form, creative power, pathos, humour, honesty, beauty, style, and a definite point of view. Some of the characters have become typical. They are solid works. Nothing flimsy about them. The themes are handled with thoroughness. What else do you want?

Then, after she had failed to learn the stiff lesson of "Romola," artistic ambition overweened in the unhappy lady, and she wrote "Middlemarch." I read a lot of "Middlemarch" not long ago, and I assert that solid it is not. Chapter after chapter starts splendidly, sinks into clever dialogue, and passes away into nothing at all, without having advanced the story one inch. Then she failed to learn the equally stiff lesson of "Middlemarch," and went and did "Daniel Deronda." It was a pity. For "Daniel Deronda" seems to have fallen down on "Adam Bede" and crushed the lovely thing deep into the earth.

But "Adam Bede" will be disinterred. I think it was "Adam Bede" that the impulsive Charles Reade pronounced to be "the finest thing since Shakespeare." A wild verdict. But Reade knew a book when he saw it. (And, by the way, he also wrote two superb historical novels, one long, one short: "The Cloister and the Hearth," and "Peg Woffington." I read the latter recently. It survived brilliantly. So did I. I am afraid to come to grips with "The Cloister and the Hearth" again, lest a horrid disillusion might darken the afternoon of my existence.) My admiration for George Eliot has been rising of late years.

There is a small but influential cult for Lord Beaconsfield. The rites of the cult are performed in private; but I have assisted at them —without actual initiation. I like Beaconsfield because he was such a grandiose adventurer, not merely in politics, but with a pen. He wrote "Vivian Grey" at eighteen, and the reader of it would guess the author's age in the first eighteen pages. As a boy I took the sketches in "Ixion" for matchless satire. I have read most of the mature novels. The trouble with Beaconsfield as an artist is that he was a statesman who diverted himself with fiction instead of being a novelist who diverted himself with politics. He created an empress, but I doubt if he created anybody else.

A fellow of terrific energy, variety, shameless flatteries, and bluff, he composed novels as he might have composed symphonies had the idea occurred to him. He revelled in his own gifts. Too often, as you read, you are inclined to complain "This Oriental artificer is not writing a novel, he is just larking around." The animadversion would be just.

His best things are his worst: glorious fustian such as the descriptions *de luxe* in "Lothair." Every few pages he gets drunk, wonders where the devil he is, and pulls himself together like a gentleman. Withal, he had moral passions and political vision, together with an informed sympathy for the under-dog. The sermons implied or direct in his novels are sound enough. None of his books is consistently good, and none consistently bad. I think that "Lothair" and "Sybil" are the most satisfactory to read *in*. Among the best is "Endymion": perhaps that was why it failed.

Another secret cult has taken possession of Captain Marryat, who must be mentioned among Victorian novelists. His worst books have an individual quality. His best are fun as gorgeous as you will find.

Lastly Trollope. Trollope is on the crest of the wave. He has been in some danger of classification as the greatest of the Victorians. He is not that. He had neither genius nor style. But he was a worker and a realist and a non-sentimentalist, and he knew what life is. His pictures of Victorian manners are far more exact and various and complete than those of either Thackeray or Dickens. There was no nonsense about him. Unfortunately when he had once begun a novel he drove right on, up hill and down dale like a Roman road, and no doubts or hesitations or artistic scruples would stop him or even slacken his speed. Four miles an hour, no more and no less, the whole time.

This is no way to write a first-rate novel. He did not write one. His dullness and his clumsiness are frequently extreme, his demands on the reader's forbearance are ruthless. His novels will not, I am convinced, survive. But for the present he insists on being read. He cannot be ignored. Possibly in fifty years our unimaginative posterity will be saying of us: "How could they read such tedious drabness?" Never mind!

I have not discussed him who is conceivably the greatest of the Victorians. Of course I mean Thomas Hardy. He lives, and is thereby spared the infliction.

Evening Standard, July 21, 1927, p. 5; July 28, 1927, p. 5; August 4, 1927, p. 5.

Explanation (1928)

About a year ago Lord Birkenhead, with that impulsive naiveté which charms and sometimes alarms his friends, galloped into the columns of the *Daily Mail* with accusations against novelists— especially H. G. Wells and myself—of dealing too faithfully with statesmen. I replied. Lord Birkenhead, accustomed to the facile triumphs of the bar and of legislative Chambers, apparently had not foreseen what would be awaiting him in an arena where conditions are absolutely equal for both parties to an encounter. I need not describe the fray. Part of it is reproduced in the present book. The only point relevant to this Explanation is Lord Birkenhead's complaint that "the imaginative novelist now arrogates to himself the right to disparage the work of men (i.e., politicians) who have done things."

Which reminds me of the year 1915, when by official request I went to the Front in order to describe British activities there for the good of the American public. A general impudently greeted me thus: "So you've come to watch other people do things!" I merely said: "Yes," but I added other remarks with my tone and my eye. The general afterwards apologised to me, quite voluntarily.

I have referred to the episode between Lord Birkenhead and myself because I wish to re-state emphatically that novelists do indeed arrogate to themselves the right to treat, disparagingly or otherwise, all mundane phenomena without exception. Novelists capable and desirous of doing so have always arrogated to themselves this right. There has been no change in recent years.

But the question is much larger than that. Novelists arrogate to themselves the right to extend their activities beyond the novel. They arrogate to themselves the right to be journalists. For myself, I began as a journalist, I have never ceased to be a journalist, and I have no intention of ceasing to be a journalist. I am often informed by journalists who cannot write novels that a novelist is not entitled to meddle in public affairs. I do not agree, and I lose no opportunity of saying so. Lawyers, doctors, other professional men, men of business, financiers, and many assorted adventurers and rascals arrogate to themselves the right to meddle in public affairs and incidentally to do quite a lot of disparagement; and I can conceive no reason why novelists alone should be debarred. I admit that it may be inconvenient for certain persons when novelists intervene who are really expert in the use of a pen; but what of that?

And the question is even larger. I hold that a novelist is entitled to handle all different kinds of topics. According to my theory, the same novelist is entitled to write on high politics and literature and the fine arts in high-brow periodicals with a select circulation, and also to appeal on common daily subjects to vast publics in news-papers with a circulation of a couple of millions. Why not? If thereby he demonstrates that he does not know what he is talking about, so much the worse for the novelist. He will pay in loss of prestige for his folly. The publicists who get angry because a writer who discusses, say, the work of Henry James dares to discuss also a prize-fighter or diet bring a smile to my face.

Many years ago I wrote a series of articles on the daily organiza-tion of time for the *Evening News*. They excited considerable interest. When I proposed to republish them in book form I was most strongly urged not to do so, and terrible prophecies were made to me of the sinister consequences to my reputation if I did. I republished them. "How to live on twenty-four hours a day" sold very well from the start; it still has a steady sale, and it has brought me more letters of appreciation than all my other books put together. I followed it up with a dozen or more books in a similar vein. And I do not suppose that my reputation would have been any less dreadful than it is if I had never published a line for plain people about the management of daily existence.

There remains the charge of pot-boiling. I have never expressed opinions that I do not hold; nor have I ever been asked to express such opinions. Life for me has many savours, which I relish keenly. Therefore many subjects interest me. I never write on a subject which does not interest me, and I always write as well as heaven permits. Nevertheless, journalists who are not novelists accuse me about once a week of pot-boiling. The argument is not stated very clearly; but it seems to amount to this: first, that a man who has written long realistic novels which have met with approval ought not, if he is a serious artist, to write anything but long realistic novels; second, that a man who can make a livelihood out of writing novels ought to confine himself to novels, because if he goes outside them he will make more money. Personally, I cannot see that a writer ought not to write what he wants to write simply because the result of his doing so would be an increase in his income. I write for money. I write for as much money as I can get. Shakespeare and Balzac did the same. I might, of course, give my articles to newspapers gratis. (I do sometimes.) But why should I? And are reviews of books pot-boilers, or are they not?

The essays in this volume are extremely various, in both subject and style. It was on the guiding principle of extreme variety that I selected them out of a large mass of essays. My wish was to show to those whom it may concern what rights a novelist is, in my opinion, entitled to arrogate to himself.

Introduction to *The Savour of Life* (New York: Doubleday, 1928).

The Born Reviewer (1930)

Constantly I am receiving advice, chiefly by letter, as to the proper way to review books. My counsellors seem (1) to be young (2) to regard me as an amateur. A few weeks ago I got a whole circular of hints (unsigned). Every hint was quite silly, except one which ran thus: "Don't be too literary and devote columns to a memoir about some long-forgotten writer (like Leigh Hunt) whom no one has ever read or wants to read." I admit that I heartily agree with the hinter on this point. But then I have never done what he ordered me not to do; and to see precious space wasted weekly on authors who though unburied are shockingly dead, exasperates me at least as much as it could exasperate my caustic anonymous mentor. While granting the validity of his complaint against the too prevalent habit of mauling corpses, I wish to inform the complainant and indeed the entire review-reading world, that I am not an amateur reviewer. On the contrary if there is a born reviewer writing to-day I am he.

Forty years ago, when I was free-lancing, I wrote a review of a book by an obscure French author and sent it in to "The Illustrated London News." Nothing more ignorantly foolish than such a journalistic proceeding could be conceived. As if editors of great papers accepted from outsiders reviews of books of no importance whatever! Still, the review was accepted. It did not appear for many weeks, and I spent a large part of my remuneration (15s.) in vainly buying issues of the paper week after week at sixpence a time; but it did at last appear.

Again, I wrote a review of Edward Carpenter's "Towards Democracy" and sent it to "The Weekly Star" (long dead). "Towards Democracy" was even then an old book. Nevertheless the review was accepted. Again I wrote stylistic news-paragraphs about forthcoming books, and sold dozens of them to "The Daily Chronicle" (at 3s. 6d.—or was it 2s. 6d.—apiece). But did "The Daily Chronicle," then the Thunderer of literature, ever invite me to do reviews for it? Did "The Weekly Star"? Did "The Illustrated London News"? No, no and no.

Nevertheless I became a reviewer for another weekly paper, and I have found my reviews quoted in books about authors a quarter of a century later. How did I get the job? Very simply. By being assistant-editor, then editor, and always a debenture-holder, of the paper. I gave the job to myself, and by the easy device of being a shareholder of another paper, I obtained another reviewing job. I have reviewed a thousand books in three years. Even the most modern reviewers, in these efficient days of large-scale rationalisation of reviewing, can hardly beat that. But did any other papers invite me to do their reviews? They did not.

Then I asked "The Academy" for work: the only occasion in my life when I have lowered myself so far as to ask any editor for any job! "The Academy" answered my prayer. My reviews were the talk of the few hundred people who call themselves "the town," and I succeeded in raising the "Academy's" space rate from half-a-guinea to fifteen shillings a column. But something sinister happened, not to me but to the paper, and I wrote no more for it.

And then arrived the marvellous day when the editor of "The New Age" called on me and implored me to write reviews for him. It was too good to be true. I am bound to say that he said he couldn't pay me anything. Still, it was too good to be true. I consented. These reviews genuinely did flutter the dovecots. So much so that people might be observed reading them while crossing Fleet Street; and the editor, who was nothing if not munificent, began to shower on me weekly cheques of one pound one shilling each. Great days! Then something sinister happened to "The New Age" also. I ought to mention that years after I republished a selection of these reviews in volume-form, and the book sold like editions of evening papers containing the winner and s.p. of the 3:30.

But did any other editors invite me to do reviews? Certainly not. So I took seriously to writing novels and plays, and the mandarins of Fleet Street told me what a fool I was to try to write fiction when my obvious bent was criticism. And now, when I have taken once more to reviewing, well-meaning persons tell me what a fool I am, and what impudence I display, to try to write criticism when my obvious bent is fiction. There is a saying that you can't please everybody. Well, I have always done all I honestly could do to please everybody: I have never succeeded; and I shall never cease this Christian endeavour. With one exception. If I displease anybody by denying that I am an amateur reviewer, I shall stoutly continue in the denial, and anybody can be as displeased as he chooses.

Reviewing has changed since the early nineties when I began. It has changed for the better. In those days it was on the whole as bad as it is to-day in most of the leading American papers. It is better informed and better written (because editors are more keen in their search for reviewers); it gets itself more talked about, is better paid, and is more punctual than of old. I can recall the spacious age when a review would appear six months or even twelve months after the publication of the book. And no one seemed to perceive anything odd in this majestic dilatoriness. The publication of a book was not news then. To-day it is news. Therein lies the literary difference between the twentieth and the nineteenth centuries. Why does the publication of a book constitute news now? Because the public is more interested—or less uninterested—in literature than it used to be. There cannot be any other reason.

I intended to write an article about the nature, scope, difficulties, influence, and general high importance of book-reviewing as a vocation. Whereas I have written only the introduction to such an article. The explanation is that when writers start to write about themselves they are always long-winded. But later in the summer, when I have cleared off the new novel by H. G. Wells and a few other major items, I shall return to the subject.

Evening Standard, July 10, 1930, p. 5. The original title was "I Am Not an Amateur Reviewer."

Appendix
Virginia Woolf's "Mr. Bennett and Mrs. Brown" (First Version, 1923)

The other day Mr. Arnold Bennett, himself one of the most famous of the Edwardians, surveyed the younger generation and said: "I admit that for myself I cannot yet descry any coming big novelist." And that, let us say in passing, is all to the good—a symptom of the respectful hostility which is the only healthy relation between old and young. But then he went on to give his reasons for this lamentable fact, and his reasons, which lie deep, deserve much more consideration than his impatience, which lies on the surface. The Georgians fail as novelists, he said, because "they are interested more in details than in the full creation of their individual characters. . . . The foundation of good fiction is character-creating, and nothing else. To render secure the importance of a novel it is necessary, further, that these characters should clash with one another," or, of course, they will excite no emotion in the breast of the author or anybody else. None of this is new; all of it is true; yet here we have one of those simple statements which are no sooner taken into the mind than they burst their envelopes and flood us with suggestions of every kind.

The novel is a very remarkable machine for the creation of human character, we are all agreed. Directly it ceases to create character, its defects alone are visible. And it is because this essence, this character-making power, has evaporated that novels are for the most part the soulless bodies we know cumbering our tables and clogging our minds. That, too, may pass. Few reviewers at least are likely to dispute it. But if we go on to ask when this change began, and what were the reasons behind it, then agreement is much more difficult to come by. Mr. Bennett blames the Georgians. Our minds

269

fly straight to King Edward. Surely that was the fatal age, the age
which is just breaking off from our own, the age when character
disappeared or was mysteriously engulfed, and the culprits, happily
still alive, active, and unrepentant, are Mr. Wells, Mr. Galsworthy,
and Mr. Bennett himself.

But in lodging such a charge against so formidable a library, we
must do as painters do when they wish to reduce the innumerable
details of a crowded landscape to simplicity—step back, half shut
the eyes, gesticulate a little vaguely with the fingers, and reduce
Edwardian fiction to a view. Thus treated, one strange fact is
immediately apparent. Every sort of town is represented, and
innumerable institutions; we see factories, prisons, workhouses, law
courts, Houses of Parliament; a general clamour, the voice of
aspiration, indignation, effort and industry, rises from the whole;
but in all this vast conglomeration of printed pages, in all this
congeries of streets and houses, there is not a single man or woman
whom we know. Figures like Kipps or the sisters (already nameless)
in the "Old Wives' Tale" attempt to contradict this assertion, but
with how feeble a voice and how flimsy a body is apparent directly
they are stood beside some character from that other great tract of
fiction which lies immediately behind them in the Victorian age.
For there, if we follow the same process, but recall one novel, and
that—"Pendennis"—not one of the most famous, at once start out,
clear, vigorous, alive from the curl of their eyelashes to the soles of
their boots, half-a-dozen characters whose names are no sooner
spoken than we think of scene after scene in which they play their
parts. We see the Major sitting in his club window, fresh from the
hands of Morgan; Helen nursing her son in the Temple and suspect-
ing poor Fanny; Warrington grilling chops in his dressing-gown;
Captain Shandon scribbling leaders for the "Pall Mall Gazette"—
Laura, Blanche Amory, Foker; the procession is endless and alive.
And so it goes on from character to character all through the
splendid opulence of the Victorian age. They love, they joke, they
hunt, they marry; they lead us from hall to cottage, from field to
slum. The whole country, the whole society, is revealed to us, and
revealed always in the same way, through the astonishing vividness
and reality of the characters.

And it was perhaps on that very account that the Edwardians changed their tactics. Such triumphs could scarcely be rivalled; and, moreover, triumphs once achieved seem to the next generation always a little uninteresting. There was, too (if we think ourselves into the mind of a writer contemplating fiction about the year 1900) something plausible, superficial, unreal in all this abundance. No sooner had the Victorians departed than Samuel Butler, who had lived below-stairs, came out, like an observant bootboy, with the family secrets in "The Way of All Flesh." It appeared that the basement was really in an appalling state. Though the saloons were splendid and the dining rooms portentous, the drains were of the most primitive description. The social state was a mass of corruption. A sensitive man like Mr. Galsworthy could scarcely step out of doors without barking his shins upon some social iniquity. A generous mind which knew the conditions in which the Kipps and the Lewishams were born and bred must try at least to fashion the world afresh. So the young novelist became a reformer, and thought with pardonable contempt of those vast Victorian family parties, where the funny man was always funny, the good woman always good, and nobody seemed aware, as they pursued their own tiny lives, that society was rotten and Christianity itself was at stake. But there was another force which made much more subtly against the creation of character, and that was Mrs. Garnett and her translations from Dostoievsky. After reading "Crime and Punishment" and "The Idiot," how could any young novelist believe in "characters" as the Victorians had painted them? For the undeniable vividness of so many of them is the result of their crudity. The character is rubbed into us indelibly because its features are so few and so prominent. We are given the keyword (Mr. Dick has King Charles's head; Mr. Brooke, "I went into that a great deal at one time"; Mrs. Micawber, "I will never desert Mr. Micawber"), and then, since the choice of the keyword is astonishingly apt, our imaginations swiftly supply the rest. But what keyword could be applied to Raskolnikov, Mishkin, Stavrogin, or Alyosha? These are characters without any features at all. We go down into them as we descend into some enormous cavern. Lights swing about; we hear the boom of the sea; it is all dark, terrible, and uncharted. So we need not be surprised if the Edwardian novelist scarcely attempted to deal with character except in its more generalized aspects. The Victorian version was discredited; it was his duty to destroy all those institutions in the shelter of which character thrives and thickens; and the Russians had shown him—everything or nothing, it was impossible as yet to say which. The Edwardian novelists therefore gave us a vast sense of things in general; but a very vague one of things in particular. Mr. Galsworthy gives us a sense of compassion; Mr. Wells fills us with generous enthusiasm; Mr. Bennett (in his early work) gave us a sense of time. But their books are already a little chill, and must steadily grow more distant, for "the foundation of good fiction is character-creating, and nothing else," as Mr. Bennett says; and in none of them are we given a man or woman whom we know.

The Georgians had, therefore, a difficult task before them, and if they failed, as Mr. Bennett asserts, there is nothing to surprise us in that. To bring back character from the shapelessness into which it has lapsed, to sharpen its edges, deepen its compass, and so make possible those conflicts between human beings which alone arouse our strongest emotions—such was their problem. It was the consciousness of this problem, and not the accession of King George, which produced, as it always produces, the break between one generation and the next. Here, however, the break is particularly sharp, for here the dispute is fundamental. In real life there is nothing that interests us more than character, that stirs us to the same extremes of love and anger, or that leads to such incessant and laborious speculations about the values, the reasons, and the meaning of existence itself. To disagree about character is to differ in the depths of the being. It is to take different sides, to drift apart, to accept a purely formal intercourse for ever. That is so in real life. But the novelist has to go much further and to be much more uncompromising than the friend. When he finds himself hopelessly at variance with Mr. Wells, Mr. Galsworthy, and Mr. Bennett about the character—shall we say?—of Mrs. Brown, it is useless to defer to their superior genius. It is useless to mumble the polite agreements of the drawing-room. He must set about to remake the woman after his own idea. And that, in the circumstances, is a very perilous pursuit.

For what, after all, is character—the way that Mrs. Brown, for instance, reacts to her surroundings—when we cease to believe what we are told about her, and begin to search out her real meaning for ourselves? In the first place, her solidity disappears; her features crumble; the house in which she has lived so long (and a very substantial house it was) topples to the ground. She becomes a will-o'-the-wisp, a dancing light, an illumination gliding up the wall and out of the window, lighting now in freakish malice upon the nose of an archbishop, now in sudden splendour upon the mahogany of the wardrobe. The most solemn sights she turns to ridicule; the most ordinary she invests with beauty. She changes the shape, shifts the accent, of every scene in which she plays her part. And it is from the ruins and splinters of this tumbled mansion that the Georgian writer must somehow reconstruct a habitable dwelling-place; it is from the gleams and flashes of this flying spirit that he must create solid, living, flesh-and-blood Mrs. Brown. Sadly he must allow that the lady still escapes him. Dismally he must admit bruises received in the pursuit. But it is because the Georgians, poets and novelists, biographers and dramatists, are so hotly engaged each in the pursuit of his own Mrs. Brown that theirs is at once the least successful, and the most interesting, hundred years. Moreover, let us prophesy: Mrs. Brown will not always escape. The capture of Mrs. Brown is the title of the next chapter in the history of literature; and, let us prophesy again, that chapter will be one of the most important, the most illustrious, the most epoch-making of them all.

Nation and Atheneum, XXXIV (December 1, 1923), 342–343.

Selected Bibliography

Bennett's principal critical writings are contained in the following:

The Author's Craft. New York: George H. Doran Co., 1914.

Books and Persons. New York: George H. Doran Co., 1917.

Fame and Fiction. London: Grant Richards, 1901.

How to Become an Author. London: C. A. Pearson, 1903.

Literary Taste: How to Form It. London: New Age Press, 1909. (A revised version was published in the United States by Doran in 1927.)

The Savour of Life. New York: Doubleday, 1928.

Things That Have Interested Me. New York: George H. Doran Co., 1921.

Things That Have Interested Me: Second Series. New York: George H. Doran Co., 1923.

Things That Have Interested Me: Third Series. New York: George H. Doran Co., 1926.

The Truth About an Author. New York: George H. Doran Co., 1911.

The following are also full of information relevant to Bennett's career as a critic:

The Journal of Arnold Bennett. New York: Viking, 1933.

The Letters of Arnold Bennett. Ed. James Hepburn. London: Oxford University Press, 1966.

Arnold Bennett and H. G. Wells. Ed. Harris Wilson. Urbana: University of Illinois Press, 1960.

Acknowledgments

I have been helped in my work on Bennett's criticism by the advice of two Bennett scholars, Professor James Hepburn and Dr. Ingo Pommerening. Dr. Pommerening's dissertation, *Arnold Bennett Als Literaturkritiker* (Giessen, 1964), is the only published work on the subject, and I have found it very useful. The reference librarian of Swarthmore College, Mr. Howard Williams, has been patient and ingenious in locating texts. Three of my students, Mr. William Nelson, Jr., Mrs. Hannah Aizupitis, and Miss Diana Royce, have helped with research. The Faculty Research Fund of Swarthmore College has assisted with funds.

Acknowledgment is gratefully made to the following persons and publishers for permission to use copyrighted material:

Doubleday & Company, Inc., for *The Author's Craft*, Copyright 1914 by George H. Doran Company; "H. G. Wells," "Meredith," "Rudyard Kipling," "Tourgeniev and Dostoievsky," "John Galsworthy," "Henry James," and "Neo-Impressionism and Literature" from *Books and Persons*, copyright 1917 by George H. Doran Company; "James Joyce's *Ulysses*" from *Things That Have Interested Me: Second Series*, copyright 1923 by George H. Doran Company; "Is the Novel Decaying?" from *Things That Have Interested Me: Third Series*, copyright 1926 by George H. Doran Company; and "Explanation," "Young Authors," and "Russian Fiction" from *The Savour of Life*, copyright 1928 by Doubleday & Company, Inc.

Mrs. Cheston Bennett for "The 'Average Reader' and the Recipe for Popularity," "Ivan Turgenev," "Mr. George Moore," "George Gissing," "The Fallow Fields of Fiction," "The Novel-Reading Public," "Frank Harris's *The Bomb*," "Galsworthy's *A Commentary*," "A Few Words on Galsworthy," "Chekhov's *Cherry Orchard*," "The Progress of the Novel," "Henry James's *Embarrassments*," "My Literary Heresies," "Some Adventures Among Russian

Index

277